SURVIVAL GAMES
PERSONALITIES PLAY

SURVIVAL GAMES

PERSONALITIES

PLAY

Eve Delunas, Ph.D.

SUNFLOWER INK ❁ CARMEL, CALIFORNIA

SURVIVAL GAMES PERSONALITIES PLAY

Published by Sunflower Ink
Palo Colorado Road, Carmel, CA 93923

9 8 7 6 5 4 3 2

ISBN 0-931104-35-1
Library of Congress
Catalog Card Number: 92-64111

Thank you, David, for giving me the tools and helping me find the courage to use them. With much gratitude, this book is dedicated to you.

TABLE OF CONTENTS

Preface   ix
Acknowledgments   xi

PART ONE: THE SURVIVAL GAMES   1

1. A Map of the Territory   3
2. The Survival Games   25
3. Identifying Personalities   45

PART TWO: TREATING THE TYPES   55

4. Stopping the Blackmail Game   59
5. Stopping the Complain Game   83
6. Stopping the Robot Game   107
7. Stopping the Masquerade Game   129

PART THREE: THE CASES   155

Case #1 Lowering Mom's Blood Pressure   161
Case #2 Teaching the Boss   179
Case #3 My Puppy   191
Case #4 The Vulcan   201
Case #5 The Solar System   209
Case #6 Your Husband or Your Son?   231
Case #7 Rocking the Boat   239
Case #8 Phoney Clues   251

Afterword   271
Bibliography   273
Suggested Readings   277
Training Activities   285
Books and Tapes   287

PREFACE

Back in the 1970s, I had the good fortune to stumble into a graduate counseling program at California State University, Fullerton (CSUF) that was truly exceptional. Designed by Dr. David Keirsey and Dr. Marilyn Bates, this program's objective was to train students to become competent in the *use* of every major treatment model and every major theory for understanding and explaining abnormal behavior. Hence, the focus of this program was on what the psychotherapist *does* in order to be most helpful. As a student at CSUF, I learned how to employ Gestalt methods, role playing, serial drawing, rational-emotive therapy, reality therapy, behavioral therapy, and many other treatment techniques that were standard at the time. To my delight, I was also trained in the use of such intervention methods as symptom prescription, interdiction, and Ericksonian hypnosis, before they had gained widespread recognition and acceptance. Thanks to Dr. Keirsey, I even had the opportunity to travel to Phoenix to visit Dr. Milton Erickson and to learn from the master himself.

In addition to acquiring a wide variety of treatment tools while at CSUF, I also discovered that I could select from any number of perspectives from which to view the same symptom. It became clear that whether I chose to explain someone's abnormal behavior in terms of a defending ego, inadequate role, dysfunctional system, negative script, reinforced response, or some other theory depended upon how *useful* that theory would be in helping me to understand and treat a given case.

The CSUF graduate counseling program also furnished me with a unique set of lenses through which to view people's actions—the Keirseyan Temperament Model. These lenses provide a way of recognizing and understanding human differences that has proven invaluable in my seventeen years of clinical practice. I find them particularly appealing because they offer useful explanations for the unusual things people do, without labeling those people as *mad, bad, sick,* or *stupid.*

In the past fourteen years, millions of people have become acquainted with Keirsey's and Bates' descriptions of the normal behavior of the various personality types through the book, *Please Understand Me* (1978). To date, however, knowledge of Keirsey's extensive work on the games the personalities play is confined almost exclusively to those of us who passed through the doors of CSUF's graduate counseling program back in the seventies and early eighties.

Over the years, I have had opportunities to teach the Keirseyan Games Model to students in university classes and to diverse groups attending professional seminars. Time after time, the response has been the same: people are intrigued with this information and hungry for more. Many of my students have urged me to write a collection of case studies so that others may recognize the practical value of this approach.

Three years ago, I began this book with the intention of including ten simple cases and some brief analyses. Over time, the project grew in length and complexity as I discovered that I had to provide some basic information on the games and on treating the types before the case examples would make any sense. What eventually evolved was a book that summarizes my approach to applying Keirsey's Games Model in my work as a psychotherapist.

This project has presented me with an opportunity to pass on to others what I have learned from the many fine teachers and extraordinary clients and students who have been a part of my life. The subject is one that still fascinates me as much today as it did almost twenty years ago when I first heard about it. I hope that you find this set of lenses as helpful and as illuminating as I do.

Eve Delunas
Big Sur, California
June, 1992

ACKNOWLEDGMENTS

I wish to thank my wonderful husband, Roger Stilgenbauer, and my dear friend Patricia Toscano for providing me with so much support and encouragement from the start of this book to its completion. As my primary editor and sounding board, Roger has offered many outstanding suggestions that have been incorporated into this book. I especially want to thank him for suggesting that I use the label *survival games* to refer to the games that I describe on these pages. I am particularly grateful to Patricia for seeing the potential in me and convincing me to write this book in the first place. She has always believed in me when I have needed it most.

Ute Bender and Barbara Nelson are two other valued friends and associates who have spent countless hours going over this manuscript and who have lent their enthusiasm, wisdom, and clarity to this project. I appreciate their contributions enormously.

I am fortunate to have an extraordinary publisher for this book who is also a gifted artist. Ric Masten not only designed this book and created the artwork for its cover, but also coordinated and directed every aspect of its publication. His assistance and expertise have been invaluable to me.

I am grateful to Laurie Jones Neighbors for her outstanding editorial assistance. Thank you also to Jerri Masten Hansen for her cover photo, to Rob Kessel for his feedback on the manuscript, and to Dr. Sue Cooper for suggesting the title of this book.

I thank my parents, Henry and Helen Delunas, for always reminding me that I was capable of doing anything that I wanted to in life. I also appreciate Cyndy and Ron Miller, Andrea and Al Mosca, Ken and Jan Delunas, Rick Toscano, Margie Stilgenbauer, and Becky Roberts for their ever-present enthusiasm and encouragement for this project.

I wish to acknowledge and thank all of the people who have been so supportive of my work as a psychotherapist—most especially, Grace Perkins, Dr. Allen King, Sharon Johnson, Dana Armstrong, Ann Massa, and Victoria Johnson.

Lastly, I want to extend my love and gratitude to all of the wonderful clients and students who have so enriched my life over the past seventeen years, and who have been a constant inspiration to me.

SURVIVAL GAMES

PERSONALITIES

PLAY

The names, locales, and identifying characteristics of all individuals mentioned in case examples have been altered to protect privacy while preserving coherence. In some instances I have combined information from two similar cases in one example.

PART I

THE SURVIVAL GAMES

Chapter 1

A Map
OF THE
Territory

In his fascinating study of twenty boys and their overprotective mothers, David Levy (1943) discovered something remarkable. While all of the mothers behaved very similarly—infantilizing their preadolescent and adolescent sons by bathing, dressing, and spoon-feeding them—the boys acted and reacted toward their mothers in two distinct ways. Eleven of them were belligerent, aggressive, disobedient, and dominating, while the other nine were fearful, passive, obedient, and submissive. What's more, Levy's investigations of the mothers' and fathers' behavior yielded nothing that would account for these differences in the sons' conduct. Here were twenty boys from very similar types of dysfunctional families, yet eleven of them were bullies, while the other nine were big babies. Why the divergence in the two groups?

The behavior of these boys makes sense when we recognize their *personalities*. People are not all alike. Each personality type has its own distinct pattern of values, needs, interests, and abilities. And each type is prone to responding differently than the others in similar situations. Dr. David Keirsey has spent the past forty years identifying those observable patterns of behavior that are characteristic of each of four personality styles (Keirsey and Bates, 1978; Keirsey, 1987). In addition to giving us detailed portraits of the ways each personality normally behaves, Dr. Keirsey has both described the game that each type is prone to play when the going gets tough, and specified the context in which each of the four personalities is most likely to resort to game playing. According to his model, the boys in Levy's study were using survival games to cope with mothers who treated them like infants and fathers who were almost invisible. But the kinds of survival games they were playing varied according to their personalities.

In my years of work as a psychotherapist, I have found that the Keirseyan Games Model provides a unique and invaluable map in the territory of changing human behavior. It does not *replace* other models of psychotherapy—rather, it *augments* them. Personality theory adds another dimension to an analysis of what is going on in a dysfunctional family system. Besides furnishing useful explanations as to why a game is in progress, it points to those therapeutic interventions that are most likely to arrest the game.

This book of cases is intended to familiarize readers with the survival games different personalities play and their reasons for playing them. In addition, it is meant to show mental health professionals and those in related fields how the Keirseyan Games Model may be used to increase one's effectiveness as a change agent. Chapter one provides descriptions of the different personalities, and an explanation of what survival games are and why people play them. Chapter two describes the survival games the different personalities play. Chapter three outlines the procedure for identifying or verifying personality types using observational clues. In part two, chapters four through seven explain how knowledge of personalities may be used for designing and implementing treatment interventions. In the third, final part of the book there are eight detailed case examples[*] followed by a discussion of the observational clues used to identify or verify client personalities, the survival games they were playing and their reasons for playing them, and the rationale for choosing particular intervention strategies.

---

[*] I have changed names and identifying details in order to protect the privacy of the individuals in the cases presented here.

The case descriptions include examples of children, adolescents, and adults, whom I have seen in individual, marital, and/or family therapy.

In order to understand how and why people play survival games, it is necessary to recognize the different needs, values, interests, and abilities of each of the four personalities. Hence, what follows is a brief review of the history of psychological type theory in general and Keirsey's theory in particular. At the end of this section is a description of the four personality types and their sixteen variations.

A Brief History of Psychological Types

In 1921, Carl Jung (1971) introduced the idea that there are different types of people and that each type tends to favor the use of certain psychological functions over others. Jung's model so fascinated Isabel Myers and her mother, Katharine Briggs, that they used it as the basis for devising an instrument that could identify a person's psychological type. Once she and her mother had developed the Myers-Briggs Type Indicator (MBTI), Isabel Myers spent the remainder of her life doing research to learn more about the different personalities. Her early findings, along with her descriptions of the sixteen types, were reported in the first MBTI manual (1962). Just prior to her death, she completed *Gifts Differing* with her son, Peter Myers (1980), and a revised MBTI manual with Mary McCaulley (1985).

The Four Dimensions

According to Isabel Myers, a person's four-letter psychological type is determined by his or her preferences on each of four dimensions (table 1). The first three dimensions were identified by Jung, and Myers and Briggs added the fourth when they developed the MBTI. While each of us has both sides to our personality, usually we prefer one side over the other, just as we tend to favor either our left hand or our right hand.

TABLE 1
THE FOUR DIMENSIONS

Those who have a preference for:

Extraversion (E) Charge their batteries through social interaction	*versus*	**Introversion (I)** Charge their batteries through solitude
Sensation (S) Focus on concrete realities	*versus*	**Intuition (N)** Focus on abstract possibilities
Thinking (T) Use objective criteria to make judgements	*versus*	**Feeling (F)** Use subjective criteria to make judgements
Judging (J) Want to have things settled and decided	*versus*	**Perceiving (P)** Want to keep options open

Thus, an individual who is an ESTJ prefers Extraversion, Sensation, Thinking, and Judging over Introversion, Intuition, Feeling, and Perceiving. In all, there are sixteen different personality type combinations possible with this model.

The Notion of Temperament

When David Keirsey discovered the work of Isabel Myers, he had already been intrigued by the temperament theory of Ernst Kretschmer, a German psychiatrist who was a contemporary of Jung. Keirsey noted that the NF, NT, SP, and SJ types described by Isabel Myers correlated with the four temperaments that Kretschmer identified in his book, *Physique and Character* (1925). Searching the literature, Keirsey found evidence of the same four types being characterized by Hippocrates in 450 B.C., Paracelsus in 1550 A.D., and Eduard Spränger and Adickes in the twentieth century (Keirsey, 1987).

Drawing from these diverse sources, Keirsey began to formulate a model of personality (or temperament) that not only described the normal behavior of the types, but also predicted how and why the different personalities would engage in abnormal behavior. Keirsey's work on the survival games the types play was particularly influenced by Kretschmer, who identified both the functioning and malfunctioning personality traits that were characteristic of his four temperament groups.

The Four Personalities

In *Please Understand Me*, David Keirsey and Marilyn Bates (1978) describe the following personality (or temperament) styles: the **Artisans**, or **SPs**; the **Guardians**, or **SJs**; the **Rationals**, or **NTs**; and the **Idealists**, or **NFs**. According to Keirsey and Bates, each of these four types of people has a different set of needs or hungers which must be met on a daily basis for them to maintain their sense of self-esteem, self-respect, and self-confidence (table 2). The four personalities and their respective needs are described in the following pages.

TABLE 2
KEIRSEY'S FOUR PERSONALITIES
AND THEIR BASIC NEEDS

ARTISANS or SPs
need to:

- Be Free to Follow Their Impulses
- Demonstrate Skillfulness
- Make an Impression

GUARDIANS or SJs
need to:

- Belong
- Do Their Duty
- Be Responsible

RATIONALS or NTs
need to:

- Achieve
- Exercise Their Ingenuity
- Demonstrate Competence

IDEALISTS or NFs
need to:

- Become Self-Actualized
- Develop Potential in Self and Others
- Be Authentic

The Artisan Personality

Artisans, or SPs, are action-oriented people—and they must be bold, graceful, and impressive in the actions they take. People of this personality thrive on being free to follow their impulses, living in the moment, taking risks, and pursuing exciting adventures. They are gifted in their ability to make and use tools, whether the tool is a jet plane, a scalpel, a bulldozer, or a potter's wheel. Ever-courageous and cool-headed in times of crisis, Artisans excel on any type of rescue team. In business, they put their tactical skills to use as entrepreneurs, troubleshooters, and stock market wheeler-dealers. Unequaled as performers and composers, Artisans are found in great numbers among Olympic athletes, dancers, musicians, composers, playwrights, poets, artists, comedians, and actors. Teddy Roosevelt, John F. Kennedy, Martin Luther King, Ernest Hemingway, Lucille Ball, and Amelia Earhart are all outstanding representatives of this personality type.

The following descriptions of Artisans of various ages depict the multitude of ways that people of this personality may express their preference for action, freedom, excitement, risk, and fun.

> Lucy, a seventy-three-year-old great-grandmother who has been married for fifty years, dresses in modern styles and bright colors, and often wears several large pieces of gold jewelry. An outspoken woman, Lucy is known for her shocking remarks and for her ability to find humor in almost any situation. Lucy's favorite pastimes are painting pictures, dancing, and downhill skiing. Recently, knee problems have curtailed her skiing. She reports that this is most irritating, because now that she is finally a senior citizen, she is permitted to ski for free at her favorite mountain resort.
>
> * * * * * *
>
> Bob is an easy-going, softspoken man of forty-five who has always loved to work on engines. Since leaving the police force while still in his twenties, Bob has worked at a variety of jobs that enable him to make use of his mechanical genius. He has successfully managed the service department of a large auto dealership, and he has also owned and operated his own automobile repair business. Bob is no stranger to hard work—it is not unusual

for him to work sixteen-hour days for months on end. He also enjoys change; in the first ten years of their marriage, he and his wife lived in fourteen different homes that he bought and sold for sizable profits. In his spare time, Bob enjoys doing odd jobs around the house and also buying and selling used cars at the wholesale car auction.

* * * * * *

Maria, an attractive and very popular sixteen-year-old, does just enough in her high school classes to get by. For years, her parents, teachers, and counselors have been telling her that she is capable of getting all As if she would only apply herself. But much to their chagrin, she always ends up with Bs and an occasional C or D. Maria frankly admits that she finds most of her classes boring and a waste of her time. The only thing she likes about school is the chance to be with her friends and to participate in drama productions. Since Maria loves to act, and she is good at it, she hopes to pursue a career in the dramatic arts. When she's not at school, Maria is talking on the phone, shopping, or out partying with her friends.

* * * * * *

Three-year-old Tyler is the most active child in the day-care playroom. He is constantly on the move, handling the toys, building, drawing, jumping, and exploring. Tyler loves physical games and is well coordinated for his age. He has always been a fairly independent child who seems to have no fear. In fact, Tyler will try almost anything should the opportunity present itself. At an amusement park, he begs his parents to let him go on the fastest and scariest adult rides. Tyler has a mind of his own, and he is always testing his parents and the teacher, to see where they will draw the line. He delights in saying things he is not supposed to and enjoys the subsequent reaction from the adults around him. When Tyler's grandfather was saying goodbye to him at the end of a visit, Tyler's parents were shocked and embarrassed to hear their son respond, "Good-bye jerkface."

The Guardian Personality

Guardians, or **SJs,** are membership-oriented people who earn their treasured right to belong by being accountable and by doing their duty unselfishly and responsibly. It is the loyal Guardian who has established and maintained all of the traditional institutions of society—the government, the churches, the schools, the banks, the hospitals. Guardians are active participants in all kinds of groups, selflessly contributing their hard work in organizations that provide service to the needy. Outstanding with logistical details and excellent at follow-through, Guardians are often found in the fields of accounting, teaching, nursing, banking, administrating, and bookkeeping. They are also exceptional when offering service to others as pharmacists, dentists, secretaries, social workers, ministers, family-practice physicians, librarians, escrow agents, and fiduciaries. Some examples of famous Guardians are: Florence Nightingale, George Washington, Harry Truman, Mother Teresa, and Queen Victoria.

The following descriptions reveal just a few of the many ways that Guardians exercise their preference for belonging, providing service, and being responsible.

> At sixty-five, Jim recently retired from his job as an elementary school principal after thirty years of service in the same school district, where he was both liked and respected by his colleagues and staff. Since his retirement, Jim has continued to work part time for the local university, helping student teachers who are in the classroom for the first time. Jim has always been active in a variety of service organizations, and also in the church he and his wife have attended regularly during the forty years of their marriage. With retirement, his involvement in these activities has mushroomed. In addition, Jim plays golf regularly with a group of retired school principals, and he and his wife have recently returned from a spectacular cruise to Alaska.
>
> * * * * * *
>
> Marla is a forty-three-year-old nurse employed at a large hospital. Since her divorce fifteen years ago, Marla has worked hard to support herself and her two children. She likes her work very much, although she finds it extremely demanding and stressful at times. Fortunately, her closest friend is also employed at the hospital, and they are able to use their daily commute to and from the job as a chance to air their frustrations. In addition to her busy hospital schedule, Marla has found time to remain

actively involved in her community church and in the Girl Scouts, where she has been a leader for many years. Marla also visits her aging mother regularly to clean her house and take her shopping. In her infrequent spare time, Marla loves to read and to knit.

* * * * * *

John is an active high school student who is treasurer for his student body. In addition to maintaining an A average, he is an Eagle Scout and a member of the school tennis team. Next year, John will be attending an Ivy League college, with a scholarship to study business management. John's goals are to join a fraternity during college, to earn his M.B.A., and then to find a job in "corporate America." Once he is out of school and financially secure, he plans to settle down, marry, and have a family of his own.

* * * * * *

Four-year-old Laura is already a very conscientious and responsible child. She especially loves to help her daycare teacher care for the younger children. One day, when all of the children at the daycare center had chicken pox, Laura handed each a blanket, assigned each a place to lie down, and instructed them all to watch the cartoon video that she asked the teacher to play for them. They did exactly as she directed. One of Laura's favorite things to do at daycare is to play "jail." Using large blocks, she constructs walls that enclose the younger Artisan boys at play. Then, she announces that they are in jail and that they will need her permission to get out. Not surprisingly, the younger boys usually comply with her rules.

The Rational Personality

Rationals, or **NTs**, are theory-oriented people who must achieve and demonstrate competence in all they do. Rationals are resolute as they strive to understand and harness the forces of nature. These calm and serious people have no competitors when it comes to their ability to be precise in thought and language. They are capable of dealing with enormous theoretical complexity as they design abstract models in the fields of mathematics, computer science, engineering, science, and architecture. As managers, Rationals put their strategic abilities to use in long-range contingency planning. Computer science, philosophy, science, technology, logic, mathematics, cardiology, research, architecture, and engineering are all fields that are likely to capture the interests and talents of this personality. Famous Rationals include Thomas Jefferson, Abraham Lincoln, Madame Curie, Ayn Rand, Queen Elizabeth I, and Nikola Tesla.

What follows are some examples of the many ways in which Rationals of all ages utilize their willpower in order to achieve and to acquire competencies in their chosen endeavors.

As a professor of history at a large public university, sixty-year-old Winston is widely recognized among colleagues for his expertise in his field of study. Winston spends the majority of his time reading history books, writing, and teaching. He is a demanding professor, known for his exceptionally difficult essay exams and heavy reading assignments. When he is not devouring history books, Winston is either out on the tennis court practicing his serve and volley, or in front of his computer mastering the capabilities of his most recent software purchase.

* * * * * *

Samantha is thirty-eight-year-old electronics engineer who works on the research and design team of a large aerospace company. She finds her job both challenging and stimulating. Samantha enjoys living on a classic wooden sailboat with her husband and cat. Besides providing opportunities for excursions to faraway places, the boat keeps Samantha busy using her ingenuity to repair the many things that can (and do) go wrong with it.

* * * * * *

Sixteen-year-old Elizabeth is more involved in her studies of math and science than she is in the high school social scene. She is bored with the small talk of most of her peers and prefers to keep to herself much of the time. Since Elizabeth is particularly fascinated with physics, she hopes to earn a Ph.D. in that subject and to eventually pursue a career in research. For fun, Elizabeth likes to work on perfecting her ability to draw three-dimensional designs on her computer.

* * * * * *

At four years of age, David never stops asking questions about why things are the way they are. And if a parent or teacher's response doesn't make sense to him, then he will tell them so. David is fascinated with outer space and with anything scientific. He implores his parents to take him to the public library several times a week, where he will check out as many books as permitted on his favorite subjects. When David was three years old and learning to count, he started at the number one and asked his mother "What comes next?" until the two of them had counted to over three hundred. Imagine her surprise when David suddenly announced, "And even God doesn't know the last number!"

The Idealist Personality

Idealists, or **NFs,** are relationship-oriented people who strive to be authentic, to become self-actualized, and to have good rapport with others. Idealists are gifted in verbal and written forms of self-expression and in inspiring people to develop to their fullest potential. With their exceptional diplomatic skills, they are able to catalyze social groups to greater levels of cooperation, harmony, and productivity. They are enthusiastic, empathic people who are interested in helping others to grow. Idealists will often be found making a positive impact on the lives of others as counselors, teachers, psychiatrists, psychologists, social workers, journalists, ministers, writers, group trainers, group facilitators, and managers. Some well-known Idealists are: Joan of Arc, Ghandi, Emily Dickinson, Abraham Maslow, and Ralph Waldo Emerson.

The following descriptions provide examples of the many ways Idealists of all ages strive to achieve self-actualization and to inspire others.

> Elena is a sixty-four-year-old Marriage and Family Therapist who has been in private practice for over thirty years. In addition to her counseling, Elena teaches part time at the local university, and she is busy writing a book. Because Elena loves her work so much, she has no plan to retire in the near future. For fun, she loves to travel, and she has managed to visit many wonderful and exotic places over the years. Wherever she goes, she is particularly interested in meeting the people and learning more about their view of the world.

* * * * * *

Since she began teaching kindergarten twenty years ago, forty-two-year-old Ann has been trying to find the most creative ways of helping each and every child in her classroom develop emotionally, intellectually, and socially. Ann has a master's degree in counseling, and she is constantly taking courses and workshops for her personal and professional development. She has a close and fulfilling relationship with her husband, who shares many of her interests. A very spiritual person, Ann strives to find the meaning in her own life and to understand herself and her relationships from a broader perspective. She paints and keeps a journal as a means of self-expression and of connecting with the deepest parts of herself.

* * * * * *

Mark is a popular high school senior who is the editor of his school newspaper and who plans to pursue a career in journalism. English literature and foreign languages have always been Mark's favorite subjects, and he excels in them. After he graduates from college, Mark hopes to join the Peace Corps in order to pursue his dream of making a difference in the lives of those who are less fortunate than himself. Eventually, he hopes to join the international staff of a newspaper, where he would like to concentrate on creating special reports to increase public awareness of the needs of those in developing nations.

* * * * * *

At four, Ryan is a very sensitive child who is well liked by the other children in his daycare class. He shows a great deal of concern for the feelings of others and encourages all of the children to get along together. Ryan has a special imaginary friend named Elizabeth who accompanies him everywhere he goes. Often when he does something he isn't supposed to, Ryan claims that Elizabeth is the one to blame. For example, when he doesn't eat his lunch, it is usually because the food being served is not something that Elizabeth likes to eat. One day Ryan saw a mouse outside the daycare center, and Elizabeth helped him design a mousetrap that would catch the mouse without harming it in any way. He took a paper plate and plastered a ring of paste around the outside of it. In the very center, he placed a mound of peanut butter. Ryan couldn't imagine why the mouse never materialized in his trap.

The Sixteen Variations

Each of the four personality types has four variants (or subtypes) with their own unique capabilities or hallmarks (table 3[*]).

TABLE 3
KEIRSEY'S SIXTEEN VARIANTS FOR
THE FOUR PERSONALITIES

Four Kinds of **SPs** or **Artisans:**

ESTP	Operator / Promoter
ISTP	Operator / Instrumentor
ESFP	Player / Performer
ISFP	Player / Composer

Four Kinds of **SJs** or **Guardians:**

ESTJ	Monitor / Supervisor
ISTJ	Monitor / Inspector
ESFJ	Conservator / Protector
ISFJ	Conservator / Provider

Four Kinds of **NTs** or **Rationals:**

ENTJ	Organizer / Marshaller
INTJ	Organizer / Planner
ENTP	Engineer / Inventor
INTP	Engineer / Designer

Four Kinds of **NFs** or **Idealists:**

ENFJ	Mentor / Group Leader
INFJ	Mentor / Diviner
ENFP	Advocate / Revealer
INFP	Advocate / Conciliator

---

[*] Most of the names that I have listed here may be found in *Portraits of Temperament*. Where I have used different names, it is because of changes that Dr. Keirsey has made since publication of *Portraits*.

What follows is a quick review of the specialized interests and talents of each of the sixteen subtypes (Keirsey and Bates, 1978; Keirsey, 1987).

Four Kinds of Artisans

The **Artisans**, or **SPs**, are comprised of two kinds of STP Operators and two kinds of SFP Players. The ESTPs are the Promoters, good at gaining the confidence of others, while the ISTPs are the Instrumentalists, excellent at making and using tools. The ESFPs are the master Performers, while the ISFPs are gifted Composers in the visual and performing arts.

Four Kinds of Guardians

The **Guardians**, or **SJs**, consist of the STJ Monitors and the SFJ Conservators. The ESTJ Supervisors excel at watching over others to be sure that they are doing what they are supposed to be doing, while the ISTJ Inspectors are good at checking to see that work has been done properly. ESFJs are the Protectors, making certain that their charges are protected from the danger of any kind of loss or harm, while ISFJs are the Providers, seeing to it that the sick, poor, ignorant, or homeless get what they need.

Four Kinds of Rationals

The two kinds of **Rationals**, or **NTs**, are the NTJ Organizers, and the NTP Engineers. The ENTJ Marshallers are outstanding at putting strategic plans into operation, while the INTJ Planners excel at devising complex contingency plans for meeting distant goals. The ENTP Inventors are capable of designing complicated machinery, whereas the INTP Designers devise better ways of doing things.

Four Kinds of Idealists

The two types of **Idealists**, or **NFs**, are the NFJ Mentors and the NFP Advocates. While the ENFJs are talented Group Leaders who can inspire large numbers of people, the INFJ Diviners are exceptional prophets who unravel the mysteries of life. The ENFP Revealers excel at locating and exposing both the good (such as undeveloped potential in people) as well as the bad (social injustice, corruption, or evil). It is the INFP Conciliators whose superb diplomatic skills can be used to help people to resolve conflicts and to cooperate with each other.

When Personalities Play Survival Games

In his book *Games People Play*, Eric Berne (1964) was the first to make a case for the utility of the game framework in explaining human behavior. Berne defines games as a series of repeated transactions (or maneuvers) that we unconsciously engage in with others in order to obtain an ulterior (hidden) payoff. According to Berne, game payoffs may be: 1) the maintenance of internal psychic stability; 2) the avoidance of anxiety-arousing situations or intimacies; 3) the procurement of strokes; and/or 4) the maintenance of the established equilibrium in a relationship. Berne emphasizes that everyone plays psychological games, and since they serve many important social functions, games are often constructive. It is only when games are destructive that they are problematic. Berne cautions us not to be misled by the words *playing games*; he stresses that these terms do not necessarily imply either fun or enjoyment. Psychological games can potentially be very serious, with very serious results.

The Keirseyan Model takes Berne's game framework one step further, by identifying the variations in game playing among the four personalities. According to Keirsey, **Artisans** play the game of *Blackmail*, **Guardians** play *Complain*, **Rationals** play *Robot*, and **Idealists** play *Masquerade*. These survival games[*] are not the same as the ones described by Berne, since most of his

---

[*] Keirsey calls them "unfriendly games."

games are more general in character and not unique to any particular personality types.

What Are Survival Games?

Survival games are just what their name implies—they are people's desperate attempts to defend themselves in overwhelmingly threatening social environments. Because many survival game tactics look so absurd, they are often mistaken as evidence of some organic pathology. But, as Berne points out, if one looks beyond the individual to the social context in which the behavior takes place, it becomes evident that the atypical behavior elicits social payoffs that have high survival value. In other words, though survival game tactics may sometimes look strange, they are actually a creative solution to a difficult, or even crazy situation.

Why People Play Survival Games

Given enough stress, anyone may play survival games. But, according to Keirsey, it is a different type of stressor that induces each of the four kinds of people to resort to game tactics. People are most likely to engage in survival tactics when they feel that something they need to retain their sense of self-esteem, self-respect, and self-confidence is in jeopardy. In other words, when people find that their basic needs are not being met or they are in danger of not being met, and they feel helpless to do anything about it, then they may begin to employ game tactics. Since each personality has different needs, it follows that each can have different reasons for behaving in these defensive, self-protective ways.

Fundamental Needs Are Not Being Met

Often individuals turn to survival game playing because their social environment seems to be preventing them from meeting their fundamental needs. This is especially true when people are not able to get what they need most at home, *nor* at school, *nor* at work. Hence, Artisans are likely to play survival games when they feel that they are not able to be free to follow their impulses *anywhere* in their lives. Similarly, Guardians are likely to employ game tactics when they feel that there is *no place* they truly belong. Rationals are likely to play games when they feel that they have *no* opportunities to achieve, while Idealists are most inclined to use survival tactics when they have *nowhere* to express their true identities. For example, an unemployed, divorced, Guardian mother whose children have all left the nest may begin to complain loudly about her depression and her numerous aches and pains whenever she finds a sympathetic ear. Her game of Complain may be seen as a way of protecting herself against abandonment by entangling others. By becoming decommissioned, she manages to be excused from her responsibilities while assuring herself of service and making certain that others do not forget about her.

Masking Inadequacy

As discussed above, each of the four personalities also needs to see themselves and be seen by others in certain ways in order to feel good about themselves. Artisans need to be *impressive* in their own eyes and the eyes of others, while Guardians need to appear *responsible*. Rationals must see themselves and be seen as *competent*, while Idealists need to be perceived as *authentic* by self and others. When individuals of each type find themselves consistently unable to act in accordance with their own values, then they experience an erosion of their self-confidence as they begin to doubt their ability to meet their needs in the future. Typically, they also start to think considerably less of themselves, feeling guilty and ashamed. At this point they may turn to survival game playing in order to mask their feelings of inadequacy from themselves and others.

The game tactics also provide them with excuses for not behaving the ways they believe they "should." Hence, Artisans often start playing games to *avoid looking and feeling unimpressive*, while Guardians employ survival tactics to *excuse their irresponsibility*. Rationals play games to *cover-up their incompetence*, and Idealists do so to *conceal their inauthenticity*. For example, the Artisan whose performances on the stage have received consistently poor reviews, and whose wife has divorced him, may begin to abuse alcohol as a way of numbing himself to the pain of being disgraced. This survival tactic also serves to keep him from putting himself on the line by performing once again. After all, what can you expect of a hopeless drunk?

Helping the Family

In addition to recognizing survival game playing as the individual's defense against loss of self-esteem, self-confidence, and self-respect, it is also possible to view it as a way of trying to be helpful to the family (see Madanes, 1981, 1984, 1990). Survival games often enable the entire system to survive as a unit. When eight-year-old Martin, an Artisan-type personality, plays Blackmail by stealing money from his mother's purse, then his battling parents suddenly unite in their concern about him and their desire to get him to stop stealing. Martin's game playing has brought a family closer together that was in danger of falling apart. Certainly, game players are not likely to be consciously aware of the ways in which their tactics are helpful to the entire family. Nor are the other family members likely to recognize or acknowledge this. But, if one looks carefully at the situation, the helpful nature of the game is always apparent. In a sense, the survival game player is sacrificing himself or herself for the good of the group. It is his or her desperate attempt to hold it all together.

Controlling the Behavior of Others

Still another function of survival games is that of putting others in a one-down position (see Haley, 1963). In a stressful, unpredictable, or unfriendly environment, getting the upper hand can be a very necessary survival tactic. Survival game players manage to control their relationships with others, while at the same time deny that they are taking control. They do this by behaving in absurd ways that paralyze others. For example, a little boy playing the game of Robot might ask repeatedly, "Is this poisonous?" at every mealtime. One can imagine how arresting it must be to his family members when they are confronted with this bizarre behavior. What do you say to a son or brother who is constantly asking if you are giving him poisonous food? Business-as-usual typically comes to a halt when there is survival game playing going on. And with the cessation of normal communications, chances are the game player finds it easier to endure an uncomfortable situation.

Sending A Metaphoric Message

There is frequently a metaphoric message (see Madanes, 1981, 1984) in the survival games that a person plays. This message may describe the feelings of the game player as well as the feelings of someone else in the family. When an Artisan teenager playing Blackmail takes an overdose of pain-killers, I look to find out whose pain, besides her own, she is trying to kill. Similarly, when an Idealist boy playing the game of Masquerade reports that he cannot swallow, and physicians cannot provide a medical explanation for this problem, then one may ask *who* can't swallow *what* in the family.

Game Tactics Are Not Conscious or Deliberate

Though survival games have many useful purposes, it is a mistake to assume that people play them consciously and deliberately. Rather, game players are likely to report that they can't help themselves, that they have no idea why they are doing what they are doing, and that they just can't make themselves stop. Game tactics are always done spontaneously and inadvertently. And people are *not* aware of the reasons why they are playing games.

Survival Games Are Not Fun

Finally, it is important to recognize that these games are not fun for anyone involved. Indeed, taken to the extreme, many of them can be deadly. Game players are certainly *not* enjoying themselves, and they may even be doing themselves great harm. Yet the pain associated with the game playing is the price they pay in order to protect the tiny remnants of self-worth that they have left, while also preserving the family system. Survival games are a frantic call for help in overwhelming circumstances. Game players have reached the ends of their ropes and do not see themselves as having any constructive options. Clearly, survival games are anything *but* fun.

The Wounds of Childhood

Individuals who have been neglected or physically, sexually, or emotionally abused as children are especially prone to survival game playing. Since survival games are used for protection in dangerous circumstances, battered and neglected children turn to game tactics very early in life, in a desperate attempt to survive a situation in which they feel both helpless and threatened (Miller, 1983). There are several reasons why adult survivors of childhood abuse often continue to engage in survival game playing long after they have left their childhood homes.

Feelings of Worthlessness

People who have been abused as children usually did not have the opportunity to develop healthy self-esteem, self-confidence, and self-respect. Children learn how to regard themselves and treat themselves by watching and listening to how the important adults in their lives regard them and treat them. If children are treated without respect, then they learn to disrespect themselves. If children are treated like worthless objects, then they learn to consider themselves as having no value. If their caregivers lack confidence in them, then they learn to doubt themselves. Instead of loving and believing in themselves, most people who have been mistreated as children are plagued with self-hatred and an overwhelming sense of inadequacy.

This pervasive sense of being worthless, defective, and not good enough—called "toxic shame" by John Bradshaw (1988)—colors almost all relationships and situations as potentially threatening. As one young woman said, "I am afraid others are going to discover the truth about me—that I am really just a worthless piece of garbage!" This woman, and others like her, use survival games as a way of keeping others from discovering their imperfect selves. Their games serve as masks that cover up the terrible shame they feel.

Protecting the Self from Additional Harm

Those who have been abused as children are accustomed to living in fear. In childhood, relationships were dangerous territory. These children never knew when or where the next emotional or physical blow would land. In adulthood, they often expect relationships to be unsafe, since that is what they have known in the past. By playing survival games, they are frequently trying to protect themselves from getting hurt again.

Mastering an Unresolved Situation

Finally, adult survivors of abuse are likely to continue playing survival games because these games are a way of continuing the cycle of abuse. Many of the survival games are either self-destructive or other-destructive. Hence, for the person who was victimized as a child, they are a means of either continuing to hurt the self, and/or of hurting others. This is not due to a conscious or deliberate desire to punish the self or another—rather, it is an individual's unconscious and inadvertent attempt to master an unresolved situation.

Stopping the Cycle of Abuse

While not all survival game players were abused as children, most adult survivors of abuse are likely to engage in some kinds of survival game tactics until the wounds of their childhood have been healed. Fortunately, as they resolve the unfinished business of their early years, they are likely to stop the cycle of abuse rather than pass it on to the next generation.

Chapter 2

THE
SURVIVAL
GAMES

According to Keirsey, each of the four personalities is most prone to play a different kind of survival game when under stress, and for different purposes. While Artisans play the game of *Blackmail,* Guardians play *Complain,* Rationals play *Robot,* and Idealists play *Masquerade* (table 4).[*] Each of these four games has six variants, and a game player may employ the tactics of any number of these variants and in any combination.

It is not uncommon for each of us to play survival games from time to time—no matter how healthy or well-adjusted we are. After all, none of us lives in a stress-free world. It is only when these games continue, and escalate in severity from the mild towards the more extreme end of the scale, that there is reason for concern. Normally, the less serious game tactics will disappear on their own over time. In fact, it is in paying a lot of attention to these minor games that we may actually create a far more serious problem (see Watzlawick, Weakland, and Fisch, 1974).

---

[*] Dr. Keirsey calls the games: Hostage for the Artisan, Plaintiff for the Guardian, Android for the Rational, and Marionette for the Idealist. The purposes of the games presented here were identified by Dr. Keirsey, with the exception of Masquerade—he maintains its purpose is to confuse others.

TABLE 4
THE SURVIVAL GAMES AND THEIR PURPOSES

ARTISANS (SPs)	
Game:	Blackmail
Purpose:	Excite Self Punish Others
GUARDIANS (SJs)	
Game:	Complain
Purpose:	Excuse Self Entangle Others
RATIONALS (NTs)	
Game:	Robot
Purpose:	Preoccupy Self Distract Others
IDEALISTS (NFs)	
Game:	Masquerade
Purpose:	Alienate Self Deceive Others

What follows is a brief review of the four survival games* the personalities play and their variants. All of these descriptions have been derived from Dr. Keirsey's extensive work on this subject.

Since all survival games can range in severity from mild to extreme, in the descriptions of the games you will find examples from each end of the continuum. For example, on the mild end of the scale, a Complain player may suffer from an occasional headache, while on the extreme end of the scale, he or she may be completely incapacitated by physical disabilities. Survival games rarely start out at the severe level, but rather escalate to that point over time. With escalation, there is often increased danger to the game player and sometimes to others as well. Certainly there is also an increase in suffering on the part of all involved, with greater feelings of frustration, hopelessness, and/or desperation. Fortunately, most of our games remain at the lower end of the continuum, without ever getting out of hand.

Often, we respond to those significant others who are playing survival games by employing game tactics of our own. Thus we may see an ISTP husband who is playing Blackmail, while his ISFJ wife plays Complain. He drinks and gambles, while she complains of being sick, tired, and depressed. Chances are that as his game escalates, hers will too.

The Blackmail Game

Artisans play the game of *Blackmail* when they fear the loss of their ability to be free, graceful, and impressive. The Blackmail player appears to be under the influence of some *uncontrollable* and *irresistible impulse* to do something that is either destructive towards the self (in the case of the SFP Players) or something destructive toward someone else's person or property (in

---

* What I call "survival games," Dr. Keirsey calls "unfriendly games." I have changed most of the names that Dr. Keirsey uses for the games, and I have deviated from his model by identifying six game variations each of the personalities play, where he identifies four—enabling him to pair one game variation with each of the sixteen personality types.

the case of the STP Operators). In effect, the Artisan game player blackmails a significant other by threatening to take away something the other values unless the other does what the game player wants. The valued item might be the game player himself or herself (in the case of suicide threats, threats of self-mutilation, or a drug binge), or it might even be the other's reputation. (For example, it can be embarrassing for a parent to have his or her child caught shoplifting.) The Artisan's payoff in the Blackmail game is *restitution*—that is, the game player *gets high* and *gets even*—excitement and revenge—both at the same time. What's more, Blackmail players do not have to be concerned about being forceful, graceful, and impressive while in the throes of an irresistible impulse. While Artisans want most of all to appear graceful, it is paradoxical that in self-defense they end up doing things that look completely disgraceful. Their immoral or illegal activities distract everyone's attention away from the fact that they are not performing impressively elsewhere. Hence, the Blackmail game ultimately protects the Artisan from greater loss of self-esteem, self-confidence, and self-respect.

Six Variations of the Blackmail Game

The six forms of the Blackmail game are: *Delinquency, Con Artist, Outrage, Binge, Shocking,* and *Empty.* Blackmail players may exhibit any or all of these variants as a means of survival by gaining restitution.

The Delinquency Variant

In the *Delinquency* variant of Blackmail, Artisans may lie, cheat, steal, and/or do anything else that is also considered immoral or illegal. Vandalism, school truancy, cheating on an exam, arson, and burglary are all forms of this game. If caught in the act, Delinquency players usually deny any wrongdoing, often blaming someone else for their misbehavior. For example, the Delinquency player who has stolen a car and gotten caught may be quick to point out that the theft was the fault of the owner, who left the vehicle unlocked. Even when caught red-handed, it is rare for Delinquency players to confess to their misdeeds. The child caught with his hands in the cookie jar may vehemently deny that he had been stealing a cookie. If confronted with threats of punishment,* the Delinquency player's standard response is "I don't care."

The Con Artist Variant

The game of *Con Artist* often accompanies the game of Delinquency. These players can be masters at convincing others to believe their phoney stories. The classic movie *The Sting* is a great example of this game in action, as is the movie *The Great Imposter*. Con Artist players know how to evoke pity, guilt, or sympathy from others when it is to their own advantage to do so, such as in the case of the student who gets herself excused from taking a final exam, or the perfectly healthy adult who manages to collect disability payments. When confronted with their wrongdoing, Con Artist players will always have a good excuse and promise anything that the other wants to hear. Of course, follow-through on the promise is highly unlikely. Con Artist players excel at gaining the confidence of others. In extreme cases, they may seduce others into entrusting them with money or other valuables, and then disappear without a trace—leaving their innocent and unsuspecting prey shocked and penniless.

The Outrage Variant

Still another variant of Blackmail is the game of *Outrage*. Here Artisans may exhibit violent outbursts** in which they hurt others emotionally and/or physically, and in which they may also damage property. After letting out their rage, these players will justify their behavior by blaming the other for "pushing their buttons." In other words, the Outrage player claims to blow up because of what someone else said or did. Thus the Outrage

---

* Indeed, punish a Blackmail player, and he or she will punish you back.
** While other personalities can, and do blow their stacks, and even become physically violent, it is the Artisans who are most likely to do this consistently, and as a way of punishing others.

player conveniently places responsibility for the verbal and/or physical violence on someone else. The child who throws a tantrum at the dinner table is probably playing Outrage, as is the adult who screams obscenities at his or her children. In its most extreme forms Outrage is a very dangerous game, causing severe physical injuries or even death.

The Binge Variant

In playing the game of *Binge*, Artisans may persistently over-indulge in substances such as food, alcohol or other drugs,* or in activities like spending, speeding, sex, or gambling. People who stuff themselves with food and then purge are playing Binge, as are the ones who buy lottery tickets rather than milk for the children with their last dollars. Binge players often vacillate between periods of great excitement and periods when they are feeling empty. Thus, the game of Binge is often played cyclically along with the game of Empty. When Binge players are on a "high," then they can be very difficult to pin down in the therapist's office, as they seem to be bouncing off of the walls in every direction at once. They talk fast, move fast, and change subjects almost with every sentence they speak.

The Shocking Variant

When Artisans play the game of *Shocking*, then they say and do things that are likely to shock others. Anything that violates social conventions is fair game. Shocking players may either mutilate or harm their bodies, or allow themselves to be consistently degraded or abused by another.** Often they present

---

* This is not meant to imply that only Artisans overeat, become alcoholics, or become addicted to illegal drugs. Certainly these behaviors may be found among each of the four personalities. However, Artisans are the *most likely* of the four temperaments to binge and purge, and also to engage in repeated alcohol abuse and to abuse illegal drugs. What's more, they are most likely to to use these behaviors as a means of exciting the self while also punishing the other.

** Most victims of repeated domestic violence are either Artisans who are playing Shocking or Guardians who are playing Doormat.

themselves as helpless victims. The student who directs a vulgar or obscene comment to the teacher is playing a mild form of Shocking, while the head-banger or the person who self-mutilates with razor blades is playing the more extreme and dangerous version.

The Empty Variant

The last Blackmail variant is *Empty*. In this game, the player complains of feeling empty, devoid of feelings and impulses. Empty players may report that they don't feel anything at all—just a numbness inside—and that the things that normally get them excited just don't do anything for them. Artisans are particularly prone to playing this game in combination with any of the others when they are feeling excessively bound or obligated in a relationship.

The Complain Game

Guardians play *Complain* when their ability to continue to be accountable, unselfish, and to belong is at risk. To play this game, they present themselves as *decommissioned* by complaining loudly of being *sick, tired, worried*, and/or *sorry*. As they immobilize themselves with fears, pains, worries, fatigue, or sorrow, the Guardians manage to *entangle* others who feel obligated to take care of them. In this way, the Guardian game player manages to change his or her position from the one who gives service to the one who receives it. Complain players may describe their aches and pains in vivid detail to all who are willing to listen. They may also voice excessive fears or worries, or complain of being too tired to even get out of bed. The game of Complain protects the Guardian's ability to belong—since it is unlikely that a loved one will abandon someone who is so depressed. In addition, the Guardian is exempted from having to be accountable or unselfish. After all, you just don't expect much of someone who is so down and out. Paradoxically, in playing Complain, the Guardian who so wants and needs to be responsible becomes irresponsible. This is necessary for the Guardian to preserve whatever remnants of self-esteem, self-confidence, and self-respect he or she has left.

Six Variations of the Complain Game

The six variants of the Complain Game are: *Invalid*, *Worried*, *Doormat*, *Poor Me*, *Depressed*, and *Nag*. Complain players may employ tactics from any of these games, and in any combination, in order to entangle others as a means of survival.

The Invalid Variant

In playing the *Invalid* variant of the Complain game, the Guardian complains of suffering from one or more aches and pains. These aches and pains are real, not imaginary, though Invalid players may at times exaggerate in their reports of the degree of discomfort they are experiencing. In the mild form of the Invalid game, players may complain of an occasional headache,* sore back, stomach ache, or of being fatigued. In the more serious and extreme versions of this game, players may become incapacitated from psychosomatic disorders such as severe headaches, ulcers, colitis, heart attacks, strokes, or arthritis.

The Worried Variant

Those who play the *Worried* variation of the Complain game are plagued with terrible worries and fears of bad things that may happen. While the bad things that they fear are real possibilities, Worried players go overboard in the number of worries they entertain and the amount of time they spend focusing on them and voicing them to others. What's more, these players worry about events that are completely out of their control. For

---

* While any of the temperaments may suffer from headaches, or any other psychosomatic disorder, it is the Guardian who is most likely to develop these physical ailments and to make others aware of these problems by complaining about them.

example, a mild form of the game of Worry is the child who worries that a parent will be killed in an automobile accident. A more severe example of the Worry game is the mother who is so fearful that something bad may happen to her son (either now or ten years in the future) that she cannot sleep at night, quits her job, and keeps him home from school and play activities so that he remains "safe" with her at all times. At its worst, the Worry player may be plagued with anxiety attacks which involve hyperventilation, heart palpitations, excessive perspiration, and even fainting.

The Doormat Variant

With the *Doormat* version of the Complain game, players repeatedly allow themselves to be stepped on by others, while behaving as lowly servants. Though they are hurting and resentful of their mistreatment, Doormat players continue to allow others to take advantage of them. These players do not stand up for themselves and set limits with others. *No* is a word that is missing from their vocabularies. Not surprisingly, many Doormat players marry Artisans who play Binge, Outrage, and/or Delinquency. At its worst, the game of Doormat is one in which players may remain in relationships in which they are the objects of physical violence*

The Poor Me Variant

In the game of *Poor Me*, players complain loudly and often about how put-upon they are. They let all the world know about the heavy burdens that they must bear. While they often verbalize their displeasure over the way in which they are being treated, these players rarely refuse to comply with the excessive demands of others. Instead, they are inclined to do exactly what their bosses, colleagues, mates, children, and/or parents want or expect them to do, complaining all the while. At worst, these individuals will complain about how bad off they are to anyone

---

* Once again—victims of repeated domestic violence are usually either Artisans playing Shocking or Guardians playing Doormat.

who is willing to listen. They will tell you in great detail about the many responsibilities that fall on their shoulders, while pointing out any and all of the people who are not pulling their own share of the load. Often those who play Poor Me also play the game of Doormat.

The Depressed Variant

Players of the *Depressed* variant of Complain report that they are filled with sadness. Everything looks dark and dreary to the Depressed player, and there is no hope on the horizon. They may experience insomnia, or sleep almost all of the time. These players often report having little or no energy and feeling greatly fatigued. Just getting out of bed and getting dressed may seem like an overwhelming task to them, and they agonize over making even the smallest decisions. Depressed players almost always let those around them know just how badly they are feeling. In mild cases of Depressed, players feel gloomy for a few days, while in extreme cases, players may feel down for months, and contemplate or even attempt suicide.

The Nag Variant

One final variation of Complain is the game of *Nag*, where players harp on others regarding what they should and should not be feeling, thinking, and/or doing. Over time, this game can escalate to the point where Nag players raise their voices, even to the point of screaming at significant others. Nag players do not forgive or forget the past, but rather, take advantage of every opportunity to drag the other's past transgressions into the present discussion. An example of a less severe case of Nag is the youngster who tries to boss her classmates around, instructing them on how they are to behave in the classroom. An extreme case is the man who tries to dictate his wife's behavior, constantly and repeatedly reminding her of her past wrong-doings, and of what she should or should not think, feel, or do. When she returns home after an outing, the first thing he does is fire questions at her about where she was and whether or not she did something she is not supposed to do. Here the Nag player behaves like a "critical parent" who is trying to set a "wayward child" straight. The problem is, that the "wayward child" is a grown adult who desires no straightening out and who demonstrates her refusal to cooperate by rebelling all the more.

The Robot Game

Rationals use the game of *Robot* when they fear a loss of their ability to continue to be competent, achieving, and resolved. In this game they manage to *distract* others by preoccupying themselves with what they *must* think or do or what they *must not* think or *not* do. Robot players act like computers who have no choice but to behave in accordance with their programming. They may spend hours performing various meaningless cleaning, counting, and/or touching rituals, or report that they cannot stop the horrible, frightening thoughts that repeatedly run through their minds. They may compulsively avoid certain places—like enclosed spaces—or obsess about simple things that they must not forget to say or do when performing—such as on a test. It is paradoxical that the Rational type behaves so irrationally when under stress. Yet, all of these forms of preoccupation attract the Rational's attention away from those areas in which he or she feels incompetent. What's more, they also keep other people from noticing where the Robot player has failed or may fail. Hence, the game of Robot enables the Rational to protect his or her limited reserves of self-esteem, self-respect, and self-confidence.

Six Variations of the Robot Game

The six variations of the Robot game are: *That's Illogical, Super-Intellectual, Nitpick, Superstition, Blanking Out,* and *Haunted.* Robot players may display tactics from any or all of these games as a way of surviving by distracting themselves and others.

The That's Illogical Variant

In *That's Illogical*, the Robot player keeps others on the defensive by asking lots of questions about what others think, want, feel, or do and why they think, want, feel, or do it. Once others begin to explain or defend themselves, then That's Illogical players accuse them of being illogical. Emotions, values, intuition, or any such nonrational reasons offered by the other are especially likely to be dismissed as irrelevant, unacceptable, ridiculous, or just plain stupid by the game player. One sees a mild version of this game where a teenager points out to her worried parents that their reasons for not letting her take the car are irrational. In a more extreme version, a man might intimidate his wife and children by dismissing their feelings and concerns as illogical and therefore not worthy of discussion.

The Super-Intellectual Variant

The game of *Super-Intellectual* is the variant of Robot in which the player behaves in a way that is very intellectual, and devoid of emotion. These survival game players appear cold, stiff, distant, and impersonal in their interactions with others. They rarely smile, and tacitly avoid any mention of feelings, or their expression. What's more, they intellectualize everything—even emotions. For example, Super-Intellectual players may say, "I believe that there were the anticipated feelings of sadness present when my mother died," rather than saying, "I felt sad when my mother died." These players may also use very sophisticated vocabulary and bring up complicated, highly abstract, technical subjects in conversations which leave others feeling distanced and uncomfortable. An extreme example of a Super-Intellectual game player might be the young person who excels in math and science in high school and is labeled as a nerd by the other students. Not surprisingly, the survival games of Super-Intellectual and That's Illogical are often played by those Rational-types who do not feel competent or comfortable in dealing with social situations or with their emotions.

The Nitpick Variant

When Robot players employ tactics from the game of *Nitpick*, then they can miss the forest for the trees. Their attention to minute details can so preoccupy them that they completely disregard the big picture. And in their drive for perfection, they may end up not completing anything, since whatever they produce is never up to their own standards. Nitpick players are rarely satisfied with their own work. Nothing is ever perfect enough, comprehensive enough, coherent enough. There are always flaws to be corrected, or something to be added, deleted, changed. An example of a Nitpick player is the graduate student who works for five years on a dissertation, but never finishes, because he must say it all before it is complete.

The Superstition Variant

The game of *Superstition* is one in which Robot players may go to extremes to avoid something—like germs. The Superstition player may refuse to touch doorknobs, steering wheels, or other objects with their bare hands. These players may also avoid particular places, situations, people, or things. In addition to, or instead of avoiding things, Superstition players may engage in repetitive rituals—like cleaning, counting, or chanting. They may also exhibit facial tics, or other repetitive body movements. Examples of Superstition are the man who washes his hands one hundred times a day, or the child who spits on each shoulder and then repeats certain phrases to herself before she enters any room.

The Blanking Out Variant

In *Blanking Out*, Robot players experience moments when they can't think of familiar words, names, or numbers. This is most likely to happen when performing—as in taking a test, giving a speech, or reading out loud in front of classmates. Blanking Out players may forget the name of a family member or friend when introducing them to a group. Students may forget the material they know the best when taking a test. In extreme cases of

Blanking Out, players may stutter or stammer. Since Blanking Out players are afraid that they will blank out, they will remind themselves over and over again not to forget anything. This has the same effect as telling themselves: "Don't think of pink elephants!" They end up doing exactly what they have been telling themselves *not* to do.

The Haunted Variant

Haunted is the last variant of the Robot game, where players cannot make certain unpleasant thoughts go away. In its mildest form, Haunted players cannot stop playing a phrase from a song over and over in their heads. At its worse, Haunted players are horrified to find themselves thinking about doing awful things to the people they love the most. And it is because they would never do what they are imagining themselves doing—like murdering a beloved child—that the Haunted player is so completely distracted by the game, and thus able to avoid noticing where he or she has failed or is failing.

The Masquerade Game

Idealists play the game of *Masquerade* when they feel they have not been or cannot continue to be authentic, benevolent, and empathic. The Masquerade player puts on a show that is strange, arresting, and captivating. These individuals present phoney problems that are likely to hide their inauthentic selves from public view. Masquerade players alienate themselves from whatever parts of themselves that are a source of shame. Their dramatic performances are meant to lead the self and others away from discovering what the Idealist is ashamed of doing, or of having done. Hence, the purpose of the Masquerade game is *deception*—of keeping self and others unaware of the Idealist's unethical behavior by acting as if something else is wrong. Paradoxically, the Idealist who most wants to avoid being phoney becomes a complete phoney when playing survival games.

These players experience remarkable changes in their sensory and motor systems—changes for which physicians can find no organic causes. They may appear to lose the functioning of one or more senses, or to see, hear, smell, and feel things that aren't really there. They may demonstrate tics, muscle spasms, or even seizures. Masquerade players can stand silently in a statue-like position for hours, or become paralyzed in any part of the body. These players differ from their Guardian counterparts, in that they do not complain about their physical symptoms. Rather, they display them in such a way that they cannot fail to attract the attention of others. They sometimes report severe lapses in memory, or claim to be someone else entirely. They may say that others are monitoring their thoughts, or trying to destroy them. All of these game tactics are effective ways of keeping others deceived, and thus unlikely to discover that the Idealist has been inauthentic. As a result, Idealists are able to defend themselves from further erosion of self-esteem, self-respect, and self-confidence.

Six Variants of the Masquerade Game

The six variants of the Masquerade game are: *Mind Reader*, *Martyr*, *Grasshopper*, *Statue*, *Forgetful*, and *Twitch*. Idealists may play any of these games and in any combination in their efforts to survive by deceiving others.

The Mind Reader Variant

Idealists are playing the game of *Mind Reader* when they claim to know what others are *really* thinking, feeling, and/or wanting. Mind Reader players frequently project their own thoughts, emotions, and/or desires onto others. They often attribute negative motives to others, claiming that the others are out to get them or even persecuting them. These players may even contend that others are reading their (the Mind Readers') minds and influencing them in negative ways. Once they have decided that others are against them, then Mind Reader players will misinterpret words and actions on the part of others in ways that support their contentions. They take everything as personal—even when another's comment actually has nothing at all to do with them. And no amount of arguing, reasoning, or explaining will convince them that they are wrong in their suspicions. The man who inaccurately accuses his wife of being angry with him because she is quiet is playing the survival game of Mind Reader, as is the woman who wrongly claims that all of her co-workers dislike her and are always talking about her behind her back. At the extreme, a Mind Reader player may claim that the FBI and other important agencies have implanted electrodes in his brain and that they are both monitoring his thoughts and putting evil ideas in his head.

The Martyr Variant

When Masquerade players use the tactics of the *Martyr* game, they sacrifice themselves for a higher cause or principle, or for the needs and wants of another. Martyr players may voluntarily endure suffering or hardship so that they may impress others with their goodness and purity and/or so that they may make others feel guilty for their own badness and impurity. Often these players sacrifice their own identities—their needs and wants—so that they may keep peace in relationships and make certain that others are happy and content. After doing this for a long time, it is not unusual for Martyr players to discover that they have completely lost sight of themselves. While Martyr players do not complain about their suffering, they do manage to make themselves very visible as they endure their extreme hardships. A mild example of the Martyr game is a man who insists on driving a beat-up car and dressing in old clothes so that his wife may have the finest sports car and wear designer clothes. An extreme example of Martyr is the anorexic who starves herself while constantly cooking for and feeding other family members. It is common for Idealists to play the game of Martyr together with the game of Mind Reader.

The Grasshopper Variant

The *Grasshopper* version of the Masquerade game is played by hopping from one topic to another in a conversation. Grasshopper players manage to keep the conversation away from sensitive issues by leaping away from them and landing on more superficial ones. They avoid talking about what really bothers them—what they feel ashamed about—by pretending to be bothered by something else. Any time the subject gets too close to the real problem, they quickly bring up another pseudoproblem to replace it, thus throwing the other offtrack. For example, a girl who feels badly about a fight she had with her friend Sue might suddenly start to complain about the amount of homework she has when her mother asks, "How is Sue?"

The Statue Variant

When Idealists demonstrate the *Statue* variant of Masquerade, they lose any degree of their motor and/or sensory functioning, and in any combination. Statue players may experience partial or full paralysis, blindness, and/or deafness. They may be anaesthetic in any part of their bodies. Some Statue players fall asleep quite suddenly and involuntarily in inappropriate places—while stopped at a traffic light or standing in line at a fast-food restaurant. The physical symptoms associated with the Statue game are paradoxical, in that they cannot be traced to any organic cause, and they do not fit the expected pattern. For example, a Statue player may be able to see everyone and everything except just one person. When that person is present, the Statue player is not able to see him or her. A more mild example of the Statue game is the little girl who is so silent and withdrawn in the classroom that she is almost invisible.

The Forgetful Variant

In the game of *Forgetful*, the Masquerade player completely forgets whatever is unpleasant. Forgetful players can forget specific events from the past or present, in part or in entirety. What's more, they are not aware that there is something they are not able to remember. In extreme cases, Forgetful players completely forget their identity and may even take on a new one. A mild example of the Forgetful game is the woman who temporarily forgets to make an unpleasant phone call that she has promised her husband she will make.

The Twitch Variant

The *Twitch* player demonstrates an unusual increase in motor activity that cannot be traced to an organic cause. Twitch players may exhibit tics of the face or neck, or spasms in any part of the body. In addition, Twitch players may demonstrate occasional verbal outbursts that are an outpouring of all of the negative thoughts and feelings which have been repressed over a period of weeks or months. Once begun, these outbursts cannot be stopped. However, they are not likely to involve any physical damage to persons or property. In the extreme, Twitch players may exhibit violent seizures that cause a loss of consciousness.

Summary

This chapter has outlined the games the different personalities play and their reasons for playing them, according to the Keirseyan Games Model. Table 5 provides a listing of the four games and the twenty-four variants which have been discussed here.

The next chapter presents a practical format for identifying or verifying personalities using observational clues. Then, in part two, chapters four through seven offer guidelines for intervening to stop the various survival games. Part three includes eight cases which provide examples of individuals who are employing survival tactics and the methods used to treat them.

TABLE 5
THE FOUR GAMES AND THEIR VARIANTS

KEIRSEYAN TYPE	Artisan	Guardian	Rational	Idealist
MYERS TYPE	SP	SJ	NT	NF
SURVIVAL GAME	Blackmail	Complain	Robot	Masquerade
VARIANTS	Delinquency	Invalid	That's Illogical	Mind Reader
	Con Artist	Worried	Super-Intellectual	Martyr
	Binge	Doormat	Nitpick	Grasshopper
	Outrage	Poor Me	Superstition	Statue
	Shocking	Depressed	Blanking Out	Forgetful
	Empty	Nag	Haunted	Twitch

Chapter 3

IDENTIFYING
PERSONALITIES

There are two ways of identifying personality types: through pencil and paper tests, like the Myers-Briggs Type Indicator (MBTI) and the Keirsey Temperament Sorter,[*] or through observation. Each of these methods has its pros and cons. While tests are easier to use than observation, they are also prone to a good deal of error. In my experience they misidentify personality types about 25[**] percent of the time in the normal population, and up to 50 percent of the time with people who are playing survival games. This is not because people intentionally falsify their result on these instruments; rather, it is because most of us are not consciously aware of our habit patterns. Since survival game players are especially troubled and confused, they are even more prone to unwittingly giving a false report of their preferences and behavior on tests. Still another shortcoming of the MBTI and the Keirsey Sorter is that the vocabulary they use is too advanced for most children under the age of twelve or thirteen.

---

[*] The MBTI may be ordered through Consulting Psychologists Press in Palo Alto, CA. The Keirsey Temperament Sorter appears in *Please Understand Me* (individual copies may be ordered through Prometheus Nemesis Books in Del Mar, CA).

[**] Guardians are particularly prone to score as Idealists or Rationals, while Artisans often score as any of the other three types.

Because personality test results are wrong so much of the time, they should be taken only as a rough indicator of personality and always followed up with careful, continued observation. Test results may only be taken as valid if they are consistently supported by behavioral data. It is best to treat them as hypotheses, which are to be supported or rejected on the basis of additional information about the person's habits. In other words, though a test says that a woman is a Rational (NT), it is important to watch her to see if she does, indeed, behave the way Rational-types typically do. If not, then chances are the test results are wrong.

Due to their inherent drawbacks, I rarely use personality tests in my clinical practice, relying instead on observation to identify personalities; this is not difficult when one knows what clues to look for in adults and children. It is fine to guess what personality type someone is, as long as one continues to watch and listen to find out whether or not the guess is on target. For example, after I speculate that Jeff is an Artisan (SP), then I observe him to see if his behavior patterns continue to match up with those of other Artisans. If so, then the label is a useful one for understanding Jeff and predicting his actions. If not, then I need to revise my hypothesis.

Using Observational Clues to Identify or Verify Personalities

This chapter provides basic guidelines for using observational clues to identify or verify personality types. The case examples in Part Three provide examples of specific clues I have used to identify the personality types of adults, adolescents, and children who are playing survival games.

Please note that the questions listed here are intended for practitioners to ask *themselves*. It is not recommended that therapists pose these questions directly to clients, because most clients are likely to provide inaccurate answers. Instead, clinicians are advised to gather information during the interview that may be used as evidence of the client's preferences.

Abstract Versus Concrete

The first question to consider in identifying someone's personality is:

Does this person seem to be more *abstract* or more *concrete* in his or her orientation towards the world?

Artisans and Guardians are concrete (also called Sensing-types, or S's), while Rationals and Idealists are abstract (also called Intuitive-types, or "N's"). How does this translate into behavior? Concrete-types are more interested in facts, while abstract-types prefer theory. Concrete-types live in the real world—focused on what can be felt, seen, heard, tasted, or touched. Abstract-types prefer to dwell in the world of ideas, which lies beyond the five senses. While concrete people have their feet solidly on the ground, abstract ones have their heads way up in the clouds.

Since there are many more concrete people than abstract ones (at least three to one), it is useful to assume that clients are concrete, unless there is ample evidence that they prefer abstractions. What are some of the clues that indicate an abstract orientation? Abstract people often like to talk at length about complicated theoretical subjects, which may range from philosophy, the social sciences, and literature, to quantum physics. While Idealists are most interested in theories about people, Rationals usually prefer theories about science and technology. Abstract types want to know *why* people or things are the way they are. They are energized by discussions about what is possible, and become bored or tired with extended conversations about mundane details. They see lots of grey areas when examining any subject, as opposed to viewing things in black and white terms. Abstract people—both adults and children—are usually avid readers, and their choice of reading may include (but is not limited to) science fiction, fantasy, historical novels, biographies, philosophy, science, metaphysics, psychology, and anthropology.

And what about concrete people? They are likely to center their discussions on such matters as food, clothing, shelter, recreation, transportation, and business. Concrete-types are primarily interested in knowing *what*, concentrating most of their attention on practical matters. Extended conversations about theory are often boring and even tiring to them. These people are prone to seeing things more in black-and-white terms. As children and adults, they may not like to read at all, or they may choose high suspense spy or horror novels, romance novels, or factual books about nature, geography, geology, health, or history.

Note that since concrete-types and abstract-types read some of the same books and discuss some of the same topics, it is important to ascertain where people focus the *majority* of their attention.

Cooperative Versus Pragmatic

After considering whether a client is abstract or concrete, the next question to ask is:

> **Does this person seem to be more *cooperative* or more *pragmatic* in his or her approach to doing things?**

While Guardians and Idealists are cooperative-types, Artisans and Rationals are pragmatic (Keirsey, 1987). Those with cooperative personalities are likely to ask, "Is it right?" before taking any action, while those who are pragmatic are inclined to consider, "Is it useful?" Cooperative-types are primarily concerned with whether or not an action is permissible by law or in accordance with ethical standards. In contrast, the pragmatic-types are more interested in whether or not an action is going to enable them to meet their immediate or distant objectives.

Sorting Through the Four Groups

On the basis of answers to the above questions, one can use the following formula to make a tentative placement in one of the four personality groups.

concrete	+	pragmatic	= Artisan
concrete	+	cooperative	= Guardian
abstract	+	pragmatic	= Rational
abstract	+	cooperative	= Idealist

Once a tentative label has been assigned, it is important to recall the basic wants and needs* associated with that particular personality type. For example, if the person appears to be concrete and cooperative, and therefore, a Guardian, one may recall that the Guardian needs *most of all* to be responsible, dutiful, and to belong. Though a Guardian may also need and want to be free (like the Artisan), competent (like the Rational), and authentic (like the Idealist), the desire to be responsible, dutiful and to belong takes precedence over these other concerns. The following questions are useful for putting one's initial guess to the test:

> **Judging by this person's *actions*, what does this person seem to value *most*?**
>
> **Based upon this person's behavior, does he or she seem to have primary values that match those of the hypothesized personality type?**

If the answer to the second question is *no*, then it is best to ask:

> **Which personality type has values that are similar to this person's primary values?**

---
* See table 2 in chapter one.

It can be misleading to ask people to state their values. People often *say* they value one thing, but they consistently make choices that point to a completely different priority. A more accurate way to determine a person's primary values is to find out what that person likes to do, and what, in particular, he or she likes about doing it. People reveal what is most important to them through the choices that they make. How do they choose to spend their time? What kind of work do they do, and what, if anything, do they like about it? What do they do for fun? What is their chosen lifestyle? What, if anything, do they like to read? What do they like to talk about? What movies do they most enjoy? What, if anything, do they study? What subjects are their favorites in school?

Now, this is not to claim that all of us always make choices that are in alignment with our primary values. In fact, it is when our most basic needs and wants are *not* being met that we are most likely to turn to survival game playing. Yet it is still possible to look at the overall pattern of a person's life choices in order to identify his or her most cherished values. Most clients are able to say what they enjoy doing, even if they aren't presently doing it. For example, many of my Artisan clients are playing survival games because they feel too tied up, bound, and obligated. Their need to be free to follow their impulses is being thwarted. Sometimes they are in boring, routine jobs. Clearly, they have made some career choices that are not fulfilling their primary needs. Yet when I ask them the kinds of things that they do and have done that they really enjoy, they describe exciting, hands-on, action-oriented activities, often involving risk. In other words, if you find out what people like to *do*, it is not hard to figure out what matters most to them.

Still another means of verifying a person's placement in one of the four temperament groups is by asking:

How does this person deal with rules?

Typically, Guardian-types are inclined to *follow* rules, without questioning them. What's more, they expect others to do the same. While Idealists try to conform to the rules, they are not opposed to *bending* rules in order to help a particular group or individual. Rational-types *question* all rules, and they may disregard those rules that seem foolish or illogical. Lastly, Artisans may break rules that get in the way of meeting their immediate goals. As one Artisan explained, "I'd rather ask for forgiveness than ask for permission!"

Directive Versus Informant for the Concrete-Types

Once clients have been placed in one of the four basic categories, then it is possible to determine which of the four subtypes they belong to. Here the questions posed are different, depending upon whether the client is a concrete-type or an abstract-type. In the case of Artisans and Guardians, key questions are:

Is this person more of a *director* or more of an *informant*?

Is this person more *impersonal* or *personal*?

According to Keirsey (1987), for Artisans and Guardians, Thinking-types (T's) are directors, while Feeling-types (F's) are informants. The director-types are comfortable in giving others directives—that is, in telling others what to do. As a matter of fact, they are likely to give directives even when someone just asks them for information. In contrast, the informant-types are more likely to offer information than directives, though the information they offer may be a subtle way of expressing what they really want another to do. For example, if a wife mentions to her husband that she's not sure where they should go to dinner, and he is a director, then he will probably say, "Let's go to Mario's Pizza House." If he is an informant, he is more likely to offer, "Well, we haven't been to Mario's Pizza House for quite some time, and they have good food. On the other hand, we could go back to The Chili Pepper again."

Artisans and Guardians who are Thinking-types* are not only more directive—they are also more impersonal and objective in the way they deal with people and events. Conversely, the Artisans and Guardians who are Feeling-types tend to be more personal and subjective in their involvement with people and situations.

Directive Versus Informant for the Abstract-Types

For Rationals and Idealists, there are three questions which may be asked in order to identify client preferences for Judging (J) or Perception (P):

Is this person more of a *director* or more of an *informant*?

Is this person more *unifocused* or *multifocused*?

Does this person prefer to be more *structured* or *unstructured*?

While the directors are Judging-types (J's), informants are Perceptive-types (P's). In addition, Judging-types often seem to be more unifocused—that is, focused in one direction at a time, while Perceptive types frequently appear to be more multi-focused—that is, focused in more than one direction at a time. It is the NTJ and NFJ who prefer to structure their time and activities, while the NTP and NFP prefer to leave things more loose, flexible, and open.

---

* It is a dangerous mistake to assume that the Thinking-types do not feel, and conversely, that the Feeling-types do not think!

Introverts Versus Extraverts

The last thing to decide for both abstract and concrete-types, is whether someone is an Introvert or an Extravert. The best way to figure this out is to note:

Does this person seem *uncomfortable* or *at ease* in talking with strangers?

Does this person seem to be energized through *interacting with others*, or through *spending time alone*?

Introverts (I's) are people who need time alone in order to charge up their batteries, while Extraverts (E's) get their batteries charged by interaction with others. Introverts are often uncomfortable talking to people they don't know, whereas Extraverts are fairly at ease interacting with strangers. Introverts are more private, and harder to get to know; Extraverts are more open, and easier to get to know.

Don't Use Survival Games For Identifying Personalities

One final word of caution: It is unwise to identify someone's personality according to the survival game the person is playing. Some survival games look similar, but different personalities play them for different reasons. Rather than being misled by using that information as a way of labeling someone's type, it is far better to follow the procedure outlined above.

PART II

TREATING THE TYPES

Introduction

People resort to survival games when they are unable to meet their essential needs. Most game players, however, are not consciously aware that they have primary wants that are not being fulfilled. What's more, they usually see no connection between their unsatisfied desires and the survival games they are playing. Yet remarkably, when clients make changes that enable them to get their basic needs met in positive ways, they often stop employing game tactics.

One of the primary tasks in stopping survival game playing is to assist players in finding successful ways of gratifying their fundamental needs. Since clients often can't say what they value most, it can be helpful to use knowledge of personality types to spotlight those essential hungers that must be filled in order for clients to feel okay about themselves.

Besides identifying alterations in behavior and lifestyle that might benefit a given client, knowledge of personality also provides a means of motivating the client to make desired changes. Each personality responds favorably to different key words, and also to different reasons for doing things. Certain metaphors and reframes are more likely to capture each of the types. And particular intervention strategies are associated with stopping each of the games. By using the Keirseyan model, clinicians can individualize their approach to clients and help them find the incentive to change.

The four chapters in this section offers some basic guidelines for treating the different temperaments. That means that methods for stopping survival game playing are not limited to those listed here. These are just suggestions, and certainly not the only way to approach treating the types. Hopefully these guidelines will serve as building blocks for devising creative therapeutic strategies.

Many of the methods mentioned in these chapters, such as Gestalt, role playing, or guided visualization, can be effective with any of the four personalities. Some of these methods are mentioned in more than one chapter, with an emphasis upon how they may be used with each particular type.

It is one thing to look at individual types, and still another to see an individual's behavior in the context of the family system. The Keirseyan model is particularly useful for getting a clear picture of relationship dynamics. While these chapters focus on each of the personalities separately, the eight cases in part three present analyses of how the types interact with each other. These detailed case descriptions are meant to show how one may integrate this information when working with couples or families made up of various personality types. They are also meant to show what observational clues may be used to identify client personalities.

Chapters four through seven also provide case examples, but they are very brief, and used only to illustrate key points. In these cases, for the sake of brevity, I label the clients' personalities, without offering the observational evidence that I used to derive those labels.

Chapter 4

STOPPING THE BLACKMAIL GAME

Blackmail players are probably the most challenging clients of all for the mental health professional. They often show up at the therapist's office kicking and screaming, having been dragged there by a parent or spouse who says, "Fix this person!" The Blackmail player will typically assure the clinician that he or she is just fine and needs no fixing at all. The games these players play can be frightening, even death defying, and impossible to ignore. The pressure is certainly on for the therapist to do something to create change, and to do it right away.

But should clinicians try to use traditional, introspective, or so-called nondirective psychotherapy with the Blackmail player, they are likely to meet with boredom, restlessness, or even stubborn resistance. Artisans are not prone to sitting around for long periods analyzing their every thought, feeling, and motive. These are action-oriented people who thrive on living in the moment and who focus their attention on whatever is captured by their immediate senses.

Where Artisans seek counseling for themselves because they truly want help, the going is much easier for the clinician. But whether self-referred or other-referred, Artisans respond best to therapy that is action-oriented, spontaneous, and exciting. Most beneficial are therapeutic exercises that capture their attention in the moment—Gestalt methods, role playing, guided visualizations rich in sensuous imagery, games, sandplay, or art therapy are all options that can be explored with this type.

Matching the Blackmailer's Attitude

Artisans are a little suspicious by nature, particularly of anyone who just wants to "help." Blackmail players are fully capable of manipulating their therapists, utilizing this desire to help to increase the Blackmail player's advantage. A bleeding heart is fair game to this type. They may say just what the therapist wants to hear in a most convincing fashion, or attempt to engage the therapist in a power struggle—challenging the clinician's ability to be effective with an attitude of "I don't care."

So how does the psychotherapist manage to be successful in working with the more resistant SPs? By being just as cynical as they are. Since Blackmail players may manipulate and control by "not caring" and by using the caring of others as bait with which to hook them, it can be very powerful when the therapist presents an attitude of *caring less than the Artisan does*. That means the clinician avoids giving the impression that it is important that the client change, get better, or do good things for himself or herself. It also means that the therapist is not attached to any particular choices that the client must make. In fact, the therapist might choose to point out the advantages of continuing to get into trouble, drink, or whatever.[*]

It is important to recognize that while clinicians may convey an attitude of detachment to the Blackmailer, they should still assure that there are negative consequences which are consistently enforced. Hence, the boy who violates curfew is *not* told that he should or must get home on time, though it is made very clear that every time he is one minute late, he loses the opportunity to go out on the next night. Whether or not he arrives home

---

[*] It is easy to see why Artisans make some of the best substance abuse counselors. They are able to recognize the Blackmailer's tactics and skillfully avoid getting hooked.

before curfew is entirely his choice: the counselor does not try to persuade him to behave in a particular way. Consequence methods are described in detail later in this chapter.

Challenging the Blackmail Player

Artisans can hardly stop themselves from responding to a challenge. Their nature is competitive, and they thoroughly enjoy proving that someone else was wrong in calling the shots. They love to win and to impress others with their unusual prowess. And they hate to be seen as losers. Clinicians can make use of this quality by challenging Artisan clients so that they can prove the therapist or others wrong by getting better. This challenge can be overt, as in "I don't think you have what it takes to do that,"* or a more subtle implication that others see the Blackmail player as a weakling or fool.

Artisans love risks, thrills, and exciting adventures. These are the mountain climbers, the hanggliders, the explorers, and the daredevils. Sometimes, just telling them that something is very difficult or nearly impossible for the average person to do is enough to make them want to do it. They love to venture into territories where others have tried and failed—for that makes their accomplishments all the more impressive.

Because Blackmail players love a challenge, it is best to be cautious about offering assurances to them that therapy is, indeed, going to be helpful. This kind of message can be an invitation for Blackmail players to prove you wrong. It is a challenge to defeat your attempts at helping them. Better to take the attitude, "I can't say for sure if this will help you. There are no guarantees. It has helped many others like you, but then again, everybody's different. It could end up being a complete waste of your time and money. It's definitely a risk." Unlike the other types, Artisans are drawn to risks, rather than frightened by them.

---

* Here, knowing the client's personality type is very important. Such a message to a Guardian or an Idealist is more likely to be taken to heart, and to discourage the client rather than to motivate him or her to change.

*Cancellation** metaphors* are a very effective way of challenging Blackmail players to change. These metaphors are used to present clients with a negative meta-image of themselves—that is, an unflattering and unacceptable view of themselves as they are being seen by others. When using cancellation metaphors, it is essential that therapists refrain from criticizing or judging the client's behavior. Instead, it is best to commend clients for doing the best they can under difficult circumstances. Rather than encouraging clients to change, therapists can challenge clients by discouraging change whenever possible, while making certain to point out all of the ways that the Blackmailers' opponents profit from their actions. The following case is an example of how I used a cancellation metaphor to challenge a client to stop her game of Outrage.

> A beautiful twenty-seven-year-old woman (an ESFP) came to me because she was stuck in an abusive relationship and didn't know what to do. She complained that her boyfriend of three years (another SP) monitored her every action and insisted that she give him an account of how she spent every moment of her time. He would frequently have fits of jealously, during which he would call her a "whore" and a "phoney." She would respond by getting furious, eventually hitting him with her fists. He would slug back as the aggression escalated. Thus, each was playing the dangerous game of Outrage with the other. The man refused to seek help either alone or as a couple, so she had come to therapy by herself as a last resort.

> I had my client do some Gestalt work, putting her boyfriend in the empty chair. After a very emotional dialogue in which she played both herself and the boyfriend, I told her that it looked like she was in a prison camp with no fences, and that she had been successfully brainwashed by her boyfriend, the prison guard. What's more, it appeared as if he felt particularly powerful when she lost control. He knew just what buttons to push to get the desired effect. I emphasized the difficulty that most people have in escaping from a prison camp, and told her

---

* Dr. Keirsey gave cancellation metaphors their label, referring to the way in which they cancel a client's ability to continue to play his or her game.

that many in her shoes wouldn't have the courage to simply take charge of their lives and regain their sense of self-control.

The woman became very angry as I spoke, and told me that she was unwilling to live in a prison camp anymore. It especially bothered her that she had allowed her boyfriend to have such control over her and her life. She was determined to change things. I reminded her that her boyfriend would be very distressed if she left his prison camp. After all, it made him feel powerful to have her there. Finally, I cautioned her to go slow and to be patient with herself. I emphasized that this problem had been with her a long time, and that if she was like most people, she would probably need to suffer for quite a while more before she would be ready to really change things. She was arguing with me on this point when the session ended.

Two weeks later, the woman arrived for her second session with a big smile on her face. She gleefully reported that she had left the prison camp, in spite of what I had told her during the last session. She had informed her boyfriend that she would no longer give him a complete report on her whereabouts. She refused to talk to him on the phone when he began to question her incessantly, and eventually his excessive questioning had stopped. She also decided that if he became verbally abusive, she would leave the scene, rather than engage in a fight with him. After acting on this several times, they had had no further episodes. I reacted with complete surprise, and told her how genuinely impressed I was with the way she had changed so quickly and dramatically. She responded with, "Well, I just decided that it was what I had to do, regardless of what you thought. I want to thank you for your help, although I don't really know what you did."

The second session was our final one. Six months later, she reported in a telephone interview that all was going well.

The metaphor of being brainwashed in a prison camp was used to reframe the client's present situation in a way that would be intolerable for an SP: Her attacks on her boyfriend were suddenly evidence that he was completely controlling her, rather than the other way around. That metaphor also provided a means of challenging her to leave the camp and take charge of her own life. I expressed some doubt that she would do this rapidly, but was careful not to say that she couldn't or that it wasn't possible. Mostly, I tried to provoke her to get angry in order to fuel her motivation to change. The sudden and dramatic changes she exhibited are characteristic responses to cancellation metaphors. Cancellation metaphors are useful for injecting all types of clients with an urgency to change in positive ways.

Fulfilling the Artisan's Basic Needs

As mentioned in chapter two, Artisans, or SPs, play Blackmail when they do not feel free to follow their impulses and to make an impression on others. Often they have lost confidence in themselves, and feel that they are bad or worthless. Hence, when clients are playing Blackmail, it is important to find or create new ways for them to meet their needs so that they may have more freedom, experience more spontaneous action and excitement, and/or make a powerful impact on others.

Often, therapists must arrange for parents and spouses to give Artisans more space, so that Artisans can get their need for freedom met. The following case is an example of this.

> An American couple living in Europe came to me for therapy because the man, Joe, had been feeling a strange, frightening, and inexplicable sense of emptiness for months. This feeling had interfered with their plans to marry, as well as with his effectiveness on the job. His girlfriend, Becky, was not only very concerned about him, but also deeply hurt and confused about what to do. In interviewing them, I ascertained that Joe was an Artisan (ISTP) who had begun to play the Empty variant of the Blackmail game shortly after Becky, a Guardian-type personality, had left her family and her much-loved job in the U.S. in order to come and live with him in his tiny European apartment. Since her arrival, Becky—normally a very self-sufficient, independent, and successful person—had depended upon him to meet almost all of her economic, emotional, social, and intellectual needs. After all, she was unemployed and virtually all alone in a foreign country

where she didn't speak the language. It was clear to me that Joe was overly bound, obligated, responsible, and tied up in this arrangement. It did not help that he was an Introvert who needed lots of alone time to charge up his batteries, while Becky, the Extravert, needed plenty of social interaction. And as Joe felt worse, Becky felt increasingly insecure, and even more needy.

The couple assured me that their five-year relationship had been wonderful, fulfilling, and exciting when they lived in the U.S. They shared many interests, and professed a deep love for each other. Neither could understand why Joe was feeling so awful, and what could possibly be done to help him. In private, Joe confessed that he felt guilty that Becky had given up a great job and the chance to see her family, in order to be with him. He felt pressured to make up to her for the sacrifices she had made on his behalf.

My interventions were aimed at getting Joe more freedom and breathing room, while helping Becky find new ways to meet her needs for security and belonging. I wanted to relieve Joe's feeling of complete responsibility for Becky's happiness. At my recommendation, Becky made some new friends, began to get out and do things with other people, and even took some trips on her own. Joe also spent more time alone, and did some traveling by himself. Within a month, Joe reported that his uncomfortable and alarming feeling of emptiness had completely dissipated. Within four months, Becky and Joe were married—with the commitment that they would allow each other lots of space in the relationship. Years later, they reported that their marriage was still thriving.

It is significant that neither Joe nor Becky were aware that Joe's fundamental needs were not being met. Yet, once changes were made that enabled him to feel and be more free and less burdened, then Joe stopped playing the game of Empty. Note also that just making Joe aware of the reasons why he was feeling empty would not have been enough to make those feelings go away. Insight is not enough to stop the game. Only a change in behavior will accomplish that.

Certainly, it was easier to create the necessary changes in this relationship because Becky was such a mature and self-confident person. A Guardian who lacked Becky's confidence would have found it very difficult to give Joe more space at a time when she was feeling insecure. Such a person might have even started playing the Complain game, in order to deal with her feelings of abandonment.

One way to help Blackmail players to get their fundamental needs met is to give them the assignment to go out and do something fun and exciting. The assignment may be vague, or more specific—identifying the activity, the amount of time spent doing it, or the day (or days) of the week that it is to be done. If the activity is specified, it should be something that the client believes he or she would like to do, or has enjoyed doing in the past. Where family members can enjoy playing together, all the better. It can be anything—hiking, fishing, biking, scuba diving, motorcycle riding, skiing, ice skating, flying a kite, or horseback riding are just a few examples. A good exercise to use with Artisan clients is to have them make a list of fifty things they love to do, and then to star all of the activities they would like to do in the next year. This can serve to make them aware of the ways in which they are *not* making the time to do the things they most enjoy.

It is also useful to get SP clients who are playing Blackmail to do or learn to do something creative. This can sometimes serve as an exciting challenge for the Artisan, as well as a positive way to make an impression on others. The creative endeavor may be dancing, photography, painting, woodworking, sculpting, graphic arts, acting, composing, choreographing, writing, gardening, playing an instrument, singing, sewing, doing handicrafts, or rebuilding an engine. It may also involve participation in a competitive sport like running, football, tennis, gymnastics, golf, or swimming.

The work arena is one more place in which it is possible to assist Blackmail players to better meet their needs. Sometimes clients are working at jobs that are more satisfying for the Guardian personality—such as routine-oriented desk jobs in large bureaucracies. Often these SPs will conclude there is something wrong *with* them, instead of recognizing that it is the job that is wrong *for* them. In cases of career mismatch, it is important to assist SP clients in finding work that is better suited to their action-oriented, spontaneous nature.

To help Artisans meet their need to be impressive, it is best to ask far less of them than what they are willing or able to deliver. As Artisans get excited about making changes, it is typical for them to make inflated promises to themselves or others that are well meaning, but highly unrealistic or even downright impossible. Examples are: "I'll never eat candy, cookies, or cake again," or, "I'll be on time for all of my classes from now on," or, "I'll raise all my grades from Fs to As next quarter." These statements are ways that Artisans unconsciously set themselves up to fail.

Counselors can redirect SPs' motivation to change in ways that set these clients up to succeed, by asking them to commit to taking tiny steps in the direction of change (see Glasser, 1965). For example, a student who wants to change his pattern of always being late for his first period class might be asked if he would be willing to be on time for just one day in the forthcoming week. Nothing is said about what he is or is not to do on the other four days. Often this arrangement enables the client to come back with impressive results to report—"I was on time for three days, which is even more than I said I would be."

In addition to helping Artisans meet their basic needs, it is wise to interdict the behavior of significant others who are trying to get the Blackmail player to reform or conform, since these well-meaning attempts at stopping the game usually have the opposite effect of keeping it going. Most of the time it is also imperative to attach some unpleasant consequence to the Blackmailer's use of game tactics. It may also be desirable to arrange for a positive consequence to follow the Artisan's demonstration of more productive behavior.

Interdicting the Behavior of Significant Others

Frequently, where the game of Blackmail is being played, parents, teachers, or spouses are at their wit's end to stop it. Often they have resorted to excessive nagging, punishing, and checking up on the Blackmailer. In addition, they are usually giving numerous *commercials*.* These are sell jobs on good behavior, like "This should teach you your lesson," or, "You had better change your attitude." All of these attempts at getting Artisans to stop their games actually have the effect of making them *worse* instead of *better*. Rather than solving problems, these attempted solutions end up maintaining them (see Watzlawick, Weakland, and Fisch, 1974).

A good example of this is the Artisan-Guardian couple in which the Guardian behaves like a critical, demanding parent, and the Artisan plays the role of a rebellious child. The Guardian's response to the Blackmail game is to criticize and nag the Artisan about being so irresponsible or bad, while the Artisan reacts by behaving even more irresponsibly or badly. In these relationships (which are quite common) it is essential to block the Guardian's critical parenting in order to stop the Blackmail game.

The best way to get parents, teachers, or spouses to stop doing commercializing or critical parenting is to give them something else to do instead. And one of the best things to get them to do instead is to set limits with the Artisan, and to enforce these limits by taking consistent, nonpunitive action when the limits have been overstepped. This method, called *deprivation* by Dr. Keirsey, and *logical consequences* by those in the Adlerian school (Dreikurs and Soltz, 1964; Nelsen, 1981), is a very effective way of stopping the Blackmail game. In Keirsey's definition, it is the removal of an abused privilege for a specified period of time, and nothing more. The use of deprivation starts with the proclamation, "From now on, when you do X, then Y will happen." For example, from now on, when you leave your bicycle

---

* Dr. Keirsey is credited with introducing this concept and calling these messages "commercials."

on the driveway, you lose the privilege of riding it for the next day. Or, from now on, when you get home late, you lose the privilege of going out on the next weekend night. A wife might tell her husband that from now on, when he is not home on time for them to leave for a social engagement, she will go without him. Very often, it is possible to stop Artisan children from playing survival games just by isolating them for very short periods of time—three to twenty minutes, depending upon the age of the child. After all, having an audience—especially an adult audience—can be the greatest payoff of all for these little performers.

After specifying a consequence, it is essential that it is employed every time the misbehavior occurs, without variation, without emotion, and without commercials. Deprivation works best when it happens like gravity.[*] Gravity is always the same. It gives no warnings, no explanations, and makes no exceptions. Gravity is not emotional or out to hurt anyone.

Blackmail players are natural gamblers who enjoy testing limits of any kind. If they know they get one warning, they will always test to see if they can get two warnings, instead. If they know they can get away with using a game tactic once in a while without any consequence, they will try to do so time after time. If they get the impression that someone is out to punish or hurt them, they will become determined to punish or hurt that person back. If they see that their game tactics have the effect of getting a significant other to blow his or her stack, they will continue the game for its powerful effect. And if they are being given commercials to sell them on behaving, they will become more determined than ever *not* to behave.

Sometimes parents of Artisan children will claim that they have tried the method of deprivation, and that it does not work with their children. Typically, this is because they have used the method improperly. If the use of deprivation is inconsistent, punitive, or accompanied by commercials, then it absolutely will not work with Artisan children. For example, one couple complained that using deprivation with their thirteen-year-old

---

[*] I first heard this analogy from Dr. Raymond Choiniere.

ESTP son was only making things worse in their family. It seems that the son was having terrible tantrums in which he would call his parents every name in the book. With further questioning I learned that the father, an ESTJ, was constantly blowing up at his son, yelling obscenities at him, and punching holes into walls and doors with his fists. After his explosions, the father would apologize to his son and buy him expensive gifts. It was clear that the father needed to learn some self-control before he could expect his son to do the same.

Still another mistake that some parents make is thinking that they can use deprivation (or any other methods, for that matter) to control what their children *think, feel,* and *want,* as well as what they *do.* These efforts are destined to be disastrous with SP children, who will fight to the end to maintain their autonomy. It is essential for parents to realize that while they cannot and should not try to regulate their children's thoughts, feelings, and desires, it is their responsibility to regulate their children's *behavior.* And that is the purpose of the deprivation method— stopping inappropriate *behavior.*

What follows is an example of the use of deprivation.

> Mr. and Mrs. Ellis brought their fifth-grader, Julie, to me because of her morning dawdling. Julie was an honor student and one of the most popular leaders of her class. However, both of her parents complained that although they reminded her many times each morning to wake up, get out of bed, get dressed, eat breakfast, make her bed, and brush her teeth, Julie was never ready to leave on time. As a result, Mrs. Ellis was usually late in transporting Julie, her younger sister, and several neighbor children to school. Julie's parents had tried bribing, coaxing, begging, pleading, screaming, threatening, and spanking, but Julie's dawdling had only gotten worse.

> At my recommendation, Mr. and Mrs. Ellis bought an alarm clock for Julie and informed her that they would no longer be reminding her to wake up, dress, eat, make her bed, brush her teeth, or anything else. They told her that she was probably tired of having them "bug" her about these things, and so they were going to leave her alone in the morning. Furthermore, they informed Julie that she

was to be ready to go at 8:00 a.m., and that if at 8:00 she wasn't dressed, her bed wasn't made, she hadn't eaten, or her teeth weren't brushed, that unfortunately, they would just have to leave without her so that the other children wouldn't be late. She could either stay home for the day, or find her own way to school (a fifteen minute walk). Mr. and Mrs. Ellis emphasized that Julie had a choice—to have a ride to school by being ready on time, or not. The first morning, Julie got up and sat in the middle of the living room in her pajamas until 8:00 a.m.. She sat directly in the line of traffic, so that her parents had to practically step on her in order to move from one room into the next. At one point she even asked her mother, "Aren't you going to remind me to get dressed and brush my teeth? It's getting awfully late!" Wisely, Mrs. Ellis just went about her business, without responding.

When Mrs. Ellis gathered the other children to leave, Julie grabbed her mother's legs, and yelled, "You can't leave me! I'll be late for school!" Mrs. Ellis responded calmly, "I'm sorry, but you're not ready to go, and if we waited for you, the other children would be late for school." Julie watched her mother and the other children leave, and then dashed into her bedroom, got dressed, and ran the entire way to school, getting there just in time for the bell. The next morning and for the next week, Julie was sitting at the door and ready to go at 7:55. She did go back to her old ways one more time, but when her mother left again without her, her morning dawdling stopped.

When using the method of deprivation with Artisan clients, it is best to *prescribe that they test the limits*. It is prudent to tell Blackmail players in the presence of their significant others that they must be sure and overstep the limits, so that their parents, teachers, or mates have the chance to practice imposing the consequences. For example, at the end of the first session with Julie and her parents, I had instructed Julie to be sure to be very late in getting ready the next morning, so that her parents would get to practice leaving without her. Julie is like most children, in that she would rather be in school than at home. Many parents are surprised to learn that even children who are performing poorly in school prefer to be there, rather than to stay home every day.* As is evident above, the deprivation method removes the payoff for misbehavior—in Julie's case, that was nonstop attention all morning long and the chance to engage her parents in a power struggle.

All children need encouragement. Artisan children who are playing survival games need it desperately. It is essential to accompany the use of deprivation with methods for encouraging the child who is playing Blackmail. When children are encouraged, then they are given courage—their self-confidence and self-esteem is lifted. How is this done? By focusing on the child's *assets* and *strengths*, rather than the child's *liabilities* and *weaknesses*. This means that the adult notices and comments on what the child does *right*, and not on what the child does *wrong* (see Faber and Mazlisch, 1980). And it means that the parent acknowledges the child's tiniest steps towards improvement. For example, if Joey used to miss fifteen out of twenty arithmetic problems, and now he misses only ten out of twenty, the adult focuses on the fact that Joey has made a big improvement—he has gone from getting five problems right to getting ten problems right.

Doing the Unexpected

In some cases, it is better to have significant others respond to the Blackmail game by doing the unexpected. This method requires that parents, teachers, or spouses do something to break their old communication patterns with the Blackmail player, without commenting on their new course of action. This not only stops the commercializing, nagging, and punishing—it also

---

* The method of Systematic Exlusion, developed by Dr. Keirsey, is based upon this premise. With this method, those children who exhibit chronic misbehavior are sent home from school upon the first infraction. Within a few weeks, they are behaving appropriately, in order to maintain the privilege of staying in school all day long. See the article by David Keirsey, *Abuse It—Lose It: A Drug-Free Method of Teaching Self Control to "Hyperactive" Children,* (Del Mar, CA: Prometheus Nemesis Book Company, 1991).

circumvents a power struggle and throws the Blackmail player off.

One unexpected action that significant others may take is to leave the field, without saying that they are leaving or where they are going. Though it is sometimes difficult to convince significant others to take this action, it can be a powerful way of disrupting the Blackmailer's game. After all, a player needs an opponent in order to play the game. In *Children: the Challenge*, Dreikurs (1964) recommends that parents lock themselves in the bathroom without comment, if that is the only place they can go to isolate themselves from their misbehaving children. Other therapists advise parents to leave home for the weekend, without telling their teenagers that they are leaving or where they are going.

A very simple unexpected action that parents and teachers may employ with young children is to take notes on the child's misbehavior rather than saying or doing anything to get the child to change. The writing gives the parent something to do on the spot instead of commercializing or punishing. Without the usual reactions on the part of the adult, the child will usually abandon the game.

Another surprising way for parents to respond to the Blackmailer's tactics is to pay the child and to say "thank you." This has been a particularly effective intervention with children and adolescents who control their parents by throwing abusive tantrums. In such cases, I tell the parents in the presence of the offender that their child is offering them a well-rehearsed and finely tuned performance, and that the child is deserving of being paid for such good entertainment. I explain that since the cost of going out to a good movie is at least five dollars, each parent is to hand the Outrage player a five dollar bill and to say "thank you," whenever he or she witnesses one of the young person's outbursts. This usually puts an end to the tantrums within several days.

One highly creative Idealist mom discovered that doing the unexpected was the key to getting her eighth grade Artisan son to keep his room neat. Having tried reminding, cajoling, nagging, pleading, and threatening—all with limited results—she decided to take a completely different approach with him. After announcing that his room and its condition were his business from now on, she managed to dirty his room almost every time she visited it. Although this was deliberate on her part, she pretended not to notice what she was doing. Her first act was to drop her almost empty soda can on the floor of his bedroom while talking with him, and to leave it there with soda leaking out onto his floor. Another time she dumped his clean laundry on the bed and "missed," apologizing, and yet not cleaning up the mess she had made. On other occasions she would leave a dirty bowl or cup on his nightstand. Much to her surprise, within a week his room looked better than it ever had. What's more, he asked *her* to stop messing it up. She complied, but wisely didn't go back to her old ways of taking responsibility for its condition.

Beneficiary Consequence Methods

The beneficiary consequence methods arrange that someone else benefits from the Blackmailer's game tactics. These turn the tables on the Blackmail player, who is out to *excite* the self and *punish* others; suddenly, his or her game tactics *help* others, instead. This effectively renders the Blackmailer's game useless.

With the beneficiary method of *restitution*, game players are given the option of doing something good in order to make up for something bad that they have done. The good deed should be done voluntarily, though the game player may be asked to choose between it and an alternative consequence. For example, a high school boy who plays the Delinquency game may be given the choice of either doing yard work for some of the older residents of the town, or serving several week's detention after school.

The method of restitution has many positive effects. Not only does it enable Blackmail players to make a positive impression on others—it also helps to wipe the slate clean of past wrongdoings. Often the spouse or parents of Blackmail players are more ready, willing, or able to stop dredging up the past once restitution has been made for the misdeeds. For example, one Guardian wife was constantly reminding her Artisan husband of the time three years ago when he lied to her about having lunch with his ex-girlfriend. Whenever she brought up that subject, his response was to get angry and then to do other things that bothered her— like refusing to pick up after himself around the house. I asked the wife what her husband could do to make up to her for the anguish that he had caused her three years before. She indicated that he could buy her a very expensive watch she had wanted for a long time. Arrangements were made that the husband would give his wife the watch, and that in exchange, she would no longer be able to mention the time when he lied to her about his lunch date with his ex-girlfriend. Hence, restitution gave the couple a fresh start.

The *designated receiver* * method is another powerful tool for stopping the Blackmail game. Here something that the Blackmail player values is held in escrow; it may be a large sum of money, or an item such as a car, computer, or stereo system. The player signs a contract that this item is to be given to a parent or spouse for that person to do with as he or she pleases, should the Blackmail player engage in a particular game tactic. It is best if the valued item goes to the person that the Blackmailer is most intent on punishing with his or her game. Cloé Madanes offers an example of how this method was used with a man who physically abused his wife (1990, 19). The man placed one thousand dollars in an escrow account, and then signed a contract agreeing that the money would go to his wife to give to her mother and children from a former marriage should he hit her again. At the end of a year, if he had refrained from hitting her, the couple would use the money to take a vacation,

Positive Contingency Methods

Artisans love a good contest. Contests are thrilling, exciting. They involve challenge, risk, competition, and an opportunity to impress others—all very appealing to the Artisan. For these

---

* This method was actually devised by Cloé Madanes and Jay Haley, though they do not use this name.

reasons, contests can also be useful for stopping the Blackmail game. And if some kind of gambling or an element of surprise can be incorporated into the contest, then all the better. It is essential that in using a therapeutic contest, there are no comments made about how the Blackmailer is to behave, for these comments distill the effectiveness of the contest itself. The emphasis is on who will win the contest—*not* on changing behavior.

In therapeutic contests, Artisans may compete with their mates, parents, siblings, or peers. One way to arrange things is to see to it that clients and their competitors earn points or a chance to win something when they behave in certain specified, desirable ways. One school psychologist* convinced high school girls who were frequently truant (playing the Delinquency game) to attend school more regularly by setting up a contest between them. Each time they attended a class, they could put their name on an official entry form and enter it in the contest jar. A positive written comment from a teacher for a class period earned them two official entries. At the end of each week, a drawing was held to determine the winner, who received a modest gift certificate from the local mall (donated by the PTA). Another school psychologist** set up a very successful system whereby Artisan students could win a day off from school by attending regularly. The students involved in this contest improved their attendance dramatically, until school administrators found out about it and decided that it was against the rules.

One mother offered her four children a chance to put a ticket in a jar every time they helped with housework, since she was tired of nagging and getting no results. She announced that there would be a drawing at the end of each week for a special surprise. The first morning of the contest she was awakened at 5:00 A.M. to the sound of the vacuum—it was her eight-year-old Artisan son, who eagerly informed her that he wanted to be sure to put some tickets in the jar before going off to school at 8:00.

---

* Thank you to Char Fouts Smith for this wonderful example from her practice.
** This ingenious method was devised by Dr. Raymond Choiniere.

An ESFJ mother complained that her five-year-old Artisan daughter was driving her crazy at the dinner table. The child would put her feet on the table, make a mess of her food, and eat with her hands. I suggested that the mother start a contest with her three children, whereby a preset buzzer would go off sometime during the meal. The mother was to say nothing more about table manners. The child or children who displayed good table manners when the buzzer went off would win a small prize. The mother reported that all three children began to behave at dinner, and that her Artisan daughter stopped all of her offensive behavior.

Another arrangement is to give each contestant the same number of dollars or points to start with, and to systematically reduce this amount each time a person displays a targeted negative behavior. The person with the most points or dollars left after a specified amount of time wins some kind of a prize. A third arrangement is to reward one's competitor with points or money each time the offender displays the undesirable behavior that has been targeted. Since Artisans are concrete, it is best to use tangible items to represent points or chances earned or lost in any contest that is established. Real money (small change or dollar bills), monopoly money, pieces of felt, or poker chips are all useful for this purpose.

> An Artisan-Guardian couple came to therapy in order to change a pattern in their relationship that was making both of them unhappy. The Artisan husband, playing a variant of Delinquency, would promise to come home from work at a certain time, but almost never made it, nor even called to say he would be late. The Guardian wife played the game of Nag, reminding, criticizing and judging him as irresponsible, immature, and stupid. Each claimed that they couldn't help themselves, though they would like very much to change.
>
> I instructed them to go to the bank after the session, and to withdraw one hundred dollars each in twenty dollar bills. The husband was told to hand over a twenty dollar bill to his wife each time he came home later from work than when he had said he would be. The wife was told to turn over a twenty dollar bill to her husband each time she nagged, reminded, or criticized him regarding the

time of his arrival home from work. Any money they
received from the other, they could spend on themselves
as they wished. Two weeks later, they had not exchanged
any money. This change in their relationship persisted
over time, and generalized to other areas of conflict where
there had been a similar pattern.

In this case, the exchange of money became a friendly competition between husband and wife, who began to laugh and make jokes on a subject that had previously been entirely negative and a source of tension. I used twenty dollars with this couple, because that was affordable and yet high enough that they would think twice about losing it. In less affluent families, I will use one dollar bills, or fives, instead of twenties.

Sometimes it is useful to reward Artisan children for starting or maintaining desired behaviors, without the use of contests. This works particularly well when rewards are given on an intermittent schedule, since it is more exciting if the Artisan never quite knows when the prizes are forthcoming. Rewards don't necessarily cost anything—for example, a child may be rewarded with the privilege of staying up one-half hour later, or the chance to spend several hours alone with a parent doing something fun.

Clients can also be taught to reward themselves, as demonstrated in the following case.

> Susan, an ESFP, came to me because she wanted to stop
> playing Outrage with her son and her daughter (both
> Artisans). Susan indicated that she constantly caught herself treating her kids the way her mother treated her, and
> that she hated it. In addition to blowing her stack at them
> daily, she would constantly compare her kids to their well-behaved cousins—just like her mother always did to her.

> The first thing I did was use an empty chair to have two
> parts of Susan dialogue—the part of her that loses her
> temper, and the part of her that wants to stop doing that.

> Next I had Susan close her eyes, relax, and go back to a
> time when she was young and her mother was yelling at
> her. Susan cried as she visualized herself as a small child
> enduring her mother's wrath. Next I had Susan, the adult,

rescue, comfort and nurture Susan, the child, in her mind's eye. After venting her anger at her mother, Susan pretended to take her child self to someplace safe.

After I had her open her eyes and return to the room, I proposed to Susan that every time she was about to lose her temper with her children or compare them to their cousins and she stopped herself, she should give herself one point. When she had accumulated twenty-five points, she was to plan to give herself something that she really wanted. She decided that she wanted a new dress as a reward, since wearing it would also remind her of her accomplishment.

Susan reported immediate success with this method. In the first month, she only yelled once at her children, and she accumulated twelve points for those times that she stopped herself from losing her temper. What's more, she reported feeling better about herself than she had in years. As she changed her ways of dealing with her son and daughter, their behavior began to improve, too. It took her four months to earn the twenty-five points needed to get her new dress, since Susan found that even the impulse to blow her stack had begun to disappear.

Championing the Inner Child

In addition to arranging for Susan to reward herself, I also used guided imagery to take her back to her childhood, where she could rescue herself from an abusive situation. This method is particularly useful for SFPs who were victimized in childhood, and who continue to play that role throughout their lives by abusing themselves or allowing themselves to be abused by others. Inner-child work enables these clients to go back and break the cycle of victimization where it first began.

John Bradshaw (1990) has written and lectured extensively on techniques for healing the wounds of childhood and championing the inner child. According to Bradshaw, by having clients return to painful childhood scenes as their adult selves, where they can defend, protect, and rescue their younger selves, clients can become their own champions. Once they have assumed that role, clients often stop allowing themselves to be abused in the present. In the following case, this method is used to help a sixty-nine-year-old ISFP who is playing the Shocking variant of Blackmail.

Sadie, a slender and vivacious sixty-nine-year-old woman, was referred for counseling by her physician, because she was unable to relax. She told me that she had always been a "hyper" person, and that she didn't know how to slow down. Unfortunately, she had recently suffered from some stress-related physical disorders, and the doctor was concerned. Sadie never complained about her physical ailments—and they certainly didn't stop her from being in constant motion.

I learned that it bothered Sadie a lot that her husband of thirty-five years was always putting her down. When she asked him to stop, he told her that she was just too sensitive. Sadie confessed that she had always felt that she was stupid and good for nothing. She wished that she had the confidence to go out and do something fun and useful. She spent most of her time helping her husband with his business and taking care of her many animals. A deeply caring woman, Sadie described herself as a real lover of both animals and small children.

Sadie told me that both of her parents abandoned her when she was a small child. Growing up in an orphanage, she was often yelled at and hit by her caretakers. She spent her teen years in foster homes, where she was sexually abused by two of her foster fathers. Sadie's first husband was an alcoholic who violently beat her. She explained that her present husband was pretty good to her, except for putting her down. Though she had requested it, he refused to go to therapy with her.

Since Sadie seemed comfortable with me and ready to work, I began in the first session with having her do some Gestalt work with her husband. She told him how badly she felt when he talked down to her. Next, I had Sadie close her eyes, and tell me exactly how it felt in her body when her husband put her down. She described a tight and heavy pressure in her chest. I had Sadie imagine herself going back to the first time that she felt the same feeling in her chest. She saw herself as a six-year-old object of ridicule and physical abuse at the orphanage. I instructed Sadie to have her adult self enter the scene and to stand up to the abusers and make them stop. She cried and screamed at them for hurting her child self. Next, I had Sadie take the child to a safe place and pretend to be her mother. She imagined nurturing the child and playing with her. Finally, I had Sadie place her child self safely in her heart, surrounded by love, and to return to the present. Sadie reported that she felt like a load had lifted from her chest. She described it as a sense of relief. I sent Sadie home with the assignment to spend two hours during the week with her eyes closed, talking to her inner child, and playing with her.

When Sadie returned a week later with a big smile on her face, her first words were, "I did it!" Apparently, she had gone home and told her husband that if he didn't stop putting her down, she was leaving him. (This took me by complete surprise.) She told me, "He knew that I meant it, too!" What's more, she reported that he had apologized and had virtually stopped his negative comments. She said that she had been much more relaxed. We spent the second session using the same inner child methods to work on the sexual abuse that Sadie had suffered in her two foster homes.

When Sadie returned for the third session, she reported that things were wonderful with her husband, that her "mind and system felt clear," and that her headaches had stopped. Friends and family had commented on how relaxed and positive she seemed. She told me that her husband was able to just kid her, and her feelings didn't get hurt. We discussed things she might do outside of the home that would be fun and challenging—like taking a college class, or volunteering to work with children. After just a few more sessions, we terminated therapy.

An action-oriented person, Sadie didn't waste any time getting right to work in therapy. She certainly is living proof that it is never too late to change. As an SFP, Sadie didn't complain to her friends and relatives about her physical disorders. While all types can suffer from physical problems, it is only the SJ who complains loudly and often about those aches and pains in order to entangle others.

Conclusion

The methods described in this chapter are particularly effective for working with Artisans. As stated earlier, many of the techniques described here can also be useful in working with the other types. Conversely, clinicians will find that some of the tools presented in the chapters for stopping Complain, Robot, and Masquerade will also be effective in stopping Blackmail.

In part three of this book, there are several case examples in which I used the therapeutic techniques described in this chapter in order to stop the Blackmail game. Those cases provide additional information about working with Blackmail players in the context of their family systems, as well as details about those observational clues which may be used to identify SP clients.

When Artisans stop playing Blackmail, then they are free to be their most playful and creative selves. Those Artisans who feel good about themselves are inclined to live life to the fullest. They are graceful, bold, and impressive in their artistry—whether building houses, running a marathon, performing music, or writing a novel. They are both excited and exciting—as they find the courage to do what others only dream of doing.

In relationships, healthy Artisans bring joy and beauty into the lives of those they love. They are open-minded, colorful, clever, generous, kind, hardworking and forgiving. Artisans remind us to enjoy the precious present, and they show us how to laugh. They brighten each day with their unshakable optimism.

Artisans who have given up their game playing have stopped trying to control others and instead have learned to control themselves. They have found ways in which they can express their impulsive nature, without going out-of-bounds. They have developed a respect for the rights and property of others, and have demonstrated a willingness to honor their commitments with others. They have learned to channel their incredible energy into constructive projects, rather than in destructive directions. They value themselves and surround themselves with those who treat them with love and respect.

Chapter 5

STOPPING THE COMPLAIN GAME

Unlike the Artisans, Guardians usually bring themselves to therapy. The difficulty with Guardians, though, is that too often they are there to work on changing somebody else, instead of themselves. And usually that somebody else is an Artisan mate or child. This isn't to say that SJs claim that they are perfect and have nothing to do with the relationship difficulties. It's just that they are so consumed with anger, frustration, resentment, or hurt over the behavior of the significant other that they cannot see beyond it. The Complain players' blind spot is their inability to recognize what they are doing to contribute to the problem.

The first challenge of the clinician in working with the individual Guardian is to shift the client's focus from the other to the self. It may be necessary to do this repeatedly in a given session, since many SJ clients will automatically launch back into a litany of complaints about the other over and over again. These complaints may take the form of stories about what the other did or didn't do, illustrating how the Guardian has suffered in the relationship. While these stories can be a useful source of information for the clinician about what is going on, it is important to help Complain players to focus on the choices they have made in these situations, and the options that are currently available to them. This helps to move the SJ from the position of helpless victim to that of someone with a modicum of control over his or her life.

When Guardians do talk about themselves in therapy, it is often to complain about their aches and pains, worries, fears, and/or depression. After all, these problems are the essence of the Complain game. While it is important to take the time to find out exactly what the SJ's complaints are, it is generally a mistake to spend the entire counseling session discussing them. In order to help the Complain player, it is essential to deal with the issues that are making the Guardian feel desperate enough to turn to survival game playing. This is not always an easy task, since the more troubled Complain players will return at the slightest opportunity to the subject of their aches and pains as a way of avoiding the more threatening topics—and sometimes, as a way of communicating metaphorically about them. For example, one client began by telling me about her excessive fatigue, and then went into a lengthy description of the gynecological problems which had plagued her for the past fifteen years, and which had made sexual intercourse impossible for her. As soon as I was able to direct the conversation to the topic of her relationship with her husband, she changed the subject in mid-sentence by saying, "and as I sit here, gazing out of that window, I have tremendous rectal pain. " Her message was clear.

Guardians play Complain when their needs to belong and to be needed are in jeopardy. Almost any major life change can leave the SJ feeling alone, insecure, abandoned, and useless; for example, the death of a loved one, divorce, moving, retirement, or having one's children grow up and leave home. In other cases, Guardians turn to game playing because they cannot continue to say "yes" to certain responsibilities, and yet, they cannot bring themselves to say "no." SJs typically pride themselves on being highly responsible, and they see themselves as earning their right to belong by doing their duty every day. But what happens when they feel weighed down with too many burdens? Rather than saying "no" to their bosses, spouses, or children, Guardians will become too sick, tired, worried, or depressed to continue business as usual. In this way, the SJ is excused from being accountable, without risking rejection. After all, no one is going to reject someone who is so down and out.

To stop the Complain game, it can be very useful to help clients find new places where they can be valued, contributing members of a group. Besides seeing to it that their basic needs are fulfilled, it is usually necessary to give Complain players permission to say "no" and instruction in how to do so. Along with learning how to set limits, they may also profit from learning how to ask for what they need and want, and how to express themselves without putting others on the defensive. It can also be beneficial to teach their significant others to say and do the things that make Complain players feel appreciated. Most Complainers are holding on to guilt, shame, and/or resentment regarding events of the past. A primary goal is to assist them in resolving their unfinished business so that they are free to live more joyfully in the present. Therapists can also offer assistance where SJs are having difficulty in letting go of people, places, and situations, as they so often do.

Finally, many Guardian clients will profit from instruction in the use of tools for reducing or controlling the symptoms of excessive anxiety and stress.

Fulfilling the Guardian's Basic Needs

There are many ways of seeing to it that SJs are able to find membership and earn their right to belong. Volunteer work with any nonprofit organization is always an option, whether it involves tutoring, mentoring, being a big brother or sister, restoring a historical landmark, or caring for the sick, the poor, the homeless, or the elderly. Service clubs and church organizations may provide excellent opportunities for Guardians to fill their need to belong and contribute. Twelve-step program support groups like AL-ANON, Co-dependents Anonymous, Overeaters Anonymous, and Alcoholics Anonymous are also excellent for SJs. Other possibilities are: professional organizations, homeowner's associations, community action groups, sports and hobby clubs, and senior citizen groups. SJs will often feel gratified by holding a specific office or title in these associations, since this is perceived as added confirmation that the Guardian does, indeed, have a place in the hierarchy. Sometimes Guardians will enjoy taking classes in areas of interest, whether art, ceramics, photography, music, floral arranging, history, or foreign language. In other cases, it is best to encourage SJ clients to take a full or part-time job, or to change jobs so they can do something that better suits their needs. Where SJ children are playing Complain it is often possible to get them involved in a service club at school, or to see to it that the teacher gives them a title and a vital job to do in the classroom.

In addition to finding new ways of belonging, it is often necessary to encourage Complain players to treat themselves better. These clients usually put themselves at the bottom of their lists— everyone else gets more time and consideration than they give themselves. They will go out of their way for family members and friends and completely neglect their own needs. For example, one client would give her teenage son eight hundred dollars a month in spending money, but she claimed that she couldn't afford to buy herself a new blouse. It is very important that clinicians encourage Complain players to begin to do for themselves that which they so easily and willingly do for others.

Another problem is that Complain players rarely give themselves an opportunity to play. Dr. David Bressler is fond of telling these clients that their "serum fun levels" are dangerously low, and that he must, therefore, prescribe massive doses of play. Often it is necessary to assign SJ clients the task of playing a certain amount each week. Play can be anything that they find pleasurable or relaxing.

The following case provides an example of an SJ who was playing the Depressed, Doormat, and Poor Me variants of Complain since her last child had left the nest.

> Carolyn was referred by her physician for counseling because of her severe, debilitating depression. Carolyn could not explain why she felt so depressed—she told me that there was nothing bothering her. When I questioned her further, however, I learned that her elderly mother was severely ill, and that her her third (and youngest) child had just moved out on her own. Carolyn, an ESFJ,

reported that she and her ISTP husband, Tom, loved each other very much, but that they spent little time doing things together outside of his mechanic's shop, where she worked part-time helping out with the bookkeeping. At home after a long day at work, Tom would watch TV and avoided conversations whenever possible. Carolyn disliked working in Tom's business; yet she continued because she felt it was her duty, and also because she feared that it was the only thing other than their children and grandchildren that she and Tom had in common. Without it, there would be even less for them to talk about.

Since Tom refused to go to counseling, I worked individually with Carolyn. When I learned that she loved small children, I encouraged her to find someplace where she could work with children as a volunteer. She found a position working as a foster grandparent. Also at my encouragement, Carolyn began to involve herself in more activities with friends, so that she did not rely solely on Tom to fill her very high need for socializing. I gave her assignments to take the time for herself to do the things that make her feel good, like getting a massage, going shopping, taking long, luxurious baths, and going out for lunch with friends. Initially, Carolyn had trouble treating herself in these ways, since she felt selfish and unworthy.

In addition, I taught Carolyn how to set limits with Tom and others—that is, how to say "no" when she felt like it. Through role playing she was able to rehearse these assertion skills, and also to practice asking for what she needed and wanted from Tom. She learned to make I statements, to be very specific, and to be brief. (As an ISTP, Tom was likely to tune her out if she was too wordy and overly emotional in her communications.)

Carolyn put these new communication skills to use by turning over some of the office duties to her husband's employees. At home, she stopped automatically assuming the responsibilities that Tom typically neglected, and she started letting him know the ways in which she felt taken for granted. Instead of expecting him to read her mind, she started to ask Tom to say or do those things that would make her feel more loved and appreciated.

Over time, Carolyn reported that she no longer felt depressed.

As an ESFJ, Carolyn needed to be giving to people who both needed and appreciated her. The work she did at her husband's office did not suffice, since it involved little interaction with people, and she felt taken for granted there. At home, she was not making her desires clear to her Artisan husband, and she was letting him take advantage of her and feeling resentful about it. Though Carolyn did not realize that her fundamental wants were not being fulfilled, she stopped using tactics from the game of Depressed once she began to get what she needed most.

It is not always easy to convince Guardians to become involved in the kinds of social and charitable activities that are likely to lift their spirits. Often, they use their depression or ailments as excuses for not going out and doing things with others. Yet, paradoxically, it is only when they find new places to belong and to be of service that they are likely to feel good.

Motivating the Guardian to Change

Troubled Guardians are often reluctant to go out and participate in a group just because it is supposed to make them feel better. Many SJs believe that doing something just to help oneself is evidence of self-absorption, and self-centeredness—and these are qualities that Guardians find repugnant. Psychotherapists can utilize this attitude to motivate Complain players to stop hibernating, by reframing staying at home as selfish, self-indulgent, or even stingy behavior. Often those who are most reluctant to help themselves will leap at the opportunity to get involved with service clubs or charities in order to demonstrate to the therapist that they are, indeed, accountable to the needs of others.

The Guardian's concern for the welfare of others can be utilized in other ways, too. Many SJ parents cannot find the motivation to stop doing something that is self-destructive, until they are reminded of the ways in which it is harming their children. Sometimes this can be enough to persuade them to quit smoking, drinking, or remaining in an abusive relationship. In the following case, I utilize a girl's concern for her parents in order to get her to stop playing a dangerous game of Invalid.

Eight-year-old Gina's parents brought their daughter, an only child, to therapy out of desperation. For over a year, Gina , a pretty and very bright ISTJ, had been holding her bowels for up to twenty-one days at a time. Nothing her parents had done to try to get her to have regular bowel movements had worked. The family physician had warned that if the problem continued, surgery might be necessary as a last resort. What's more, since Gina did not have regular bowel movements, she ended up soiling endless pairs of panties with involuntary "leakage." She was embarrassed about the way she smelled around her peers. And when she finally did have bowel movements, it was often enough to stop up the bathroom plumbing.

It was clear from the start that Gina's problem was designed to be helpful to her parents, who were estranged from each other, though living together in the same home. It was also clear that she saw me as more of a threat than an ally, regardless of what I said or did. During our sessions, both with her parents present and alone, she spoke very little. At home, she would often tell her mother that she was determined not to allow me to help her. What's more, she would attempt to convince her mother that I was only trying to break up their close relationship.

Over the first four sessions, I convinced Gina's mother, another ISTJ, to be less involved with her, and her father to be more involved. One way I did this was to congratulate her father (an ISFP) for being more like a brother than a father to her. I also supported Gina's mother when she began to separate herself more from Gina, and to take better care of herself. I stopped their commercials and endless discussions and questions about Gina's bowel movements, and made Gina responsible for her own body and for cleaning her own underwear. I encouraged the parents to employ logical consequences when Gina would walk around the house smelling badly.

Much to my dismay, Gina exhibited almost no improvement during this time. Thus, in the fifth session, I decided to try a new intervention. In the presence of her parents, I told Gina that I thought I knew why she didn't have regular bowel movements—it was because she had bad parents. I implied that if her parents were as bad as I suspected that they were, that there would be some kind of severe consequences involving county authorities. (I was intentionally vague on this point.) I told her that I wasn't sure if *both* of her parents were bad, or just one of them, so I needed to do a little experiment over the next three weeks to find out. For the first ten days, her mother was to try to get her to have bowel movements. If she had none, then we would know that her mother was, indeed, a bad parent. Then during the next ten days, her father was to do everything possible to try to get her to have a bowel movement. Once again, if she had none, then he would be identified as a bad parent. While I was giving these instructions, Gina looked quite shocked. Her parents also looked at me with surprise, not knowing if they should believe what I said, or not. Without giving anyone a chance to comment, I ended the session.

Three weeks later, Gina reported that she had had two bowel movements during the first ten days, and two during the second ten days. After that, she stabilized at one to two bowel movements a week. She still soiled her panties occasionally, but much less often. As Gina improved, her parents started to complain about her "talking back" to her mother. Indeed, Gina had stopped holding back in more ways than one.

Teaching Doormat Players to Say "No"

Doormat players usually need a lot of practice, as well as permission, before they are willing to say "no" to others. Typically they are afraid that if they say "no," then others will get angry or reject them. In order to keep peace and harmony, they swallow their feelings instead of speaking up. As a result, they often end up doing things they don't want to do, while carrying around feelings of burning resentment, frustration, hopelessness, and helplessness. After a while, these unexpressed, yet unacceptable emotions may end up causing psychosomatic disorders like high blood pressure, colitis, ulcers, or even cardiac arrest (see Alexander, 1932).

Role playing is an excellent way of teaching Guardians how to set limits and say "no" to others. Once this has been practiced in the office, these clients can be given the assignment of saying a certain number of "no's" per week where they would normally be saying "yes." These "no's" can be little ones, even to strangers, like store clerks. The important thing is that the SJ gets good practice in putting the word to use. Since Guardians are usually willing to read books that will help them accomplish their goals in therapy, it is helpful to assign the book *Softpower: How to Say No and Set Limits Without Losing Your Lover, Your Job, or Your Friends,* by Maria Arapakis (1990), as homework. Another very useful title for this purpose is *The Dance of Anger,* by Harriet Goldhor Lerner (1985).

Reframing Responsibility

It is very difficult for Complain players to avoid taking on those obligations that family members or colleagues ignore. For example, an SJ mother is likely to see to it that her son carries his completed homework to school, fearing that he might forget it if left to his own devises. Here Mom has taken this responsibility away from her son—to whom it rightfully belongs—and placed it on her own shoulders. This puts the son in the ideal position of playing games with her, utilizing her willingness to bear the burden of his fulfilling his scholarly obligations. The mate, co-workers, and children of a Guardian often learn that if they only delay long enough in doing their duty, then the Guardian will do it for them.

The easiest way to get Guardians to break this pattern, is to define it as *irresponsible.* When one emphasizes that the responsible thing to do is to teach others to take responsibility by refusing to do it for them, then SJs are usually willing to entertain a change in their behavior. The hardest part for them is initially, when they must watch significant others ignoring their obligations *without stepping in or commenting.* It is best to explain that any comments about what others *should* or *must* do only indicate that the Guardian has not yet let go of responsibility for the other's actions. The following case is a good example of how a mother who was playing Doormat, Poor Me, and

Worried was persuaded to stop rescuing her adult daughter, who was playing Blackmail.

> A distraught mother (an ISFJ) named Janice came to me because she didn't know what to do about her twenty-two-year-old ESTP daughter, Karen. Though Karen had moved out on her own three years before, she would constantly call and hound her mother for money. Karen rarely worked, and she was often in financial trouble. She was demanding, rude, abusive, and threatening on the phone. If Janice tried to say "no" to her, then Karen would tell her that she was starving, and that she would be thrown out into the streets unless she had the money to pay the rent. She threatened that she might need to turn to prostitution to get the money she required. Finally, she would accuse Janice of not really loving her. By this time in the conversation, Janice always gave in and sent the money Karen requested. She told me that she worried about her daughter, and that she was afraid of what would happen to Karen if she didn't send her the money. She tried to tell her daughter that she needed to be more responsible, but no amount of talking seemed to make a difference.
>
> Janice was furious with her daughter and fed up; yet she felt terribly guilty and afraid whenever she even thought about saying "no" to her. Clearly, Janice was playing the Doormat, Poor Me, and Worried variants of the Complain game, while Karen was playing Blackmail.
>
> I began by accusing Janice of being an *irresponsible* parent. After all, she had assumed responsibility for her daughter's financial affairs, rather than allowing her daughter to learn to be independent. Until she gave up that responsibility, her daughter would not have the opportunity to take hold of it. The only way her daughter could grow up would be if she refused to treat her like a little girl anymore. In other words, it was time for her to start behaving like a responsible parent by saying "no" to her daughter.
>
> Next, I told Janice that it was also irresponsible of her to allow her daughter to verbally abuse her. This was only teaching Karen that it was okay to manipulate people by being cruel.

Janice agreed with me, and even seemed relieved as I spoke. We used role playing to rehearse how she might talk to Karen adult-to-adult, rather than parent-to-child. This meant saying "no" to Karen, stopping all critical and judging messages and all statements about what Karen "should" or "must" do, and communicating confidence in Karen's ability to manage her own life. It also meant hanging up the telephone should Karen become verbally abusive.

When Janice commented that this was difficult for her, I suggested that she pretend that she was not Karen's mother anymore, and that she imagine herself to be a distant acquaintance, instead. I also talked about the *"no" muscle*, and how it is strengthened every time we practice using it. I warned her that Karen would probably put the pressure on even harder when Janice refused her. Finally, I told her a story about a forty-year-old heroin addict I know whose mother is still supporting him and bailing him out of jail every time he is arrested.

Janice returned three weeks later to report that things were much improved. She said that she had actually refused Karen's recent request for money without feeling bad or guilty, since she knew that it was the best thing for Karen in the long run. We spent the second session, which was our last, doing some more role playing to practice the communication techniques which were introduced in the first meeting.

Chances are very good that once Janice stops rescuing her, Karen will start taking better care of herself—but not before she escalates to see if she can once again seduce her mother into taking on the role of her caretaker.

Stopping the Game of Nag

Unhappy Guardians are prone to sounding like critical parents when communicating with their children or mates. In their best efforts to try to be helpful or to convince others to change, they tend to offer lots of "should's" and "oughts." They are also predisposed to asking too many questions about what the other has been thinking, feeling, or doing. What's more, they are inclined to criticize and judge the behavior of others as bad or unacceptable.*

Most of the time, the Nag player's judgements, probing, and unsolicited advice are met with defensiveness on the part of significant others. Artisans respond to critical parenting messages in passive-aggressive ways, or by behaving like rebellious children. Rationals tune them out. Other Guardians respond with critical parenting messages of their own. And Idealists insulate themselves against the hurt they feel from such communications by distancing themselves, and eventually ending the relationship.

A good way to stop the game of Nag is to teach players to use "I" statements, instead of "You" statements. By beginning each sentence with "I," Nag players can learn to open, rather than close, the channels of communication with significant others. It is one thing to say, "You are insensitive and should learn to be more considerate of people's feelings," and still another to say, "I feel hurt when you make fun of me." "I" statements are messages about oneself, rather than criticisms of the other. Instead of putting others on the defensive, they make it easier for each person to really hear what the other is saying. One note of caution, however: Avoid following the words *I feel* or *I think* with the word *that*, since "I feel that" or "I think that" is just another way of making a "You" statement.

It is also useful to teach Guardians to use active listening, or mirroring. This gives them a way of being helpful to their significant others without offering advice. *Getting the Love You Want*, by Harville Hendrix (1988) is a good resource for teaching couples this technique, while *Parent Effectiveness Training*, by Thomas Gordon (1970), and *How to Talk So Kids Will Listen, and Listen So Kids Will Talk* by Faber and Mazlisch (1980) are excellent books for parents. When teaching SJs the method of active listening, it is best to do extensive coaching and practicing in the office, sometimes over the course of three or four sessions. The

---

* However, Guardians are not the only offenders here. Both Rationals and Idealists may also be inclined to do some critical parenting of their own.

office rehearsal can be followed up with assignments to practice the new skill for so many minutes each week.

Sometimes the best way for a counselor to stop someone's nagging, probing, and advising is to declare that certain subjects are off-limits for a couple or family. For example, in the case of Gina, described earlier in this chapter, I put a moratorium on questions or comments about the girl's bowel movements among family members. Where it is necessary to justify this kind of assignment, one can say: "I want to see if you can find other things to talk about with each other." Alternatively, the therapist can frame this intervention as an experiment, or as a means of obtaining more information about the root of the problem.

Finally, it can be beneficial to teach Guardians how to use the method of deprivation as a way of disciplining effectively without resorting to critical parenting messages. This method is described in detail in chapter four.

Helping Guardians to Feel Appreciated

As traditionalists, birthdays, holidays, and anniversaries mean a great deal to Guardians. People of this personality type will usually go out of their way to demonstrate their appreciation for others on those occasions. And it is very important to SJs that others do the same for them. When they feel overlooked or ignored by family members on special days, then Guardians are likely to feel deeply hurt. And eventually, Guardians who feel taken for granted by the important people in their lives will resort to survival game playing.

Guardians need to know that they are valued. Complain players are crying out to loved ones that they feel unappreciated, unloved, and unnecessary. Usually, where Guardians are playing a variant of Complain, their significant others are not conveying their appreciation of the Guardian in ways that are meaningful to this personality. It is sometimes necessary to teach the children and mates of SJs that when it comes to this type, it is often the little things that matter most. As concrete types, Guardians respond particularly well to *tangible* evidence that they are loved and appreciated. Flowers, cards, special meals, parties, and traditional gifts, like jewelry, are all ways that Guardians are likely to get the message that they are special. Additionally, it doesn't hurt for them to hear the words (and often) that tell them how much others care about them. A little thoughtfulness goes a long way towards helping Guardians feel that they really do matter to others.

Resolving Unfinished Business

Complain players almost always have unfinished business with significant others that is weighing them down and keeping them stuck. These unresolved relationships usually evoke feelings of bitter resentment, hatred, or anger in the client. What's more, since Guardians find these emotions unacceptable, they usually feel guilty and ashamed for having them, and they judge themselves as bad and wrong for doing so. They deny their negative emotions, and thus end up holding on to them, rather than resolving and releasing them. According to Franz Alexander, over time these individuals end up experiencing physiological disorders that are the natural accompaniments of unexpressed, unrepressed, and unresolved emotions (see Alexander, 1932). Some of the psychosomatic illnesses that may result from this pattern include: hypertension, heart attacks, colitis, arthritis, and ulcers.* While Guardians do *deny* their emotions to themselves and others, they do not *repress* them, like Idealists do. With denial, a person is consciously aware of the emotion, yet trying to push it away. This is very different from repression, where the emotion is no longer in one's conscious awareness. Hence, Guardians who experience resentment are consciously aware of it, but they are often ashamed of themselves for feeling that way. They may try to push the resentment away, and report that they feel no bitterness, but the feeling remains. Should they stew in their own juices long enough, they are likely to develop an ulcer.

---

* Certainly Guardians are not the only type to experience these physical disorders; however, these particular disorders tend to be most prevalent among Guardians.

It is essential to assist Guardians in resolving their unfinished business, in order to stop the Complain game and to help them to attain better physical health. The best way to locate the issues that need to be addressed is to notice those topics that seem to be most emotionally charged for the Complain player. Sometimes they will begin to cry when they talk about a person or a memory from the past. At other times, they will reveal glimpses of strong anger or resentment. Since Guardians are often ashamed of these feelings, they may deny what they are feeling right after they express the emotion. It is important that the clinician recognize this pattern and assist the client in owning up to his or her feelings, so that they can be dealt with once and for all.

Once the unresolved relationship issue has been uncovered, therapists may wish to give Complain players permission to have and express their feelings. Gestalt exercises utilizing an empty chair are an excellent means of assisting Guardians in exploring and resolving their unfinished business with significant others. Writing letters that may or may not be sent is another way of helping SJs to release the past. So are guided visualizations, in which they encounter significant others in their imagination, and have conversations with them. The following case is an example of how these methods were used to stop the Doormat and Invalid variants of the Complain game.

> A soft-spoken sixty-year-old ISTJ client, Martha, was referred by her physician because she had high blood pressure, was experiencing extra heartbeats, and was addicted to painkillers. Martha was working as a secretary for her husband (an ESTJ), a very powerful businessman in the community. I learned that she feared her husband, and that she rarely voiced her needs to him. At home Martha felt ignored and unimportant. She was miserable at work and wanted the two of them to retire, but he was planning to continue working indefinitely.

> I used Gestalt to assist Martha in learning to express her feelings to her husband and to verbalize her needs and wants. When she found the confidence to tell him these things in person, his response was very positive. Together, they developed a plan to retire in just two years. He began to share more of the responsibilities around the house

with her. They found more time to play together. And Martha felt more like his wife, rather than his secretary.

I learned from Martha that she had been emotionally and physically abused and neglected as a child by her mother. During her first marriage, Martha lived with her husband, her adopted son, Donald, and her mother. Martha's mother was in complete control of the household. After six years, Martha escaped by running off with another man, who ended up being physically abusive with her. She confessed to me that she had never forgiven herself for leaving her adopted child twenty-five years ago, and that though it had been very painful for her, she had not seen Donald since that time, because she believed that it would be easier on the boy.

We spent several sessions focusing on Martha's unfinished business with her mother. Using Gestalt, Martha spoke up to her mother for the first time in her life. With visualization techniques, Martha was able to go back as an adult to her childhood and rescue her wounded inner child. She nurtured her inner child, and began a process of reparenting herself. She rewrote the scenes of her past, and changed old decisions she had made about herself and her life.

Next we worked on Martha's relationship with her son. Using the empty chair, Martha began to release some of the guilt, shame, and sorrow that she had been carrying around in her heart for so many years. Then I had her sixty-year-old self dialogue with her thirty-five-year-old self, using the empty chair method. To her relief, Martha found that after twenty-five years, she was finally willing and able to forgive herself. She decided to write a brief letter to Donald (now twenty-eight years old), offering him the opportunity to meet if he wanted to, but also making it clear that she would understand if he wanted no contact.

After the above sessions, Martha reported that both her heartbeat and her blood pressure had normalized. Though she never heard from Donald, Martha indicated that—for the first time in her life—she felt peaceful inside when she thought about her son and her past.

As she slowly reduced her dosage of painkillers (while monitored by her physician) Martha noticed that she missed the pills the most every day after work, when they had given her a high feeling. I reframed the situation, and said that she was using the pills to kill the pain of boredom. Together we explored some alternative ways in which she could kill the pain of boredom. She began to vary her schedule more, to participate in environmental club outings, and to spend more time with friends. We terminated our therapy after eight sessions, since Martha had accomplished all of her goals.

Assisting Guardians in Letting Go

Sometimes Guardians play Complain because they are having difficulty letting go of people, places, or situations. SJs place a high value on security, and they often fear changes that disrupt the status quo. Once they become attached to a relationship or a job, they may avoid leaving—even if the situation is unhealthy for them. And long after a relationship has ended they may still be clinging to the hope that it will be restored, in spite of all that the former mate says or does to indicate that it is truly over.

Passport metaphors are a wonderful tool for helping reluctant Guardians to let go, since they send the message that something good is possible. In a sense, they are a way of handing clients a passport to change.[*] They encourage clients—that is, instill them with courage. They convey hope for the future, often by building on a client's past successes. There is no limit to the stories, situations, and symbols which can be used for helping Guardians to let go (see Haley, 1973; Rosen, 1982; Wallas, 1985, 1991). For example, nature alone offers endless possibilities for metaphor topics. One may describe how a tree lets go of its leaves in the fall in order that there can be new growth, blossoms, and fruit in the year to come. One might also talk about a seed that is carried off to a new place by the wind, where it lands in fertile soil and grows strong, healthy roots that stabi-

---

[*] It is for this reason that Dr. Keirsey chose to call them passport metaphors.

lize it and enable it to drink in nourishment from the rich soil. Still another option is to talk about the frightened baby bird that must be pushed from the nest so that it might discover its wings and learn to fly.

ISFJ parents, the Provider type, seem to have the hardest time letting go of their children as they grow up. Often, they are fraught with terrible worries about what will happen to their children as they leave the nest and venture out in the world. They want desperately to keep their children safe, and sometimes find it is terribly difficult to set them free, even as their offspring reach young adulthood. In the following case, I used a passport metaphor to help an ISFJ mother who is playing the Worry game to begin the process of letting go of her ISFJ daughter.

> Kimberly, a pretty fifteen-year-old girl, and her youthful mother, Lori, came to me for counseling because Kimberly had been too anxious to leave the house for many months, except for very short periods of time with her mother. The problem all began when Kimberly got very sick, and was unable to attend school for several weeks. Since then, Kimberly had avoided going places like school, friends' homes, or shopping malls, because she was afraid that she would become nauseous and need to throw up in these places. Kimberly was very concerned about this problem, since it kept her from spending time with friends and had also kept her from attending a portion of her ninth-grade year in high school. She was terrified that she would never get better, and that she would be unable to begin her second year of high school in September. And she was tired of spending most of her time at home, alone or with her mother, watching TV or talking on the telephone.

> I learned that Kimberly had just one sibling—an older brother who was away at college. Kimberly's parents were divorced, and she lived with her mother, who was employed as an administrative assistant.

> I worked with Kimberly on stopping her awfulizing thoughts by teaching her to use deep breathing, progressive relaxation, and positive mental imagery (see Borysenko, 1987). We used role playing with the empty

chair to rehearse how she might deal with friends when they made comments or asked questions about her school absence that made her feel uncomfortable. I assigned her the task of going to a shopping mall three times a week, and of staying for no longer than ten minutes, even if she wanted to stay longer, or thought she was able to do so.

After the first two sessions, Kimberly began to complain that her mother was often questioning her, advising her, coaxing her, and telling her how she should feel about her problem. In a session with Lori, she confessed to me that she was beside herself with worry about her daughter. She felt weighted down with the responsibility of assisting Kimberly in overcoming her problem, and she was willing to do anything that might help her daughter. Lori also confessed that she was having a lot of trouble with the idea of Kimberly growing up—perhaps because she was her youngest child. She was terrified that something bad would happen to Kimberly. She didn't want to let go, but she knew she had to.

To help Lori, I reminded her of how she had once enabled Kimberly to learn to walk by letting go of her hand. I talked about how difficult it must have been to watch her daughter take a few steps and then fall, and credited her with knowing, even then, that Kimberly needed to gain confidence in her own abilities by picking herself up and trying again. I emphasized how important it had been for her to be there to encourage Kimberly, to love her, and to celebrate her successes with her. As I spoke, she cried, and nodded her head in agreement.

Next, I commended her on the excellent job she had done in raising her daughter. I told her that Kimberly presently needed to know that her mother had confidence in her to handle life's challenges. I asked Lori if she would be willing to tell Kimberly, in my presence, that she had faith in her ability to handle her own problems. Lori agreed to do so.

Finally, with both Lori and Kimberly present, I declared that Kimberly was fully capable of handling her own problems, and I placed Kimberly in charge of her own recovery. I told her that she knew what was too fast and what was too slow and what was just right for her better than anyone else. At my request, Lori announced to Kimberly that she, too, had confidence in her daughter to solve her own difficulties. On that basis, I suggested that Kimberly and her mother have no further discussions about Kimberly's problem. Kimberly could make comments, but Lori was not to respond to them. And Lori was to go out and start doing the things that she had avoided doing since Kimberly had been home all the time.

Two weeks later, Kimberly and Lori came back to report lots of positive changes. Both had lived up to their agreements. Kimberly had spent ten of the past fifteen days with friends, doing things she had previously been unable to do and visiting places she had previously been unable to visit. Lori told me privately that she had thought a lot about how it was when she helped her daughter learn to walk. As she stopped trying to take care of Kimberly, she felt as if a big burden had been lifted off her shoulders. She was enjoying the opportunity to go out on some evenings and weekends with her friends.

Lori and Kimberly and I continued to meet periodically as both made the adjustment to Kimberly's second year in high school.

The passport metaphor I used with Lori was fairly obvious to her in its message and intent. Often, when passport metaphors are used, it is necessary to disqualify their purpose so that clients do not consciously resist them. The counselor offers a metaphor with a message for the client that is not directly apparent, and avoids any discussion of the metaphor by quickly changing the subject after delivering it. In this way, the metaphor is like a seed planted in the fertile soil of the client's unconscious mind. This circumvents conscious resistance, and it allow clients the freedom to make use of metaphors in whatever ways are best for them.

Still another excellent tool for assisting Guardian clients in letting go is the therapeutic ritual (see Imber-Black, Roberts, and Whiting, 1988). Rituals are an essential part of the life of the Guardian. More than any other type, Guardians are dedicated to preserving society's rituals and seeing to it that they are passed on from one generation to the next. Hence, therapeutic rituals are

an ideal way of helping Complain players to make life's transi-
tions. Where there are no culturally defined ceremonies for
dealing with the changes in our lives—for example, in the case
of a divorce—therapists can assist Guardian clients in creating
their own ceremonies. These ceremonies can be formal or infor-
mal; they can take place in or out of the therapist's office. The
may involve writing, speaking, announcing, presenting, eating,
drinking, building, creating, burning, burying, planting, cleaning,
gifting, or journeying—and even flushing a toilet.

In one case, an ESFJ Protector-type client became extremely agitated and depressed as she approached the first Mother's Day
since her own mother's recent death. To help her, I encouraged
her to establish a ritual on Mother's Day in honor of her mother,
whereby she would do an anonymous good deed for a mother-in-
need on that special day. She loved the idea, and said that
doing it gave her a wonderful feeling of relief and joy.

Another Complain player worked extensively with me on completing unfinished business related to her alcoholic father, who
abused her physically and sexually. As a means of completion, I
asked her to bring a box to therapy filled with small items that
reminded her of her father.* We discussed the significance of the
various items that she brought, and then talked about what she
wanted to do with the box and its contents. The client decided to
burn the box and most of the items, and to bury the rest in her
father's backyard. Later, the woman reported that as she carried out the ritual, she felt something lift, leaving a noticeably
lighter feeling in her chest.

Breaking the Anxiety Cycle

Guardians who play the Worried variant of the Complain game
are particularly prone to becoming trapped in the anxiety cycle
that Joan Borysenko describes in her book, *Minding the Body,
Mending the Mind* (1987). These players become caught up in
catastrophic thinking that mobilizes the fight or flight response
in both the autonomic and musculoskeletal systems. As they ob-

---

* I credit my husband, Roger Stilgenbauer, for this suggestion.

serve the body's heightened state of arousal, they often perceive themselves as even more threatened, which only intensifies their body's visceral response and the degree of muscle tension they experience. Eventually, this cycle can lead to feelings of complete panic and utter helplessness. For example, Joyce is afraid she will have a panic attacks if she goes to the grocery store. She begins to think about going to the store, and she imagines the worst. Joyce tells herself that she is likely to panic once she is in the store, and she pictures the embarrassment, fear, and shame that she will feel in such circumstances. Since Joyce's body does not know the difference between a real and imagined situation, it responds as if she is truly in danger. Her pulse increases, her palms sweat, her mouth dries, her breathing becomes shallow, and she feels light-headed. The muscles of her back, neck, shoulders, and face begin to tense up. As Joyce feels these changes in her body, she becomes even more frightened and her physical symptoms are intensified. Eventually, she is too panic-stricken to move.

It is possible to teach people like Joyce how to use various tools for breaking this debilitating cycle of anxiety. Guardians are often willing to learn these techniques when they are told that these are *practical* ways of controlling stress, since Guardians place such a high value on practicality. In her book, Dr. Borysenko offers excellent instruction in the use of deep breathing, stretching, progressive muscle relaxation, and meditating. While deep breathing is a way of calming the visceral nervous system, stretching and progressive relaxation are ways of releasing tension in the muscles. Meditation provides an opportunity to practice being present in the moment, quieting the mind, finding inner peace, and tuning in to the wisdom within us. It is often helpful to teach these methods to Worry players, and to recommend that they read *Minding the Body, Mending the Mind* in conjunction with therapy.

One additional method I use to help clients stop the cycle of anxiety is guided visualization. With this technique, I teach clients to use their imagination to picture themselves becoming increasingly relaxed, to create tranquil scenes in their mind's eye, and to experience themselves being successful in whatever ways they want to be. Usually, I instruct clients on how to use these methods in the office, and then I record personalized guided visualizations on audio tapes that they can listen to at home at a time when they are free from distractions and able to relax deeply.

Conclusion

The methods covered in this chapter are just a few of the ways to stop the Complain game. Many of the tools described in chapters four, six, and seven will also be applicable for working with Complain players. And, a number of the techniques described in this section may also be helpful in stopping the other three games.

The cases in part three include some Guardians who were seen individually and in marital and family counseling sessions. Those case examples are meant to demonstrate the applications of the methods discussed in this chapter, and also to point out those observational clues which may be useful for identifying SJ clients.

As Guardians give up their Complain game, they become once again their most thoughtful and responsible selves. Guardians with healthy self-regard are usually brimming with concern for others—and particularly sensitive to those who are in need. They are extremely generous with their time and energy, participating unselfishly in numerous projects designed for the welfare of others. Their ability to organize hundreds of details as they coordinate huge events is nothing short of amazing.

At home, healthy Guardians provide a nurturing and secure environment for their loved ones. Ever devoted to making the home a comfortable place, they focus their energies on tending lovingly to the needs of the other family members. Loyal, dependable, kind, stable, hardworking, dedicated, fair, conscientious, and honest, SJs are the backbones of our families and the foundation that our society's institutions are built upon.

Guardians who have stopped playing Complain have managed to let go of the past and to forgive themselves, as well as others. They are kind and loving to themselves—and they are good at seeing to it that others do not take advantage of them. They are able to set limits and say "no" when they want to, without feeling guilty. And they are able to express their thoughts, feelings, and desires without being critical of others. They have found a place to belong—and a way of contributing their time and energy toward making this world a better place. They know how to relax, and they give themselves lots of opportunities to play.

Chapter 6

STOPPING THE ROBOT GAME

Robot players are the least likely of all four of the types to be seen by a therapist for two reasons. First, it is estimated that they make up only about 5 to 12 percent of the population,[*] so they are greatly outnumbered by the other types. Second, many Rationals resist getting help since they perceive that as a sign of weakness and a source of shame. Robot players often believe that they should be able to apply the right formula of willpower and reason in order to solve their own problems. And even when all formulas fail them, they are inclined to persist in trying to handle their difficulties on their own.

When adolescent or adult Robot players do go to therapy, it is usually only after prolonged efforts to help themselves have produced little success. Yet, in spite of whatever desperation they feel, these clients are likely to be skeptical of most of what that the mental health practitioner says and does. After all, it is the Rational's nature to question, to put everything to the test of reason. These clients are most unlikely to nod their head in blind agreement with the psychotherapist's words and actions.

---

[*] Dr. Keirsey has lowered his estimate of NT's in the general population from 12 percent to 5 percent since the publication of *Please Understand Me*.

Rather, they are far more prone to ask why, and to point out what they perceive as discrepancies in the therapist's messages. What's more, they are often inclined to argue on general points and to disagree with the clinician's use of particular words.

This is not to say that Robot players are uncooperative clients. Where they judge the therapist as competent and the therapist's methods as reasonable, NT clients can be most cooperative. But that doesn't mean that they ever stop questioning or correcting the clinician where they deem it necessary.

Taking Over the Nitpick Game

While it is natural for Rational clients to be skeptical, it is important that psychotherapists do not permit them to engage in the Nitpick game as a way of avoiding uncomfortable personal issues in therapy. Those NT clients who feel the most threatened may attempt to control the clinician and the content of the clinical sessions by initiating endless debates about therapeutic methods and the meanings of words. Where Robot players persist in playing Nitpick in spite of the therapist's best efforts to repeatedly direct the session back to the issue at hand, it may be necessary to prescribe the NT's game as a way of taking it over.

In prescribing the game of Nitpick, the therapist directs the client to argue, find fault, criticize, and just plain disagree. For example, a counselor may take over the Nitpick game by telling a Rational client, "Of course, you will probably find much that is questionable in what I say and do and I encourage you to bring all of your criticisms and concerns to my immediate attention." When presenting a new idea to NT clients, therapists may disqualify their message by saying, "Chances are that you will disagree with what I am about to say." By directing Robot players to play their game of Nitpick, clinicians are likely to maintain therapeutic control of the sessions and to keep the NT's resistance to a minimum.

STOPPING THE ROBOT GAME / 109

Fulfilling the Rational's Basic Needs

Rationals play the game of Robot when they feel like failures and when they fear that they are incapable of future successes. Sometimes they feel blocked in their efforts to achieve by circumstances at home, at work, or at school. Typically, these clients have fallen short of meeting their own very high standards of performance in some important area of their lives. The arena in which they believe themselves to be incompetent may be academic, social, athletic, sexual, or professional. Feeling ashamed, and having lost confidence in their ability to succeed, Robot players begin to protect themselves from looking and feeling even more incompetent, by distracting themselves and others with their survival game playing. In some cases, they end up stopping even those activities in which they have consistently demonstrated high levels of achievement. With no way of meeting their need for competence, their supply of self-esteem, self-respect, and self-confidence diminishes to almost nothing, and their survival game playing escalates.

To stop this self-defeating cycle, it is essential that clinicians find ways of helping Robot players to achieve again. This, however, is not as simple as it may seem. Since Robot players are intent on avoiding failure, they are reluctant to take the risks necessary for attaining success. The Rational student who feels like a failure in physics is likely to find lots of reasons to avoid completing a final project for the course. While she just might receive rave reviews on the project, she probably lacks the confidence that is necessary to turn the project in to begin with. Since it also opens her up to the possibility of more failure, it is just too risky.

Yet, when Robot players finally begin to experience success, they usually stop employing their survival tactics. The following case is an example of a forty-two-year-old INTP who stopped playing the Haunted variant of the Robot game once he began to achieve socially and academically.

> Art came to counseling because he was terrified by horrifying images that he couldn't seem to get out of his mind. Though he swore that he had absolutely no desire or intention to do himself or anyone else harm, Art found

himself confronted daily with images of himself hanging dead on a rope suspended from a ceiling. What's more, he also would often see himself throwing his adolescent daughters off of the balcony of a tall building. This scene particularly disturbed Art, since he claimed to love his family more than anything in the world, though he believed himself to be an incompetent father and husband.

Art told me that he hated his job as the manager of a logistics department in a large manufacturing firm. A serious man who almost never smiled, Art had no friends at work and felt alienated from his colleagues. Since he was convinced that nobody liked him, he tried to avoid interacting with people at work whenever possible. In response to my questioning about what he did for fun, Art indicated that he spent most of his free time reading, flying radio-controlled model airplanes, and working with his personal computer.

Art confessed that he had always wanted to be a high school mathematics teacher, but he lacked the confidence to enroll in a four-year college. Art's father had always told him that he was too dumb to go to college, and that it would be a waste of his time and money. Although Art almost failed high school, he received outstanding scores on the college entrance exam. His father discounted those scores as merely a sign of his son's ability to make good guesses. After some technical courses at a community college, Art had gone to work for the same company where his father was employed, eventually even working in the same logistics department as his father. In spite of his unhappiness there, Art was certain that he would not be able to succeed elsewhere. Sometimes he thought about going back to college, but he was terrified that he wouldn't do well.

The first thing I did was to teach Art to smile, and to assign him the task of smiling three times a day at anyone he chose. Art was astonished to report that people he had seen at work for ten years and with whom he had never spoken, suddenly initiated friendly conversations with him after he had smiled at them. Next, I introduced Art to the "technology of social interaction." He practiced basic conversational skills using role playing, and I taught him how to offer positive comments to his colleagues and subordinates when he noticed them doing their jobs well. Art's relationships at work improved considerably, as he became increasingly comfortable interacting with his co-workers.

I introduced Keirsey's model of personality types to help Art recognize that he was an NT doing the kind of work that is most satisfying to SJs. Using Gestalt exercises, Art began to deal with his unfinished business with his Guardian father. He was able to express his anger and resentment, and to refute his father's consistent put-downs.

After several sessions, I suggested to Art that he take just one mathematics class at the community college as an experiment, just to see how much he liked or disliked it. I told him, however, that before he signed up for the class, I wanted him to commit himself ahead of time to getting no better than a C in the course. He could feel free to enjoy the class as much as he wished, and to learn as much as he wanted, as long as his grade was a C or lower. In this way, we would know that how he felt about the class was independent of the grade that he would receive.

Art readily agreed to this experiment, although he broke his promise and got an A in the class, telling me that he just couldn't help himself. On the basis of that experience, he ended up going back to school full time in the evenings to get a B.S. in Mathematics, and then to earn his secondary teaching credential. Fortunately, Art's wife, an Idealist, was very supportive of her husband's decision to return to college. Both she and Art reported that their marriage improved while Art began to pursue his lifelong ambition. Art also reported, with relief, that his horrific images had completely disappeared within a few months of his beginning therapy.

Art was playing the game of Haunted to prevent himself from noticing all of the ways in which he felt like a miserable failure. It is important to remember that Haunted players are not dangerous. Art's images of throwing his daughters off of the balcony were not indicative of repressed anger towards them, nor of an unconscious desire to do them harm. On the contrary—he imagined himself hurting the two people towards whom he felt no malice at all. Hence, the images were that much more effective in distracting Art from feeling incompetent. As with all of the personality types and the survival games they play, Art never saw the connection between his horrific images and his feelings of inadequacy. Yet, once he began to experience some interpersonal and academic success, Art stopped playing Haunted.

Teaching the Technology of Social Interaction

Many introverted Rationals who are employing survival tactics lack basic social skills. These clients frequently report that they find small talk painful, and they often unwittingly turn others off with their serious-looking exterior alone. To cloak their own discomfort, these NTs may play the game of That's Illogical, in which they first interrogate, and then discount their conversational partners with comments like, "That's a really stupid idea." If they are playing the game of Super-Intellectual, they may also appear cold and unfeeling, and take every opportunity to lecture about very complicated subjects that turn their listeners off. These Rationals are not trying to be offensive—and often, they cannot understand why others seem to avoid them. They simply do not know how to talk to people of other types without affronting them.

A good way to motivate Robot players to learn and practice alternative social skills, is to talk about those behaviors in a language that the Rational type finds appealing. Since NTs are often attracted to science and technology, they usually respond with great interest and enthusiasm when they are offered the opportunity to acquire the "tools" that are associated with the "technology of social interaction." These tools—smiling, using a person's name, asking open-ended questions, listening for free information, offering free information, active listening, giving compliments—may be rehearsed in the counselor's office, and then practiced as homework (see Smith, 1985). It is important to keep any homework assignments small, so that clients can safely carry them out and begin to experience some little successes. For example, in the first case above, Art was asked to smile just three times a day. The immediate and very positive response that he received from co-workers is not uncommon when INTs begin to smile. One handsome twenty-three-year-old INTJ who claimed to have difficulty meeting young women left the session and began to practice smiling at people right away. Within two hours, a very attractive young woman he had seen, but never spoken to, had asked him out on a date.

It is very important for Rationals to learn to be redundant when it comes to saying positive things to family and associates. Since most NTs feel silly repeating themselves and stating the obvious, they are inclined to offer much-needed compliments or expressions of affection far too infrequently. Rationals are likely to assume that the absence of negative comments is enough to let others know they have positive feelings about a given relationship. Too often, the spouses, children, and employees of Rationals come to feel unloved, unappreciated, or inadequate because they have falsely misinterpreted the NTs' silence as a bad sign.

The following case of a Guardian and a Rational who are business partners demonstrates the misunderstandings that can arise between the types when they do not recognize and appreciate each other's differences.

> Two men came for counseling to resolve the difficulties they had experienced in working together in the large computer software company they had co-founded. Both indicated that they wanted to find a way of communicating with each other at the office without fighting. I learned that Jerry, an INTJ, was responsible for designing the computer software the company produced and marketed. Paul, an ISTJ, took care of logistics, writing procedure manuals for the company, and overseeing general office operations and production. An Artisan who did not attend the sessions was in charge of their marketing department.
>
> While major decisions were made jointly by Jerry and Paul, it was the little decisions that were causing a problem. Paul complained about the questions Jerry fired at him about every little business move that he made. With twenty years of managerial experience under his belt,

Paul felt discounted by these questions, as if Jerry didn't respect his business acumen enough to trust his decisions. Usually, Paul got defensive in response to Jerry's questions, and the two would end up battling. Paul also noted that Jerry was quick to point out any errors that he made, but slow to make positive comments about Paul's contributions to the business. Paul's final complaint was that whenever he asked Jerry a simple question about the computer, Jerry would launch into a lengthy technical explanation which included ninety percent more information than what Paul needed or wanted. Sometimes these lectures would go on for over an hour, regardless of Paul's protestations.

Jerry indicated that his work in solving complicated software problems required his complete, undivided attention, and that he resented Paul's frequent interruptions to ask questions that could wait until later. In addition, he was tired of hearing Paul's complaints about being burdened by numerous problems at the office.

When I asked him to respond to Paul's concerns, Jerry said that he only asked questions of Paul in order to learn from him. He probed for the reason behind every decision, in an effort to gain knowledge, and not because he was challenging Paul or doubting his judgement. In fact, Jerry said, he wouldn't have gone into business with Paul to begin with, if he didn't believe him to be highly competent.

My first intervention was to talk to Paul and Jerry about their personality differences, using the Keirseyan model. I pointed out that the two of them made an excellent team, since their strengths and talents were in such different arenas. Then I emphasized that Jerry's extensive questioning of Paul was clearly his way of complementing his partner, whom he considered an expert on business matters, and someone from whom he could learn a great deal. I stressed that Rational types have a hunger to understand everything, and that a person like Jerry would not be asking such questions of someone that he did not respect.

Next, I taught Jerry how to use "I statements" instead of why questions as a way of getting Paul to explain things to him. Paul had the opportunity to practice responding to Jerry's comments or questions by buying time, rather than feeling put on the spot. This means that Paul would decline to answer Jerry's questions at the moment, but offer to do so at a later time. And I assigned both of them the task of telling each other daily at least one thing that they appreciated about working with the other.

Paul agreed not to ask questions of Jerry, except at certain hours of the day that were mutually established. Paul also said he would stop voicing his worries so often at the office. And Jerry agreed to try to curb his natural Rational propensity to provide answers that are much more complicated and detailed than what his Guardian partner required.

Three weeks later the two returned to their second session to report that all was going very well between them. Paul no longer felt disrespected by Jerry, and Jerry was glad to have learned some new ways of communicating with others. In several follow-up sessions, they continued to report smooth sailing.

Introducing New Models

Clinicians are likely to win the interest and cooperation of Robot-playing clients when they offer them coherent models for understanding human behavior. As is evident in the case of Jerry and Paul, Rationals can often benefit greatly from learning about personality types.* Because they are such a small segment of the population, Rationals rarely meet people who are just like them. And many NTs report feeling puzzled and uncertain when it comes to dealing with the other three kinds of people. The Keirseyan model provides the Robot-player who feels incompetent in social situations with a map of human behavior. That map enables the Rational to function more confidently and safely in what was previously dangerous territory.

---

* While other types may also benefit, it is almost always helpful to explain personality theory to Rational clients. Conversely, Artisan types are the least likely to find information about personalities interesting or useful.

Personality theory can also help Rational parents to recognize the ways in which their children are different from them, and vice versa. For example, an INTP father—a college professor—and his fourteen-year-old ESFP son were often at odds with each other. The father complained that his son was a disappointment to him because he was not involved in extracurricular activities, he did not excel in athletics, and his grades were not particularly outstanding. In fact, the boy was almost failing the very subject that was his father's field of expertise. What's more, the boy was extremely bright, and capable of all As if he applied himself. Yet, the more Dad tried to convince the boy to apply himself, the worse things became. It was apparent that the son felt angry and hurt that his father was always telling him he wasn't good enough. In typical Artisan fashion, he responded to Dad's attempts to get him to do more and try harder by doing even less.

Using type theory, I was able to explain to the father that his son was completely different from him, and that he could not expect his son to follow in his footsteps. As he backed off from pressuring the boy into being just like him, and as he began to appreciate his son for being himself, the son's grades improved significantly, and he became more involved in using his artistic talents.

Naturally, temperament theory is not the only model that may be useful with Robot players. Another that is sometimes helpful is the ABC model from Rational-Emotive Therapy, which stresses that emotional reactions stem from irrational ideas, and not from events themselves (see Ellis, 1962). Not surprisingly, Rational types respond favorably to an approach which is based upon identifying and dispelling irrational beliefs. I once had a troubled seventeen-year-old INTJ client bring a typed list of Albert Ellis's ten most common irrational beliefs to therapy, and hand them over to me, saying, "I found these in a book, and I think you should know that I believe every one of them!"

Still another model that can be effective for stopping the game of Robot, is the ego state model from Transactional Analysis (TA) (see James and Jongeward, 1971). Robot players are prone to giving themselves lots of critical parenting messages about how they should be perfect, and about how awful they are for being imperfect. While the intent is to motivate themselves, the actual effect of these messages is self-paralysis. Yet, instead of stopping the negative self-talk, the typical response of Robot players is to *increase* it as they find themselves succeeding less and less.

It is usually necessary to explain to clients that there is a difference between noticing things that one might want to improve about oneself, and judging or criticizing oneself. While making an observation about one's own shortcomings is fine, judging oneself as bad, stupid, or worthless because of those foibles is something entirely different. In the end, those criticisms only make things worse instead of better.

The empty chair exercise is a good way of getting Robot players to verbalize their internal negative self-judgement. By directing them to pretend to be their critical parent, the counselor can prompt clients to say all of their exaggerated self-criticisms out loud, so that they can hear the things that they have been telling themselves. It is also helpful to have them imagine that their other ego states—for example, the nurturing parent, the adult, or the rebellious child—have the opportunity to respond to the critical parent's messages. This method can also assist Robot players in getting back in touch with the spontaneous, joyful, playful self that is characterized by the free-child ego state.

Using the empty chair exercise, one INTP client, Anne, revealed that she had been telling herself horrible things all day long about how worthless, fat, ugly, and stupid she was. Rather than provoking herself to lose weight and find a job, her critical parenting messages had the reverse effect. For one year, Anne had been gaining weight rapidly, and she had taken no steps to find a job. Yet, she honestly believed that this was the best way to motivate herself.

I told Anne that feeding herself those messages was like feeding herself a poison that destroyed any motivation she might have. I suggested that she try an experiment in which she stopped trying to motivate herself with critical parenting messages for one day. Anne reluctantly agreed. To my complete surprise, she returned three weeks later to report that she had lost seven pounds, joined a health club, attended fifteen exercise classes, and sent out resumés to several prospective employers.

When I asked Anne to explain what happened, she told me that it was difficult to stop the critical parenting messages at first, but that by the end of the first day she felt so good that she decided to try it for another day. On the second day, she suddenly felt a burst of energy, and decided to go out and join a health club. By the third day, she felt strongly motivated to work on her resumé. Having experienced such a dramatic shift, Anne resisted the temptation to fall back into her pattern of negative self-judgment when it would present itself.

Prescribing Poor Performances

Robot players must experience success if they are to relinquish their survival tactics. Yet in their determination to avoid failure, these clients also end up avoiding those actions that could enable them to achieve. The best way for therapists to assure that Robot players will be successful is to prescribe that they perform badly.[*] By directing Robot players to make mistakes or mess up performances, clinicians are actually setting them up in paradoxical win-win situations. If they do what their therapists have asked them to do, and perform poorly, then these clients are successfully completing their assignments. And if they don't do as their therapists have asked, then they are performing well—another form of success. In prescribing that Robot players make errors on purpose, clinicians give them a fail-safe opportunity to practice new behaviors.

It is not a good idea to tell Robot players that they are being asked to perform poorly so they will end up feeling successful, since that can dilute the effectiveness of this kind of intervention. Of course, Robot players do want a good reason for making

---

[*] Dr. Milton Erickson's cases are filled with examples of his masterful use of this technique with all four types of personalities (see Haley, 1967, 1973; Rossi, 1980).

intentional mistakes. Since NTs usually have an affinity for research, they will often be willing to perform poorly on purpose if clinicians tell them that they are participating in some kind of *information gathering*, or an *experiment*.

For example, in the case of Art described earlier, I persuaded him to enroll in a college mathematics class as an experiment designed to provide information about his likes and dislikes, rather than as a means of testing his academic competence. In fact, he was to earn no more than a C in the class, so that he could be certain his opinions were not colored by a favorable grade. Under those circumstances Art felt no pressure to perform, and he ended up earning an A after all.

In another example, a high school girl named Cecilia who was playing the Blanking Out variant of Robot, avoided making presentations in front of a group because she was afraid that she would completely forget what she had planned to say. Her fear was so strong that she didn't even feel comfortable raising her hand in class to ask a question. She also shied away from participating in conversations in groups of three or more people. I told Cecilia that before I could help her, I needed more information about the way in which other people responded when she would blank out. I asked if she would be willing to participate in an experiment that would help me obtain this valuable data. I explained that her part in the experiment was to collect information by intentionally forgetting a word or a sentence once a day in the presence of any two people, and then later recording their responses on a report form. Though she claimed to feel silly in doing so, Cecilia reluctantly participated in our experiment. Almost immediately she began to feel increasingly comfortable in conversing with classmates, and considerably less fearful of blanking out.

Often Robot players will report that they are afraid of initiating friendships with the opposite sex for fear of rejection. In such cases, I will talk about the importance of being competent at receiving rejections. I emphasize that successful people are always good at getting rejected, since no one has ever reached the top without having that happen many times along the way. For homework, I direct the client to go out and collect a certain number of rejections per week, ostensibly so that the client might become more competent at handling negative responses from others. Naturally, what almost always happens is that the client comes back to report that in spite of his or her best efforts, no rejections were forthcoming. What's more, the client often reports receiving very favorable responses from those approached. Where the client has managed to be rejected, then that is celebrated as an achievement, and another positive step in the direction of increasing competency.

In the following case I used paradoxical directives with a twenty-six-year-old ENTJ who was playing the Superstition and Haunted variants of Robot.

> Shirley came to therapy because she was obsessed with the notion that she might be crazy. Shirley had access to a copy of the Diagnostic and Statistical Manual (DSM) used to make psychiatric diagnoses at her place of employment, and she could not stop herself from spending endless hours pouring over the pages, seeking evidence of her own insanity, and yet fearing that she would find it there. Besides feeling compelled to read and re-ead the DSM, Shirley reported that she would engage in certain mandatory, repetitive behaviors throughout the day, like touching her desk on one side a certain number of times, when someone else had touched the other side. Shirley was most disturbed and frightened, however, by the horrible thoughts she had of cutting off her two-year-old son's head with a large butcher knife. She adored her son, Todd, and had never done anything to hurt him. Nor did she have any intention or desire to do him future harm. Yet, she constantly imagined herself chopping off his head. It's no wonder she feared that she was losing her mind.

> I learned that Shirley's Artisan husband, Jack, had been out to sea with the Navy for four months. During that time, Shirley and Todd had been living with Jack's Guardian parents in order to save money to pay for the new house they were purchasing. Shirley's problems had begun about a month after she and Todd had moved into Jack's parents' house, where Shirley felt completely unwelcome. Jack's parents were highly critical of Shirley. Among other things, they would often make derogatory

comments about her housekeeping, cooking, and parenting. Shirley responded to their criticisms by getting angry, and then trying even harder to demonstrate that she was a good housekeeper, cook, wife, and mother.

Jack's mother watched Todd during the day, and often refused to follow the instructions Shirley gave her regarding the child. Shirley missed Jack terribly, and looked forward to his return in two more months, at which time they would move into their new house.

At work, Shirley was also under enormous pressure. Over the past six months, she had been trying to do the job of three people. She tried hard to be the perfect employee, but she felt like a failure.

Shirley's mother was her best support system—more like a close friend than a parent. Whenever she was having an episode of DSM reading at the office, she would call her mother, who worked in another department, and her mother would come over to comfort her and assure her that she was not crazy. In the evenings, Shirley would often go to her parents' house when she was feeling her worst. Shirley would ask her mother up to fifty times a day, "Am I crazy?" Her mother would spend hours offering support and encouragement to her only daughter.

I told Shirley that it was evident that she was trying to do an A+ job at work and at home, and that it was more than any human could possibly do. I wondered if she would be willing to do an experiment, in which she would do a perfect C+ job as an employee, a houseguest, a wife, and a daughter-in-law—and just focus her energies on being an A+ mom. Shirley smiled in response to this assignment, and readily agreed.

I also told Shirley that she was obviously very concerned about how well her mother was able to handle their separation. Since she was married, Shirley had always lived right down the street from her mother. Now her new house would be almost an hour's drive away. I commended Shirley in finding a great way of making certain that her mother would not feel rejected, and seeing to it that her mother could feel needed. I told Shirley that it was important that she continue to pour over the DSM daily at work, so that she could tell her mother about her fears. I assigned her the task of going at least once a day during work hours to tell her mother that she was fearing insanity, and of asking her mother at least thirty times each day if she (Shirley) was crazy. This was, after all, a way in which she could keep her mother involved in her life. Without Shirley's problems, I speculated that she and her mother might not know what to talk about. Shirley argued back that she was making her mother a nervous wreck, rather than helping her. She also declared that there were lots of other things she and her mother could talk about—like childrearing, for example.

Within several weeks, Shirley returned to tell me that she had asserted herself with her mother-in-law regarding Todd's care, and that Jack's mother responded favorably. Shirley claimed to enjoy doing a C+ job at work and at home so much that she planned to continue. She also found that she had much more energy to spend with her son doing positive things.

Shirley had refused to ask her mother "Am I crazy?" thirty times a day, though she still asked her around fifteen times, and she still read the DSM and did repetitive touching on her desk. She reported that she and her mother had begun to talk about other things together. She also said that her horrible thoughts about cutting off her son's head were diminished somewhat, but by no means gone.

Over the next two months, Shirley continued to show good progress. But it wasn't until Shirley, Jack, and Todd were settled in their own home and Shirley had found a new job, that she ceased using Robot tactics.

Prescribing Ordeals

One more way to stop the Robot game is by prescribing ordeals. While ordeals may at times be useful in stopping the other three games, they are particularly effective with NTs.[*] Dr. Milton

---

[*] In *Love, Sex, and Violence*, Cloé Madanes points out that ordeals are particularly useful for obsessions, compulsions, and self-inflicted

Erickson originated this approach, which is described in detail in the book *Ordeal Therapy*, by Jay Haley (1984). To use this method, clinicians prescribe that Robot players do something that is unpleasant, and yet good for them, every time that they engage in certain specified Robot game tactics.

For example, Barbara is desperate to stop playing the Superstition variant of Robot, whereby she washes her hands over one hundred times a day. The therapist learns that Barbara wants to limit her hand-washing to just ten times a day. To prescribe an ordeal in this case, the therapist begins by asking Barbara to list those good things that she thinks she *should* be doing, but she *isn't* doing. Barbara mentions activities like pulling weeds, studying foreign languages, organizing her files, and cleaning her closets. Next, the therapist reminds Barbara of her trustworthiness, by saying, "I know that you are a woman of your word. Once you give your word, I know that you can be trusted to honor your commitments." Finally, the therapist tells Barbara: "I have a guaranteed solution to your hand-washing problem; however, you must promise to follow my directives before I tell you what that solution is. All I can tell you now, is that the solution is good for you." The clinician absolutely refuses to reveal the solution until Barbara has given her promise that she will do exactly as instructed. Rather than pressuring Barbara to give in, the counselor suggests that Barbara take several weeks to think about it.

Since Barbara is curious and anxious to hear about and employ this guaranteed solution to her hand-washing problem, she agrees to follow whatever directives the therapist will give her. Once Barbara has given her word, the therapist tells her that from now on, when she washes her hands more than ten times a day, she must get up at three in the morning and spend time cleaning her closets. For every ten extra times she washes her hands in a day, she must do one hour of cleaning. Since she has already agreed to carrying out the ordeal, Barbara compulsively follows the clinician's instructions. After a few nights of

violence. They are not recommended for substance abusers and depressed people (1990, 21).

unpleasant closet cleaning, she abandons her excessive hand-washing.

Ordeals are only effective when clients are sufficiently moti-vated to carry them out. For this reason, it is important to follow the procedure outlined above. It is also important to prescribe ordeals that are unpleasant enough to motivate clients to stop employing their game tactics. For example, cleaning one's closets in the daytime might not be uncomfortable enough—doing the same at 3:00 A.M. is far more likely to have the desired effect.

In her book, *Love, Sex, and Violence*, Cloé Madanes (1990) describes an ordeal she used with a woman who was procrasti-nating on completing her doctoral dissertation. For every day that the woman did not write four pages, Madanes instructed her to send a check for $100 dollars to a stepsister she did not like, with a note that expressed her love. The woman never sent a check, and completed her dissertation in just a few months.

In the following case, I also prescribed an ordeal to help a thirty-year-old man who was having trouble completing his dissertation.

> Carl was a kind and sensitive INTP who came to therapy because he was frustrated with his inability to finish his doctoral dissertation. Although Carl had been working on his dissertation for many years, he still had most of it left to write. He was highly critical of himself for not yet finishing—but he just couldn't bring himself to complete it. He worked on the dissertation almost every day, but never seemed to get very far.
>
> As I got to know Carl better, I learned that he had a very limited social life. Since he had been deeply wounded over the sudden and unexpected ending of a long-term intimate relationship with an ESFP five years before, Carl had completely avoided close relationships with women. The very thought of going out on a date made him extremely uncomfortable. He was afraid of saying the wrong things, of being a bore, and of looking and sounding foolish. What's more, he was afraid of getting hurt again. He blamed himself for being stupid the first

time, and he wasn't going to make the same mistake again.

I worked with Carl over a long period of time dealing with issues ranging from the severe emotional abuse he suffered as a child, to his current relationships with parents and adult siblings. Through working with his inner child, Carl was able to nurture and reparent himself, and to make new decisions about what was possible for him. He practiced new assertion skills that he employed at work and with his parents during their infrequent visits.

To get Carl moving forward on his dissertation and in his social life, I prescribed an ordeal. Carl was to complete ten pages on his dissertation in a week. The work could be a first draft, and even poorly written, but it had to be ten full pages on his computer. (Carl had told me that ten rough draft pages in a week was a reasonable goal for himself.) If Carl did not complete the full ten pages within a week, then he would have to have a date with a woman. It was up to him to find someone who was willing to go out with him. Carl squirmed and protested when I described the ordeal, but I reminded him that he had already given his word, and that I knew I could trust him to honor his commitment to me.

Carl returned two weeks later to report that he had only completed nine and a half pages of his dissertation the first week and ten the second week. In accordance with our agreement, he had already been out on a date—which was surprisingly fun. I assigned a continuation of the ordeal for the following two weeks.

Once the ordeal got Carl dating again, I gave him assignments to collect certain numbers of rejections, and also to go out on a date and to intentionally look and sound as foolish and boring as he possibly could. As Carl followed through on these exercises, he began to gain confidence in his ability to relate to women. By working with the Keirsey model, he also became more aware of the different personality types, and able to better predict and understand the behavior of those unlike him.

During this time Carl's dissertation work proceeded slowly, but favorably. When we terminated therapy, he was working steadily on finishing it. Eight months later, he wrote to tell me that he was on the verge of completing his dissertation, and that he had established a very satisfying relationship with a special woman.

Conclusion

This chapter reviews some methods which are often effective for stopping the Robot game. There will be times when these techniques may also be useful for working with Blackmail, Complain, and Masquerade players. Conversely, therapists may find it appropriate to utilize some of the tools described in the other three chapters with NT clients.

Part three provides more detailed examples of how to recognize NT clients and how to employ effective intervention strategies for stopping their games.

Rationals who have stopped playing Robot are ingenious and achieving. They are wonderful independent thinkers, who utilize their incredible powers of reason to solve complicated problems—whether curing diseases, managing multinational corporations, designing computer hardware and software, or inventing ways of exploring other galaxies. NTs who feel good about themselves are not only intent on acquiring new knowledge; they are also apt to share it with others through their writing and/or teaching. Often ahead of their times, Rationals are the intellectual pioneers who explore uncharted scientific territories.

In families, Rationals bring curiosity, stimulating ideas, and a love of learning. NTs are reasonable, objective, clever, fascinating, achieving, honest, hardworking, autonomous, and kind. They are courageous role models, teaching us to stand firm behind our principles and convictions, encouraging us to think for ourselves.

Rationals who have given up their Robot games are humble. They are aware of their strengths and also their limitations. NTs with healthy self-esteem are willing to take risks, as they pursue those avenues of achievement that interest them. They are actively involved in learning, in acquiring new competencies. And they demonstrate exceptional willpower in the accomplishment of their goals. In relationships, successful NTs are more aware of the concerns and feelings of others, and more likely to be redundant in expressing their love and appreciation. They are able to be playful and spontaneous, and they maintain a balance in their lives between work and recreation.

Chapter 7

STOPPING THE MASQUERADE GAME

Though they make up only a small percentage of the population—from 10 to 12 percent[*]—Masquerade players are seen in great numbers by mental health professionals. This isn't because Idealists have more problems than the other three personalities; rather, it is because they are so interested in self-growth. Idealists are on a lifelong path of self-discovery, an eternal quest to become self-actualized. Typically, they are drawn to those books, classes, workshops, and individuals who will offer them guidance along their path. For NFs, therapy is an opportunity to receive assistance in uncovering and becoming their true selves, as they let go of the disguises they have been hiding behind—disguises that were designed to win the approval and acceptance of others.

More than any other type, NFs are prone to seek validation from others that they are, indeed, okay. Relationships are the center of their lives and the source of their deepest feelings about themselves. When things go wrong in relationships, these clients are especially prone to conclude that it is because there is something wrong with *them*. Taking everything personally, they de-

---

[*] Since the publication of *Please Understand Me*, Dr. Keirsey has revised his estimate of NFs in the population from 12 to 10 percent.

cide that the problems in their relationships are due to their own terrible defects. Where they have been inauthentic in an effort to maintain rapport with others, they are likely to feel even more ashamed of themselves. Hence, Masquerade players end up using their game tactics to keep others from discovering what they believe to be the painful truth about themselves—that they are worthless phonies.

Stopping the Game of Grasshopper

Clinicians may expect that Idealist clients will unconsciously employ the Masquerade game during psychotherapy sessions, in spite of their high level of motivation to work on themselves. For, as much as these clients want to grow, they are also terrified that the psychotherapist will discover their most shameful selves. Therapists must be alert so that they are not thrown off the track by the Masquerade player's deceptive tactics. Most notable among these will be the tendency to present pseudocomplaints. Often, NF clients will talk about problems with the therapist that are just minor frustrations or irritations, rather than discussing those issues that are especially troublesome and emotionally charged. What's more, they will avoid getting specific about anything, even when questioned for concrete examples. And, should the topic get dangerously close to the issue that is really bothering them, Masqueraders will play the Grasshopper variant of their game, hopping suddenly onto a "safer" subject. For example, a woman who is deeply distraught over her relationship with a married man, may briefly mention that topic and then claim that she wants to talk about her relationship with her daughter. Whenever the topic of her affair is raised, she quickly changes the subject.

There are several things that clinicians can do to assure that sessions with Masquerade players will be as helpful as possible. First of all, it is essential to assist NF clients in setting clear, specific, concrete goals for therapy. Of course, this is important to do with all clients; it is just a little more difficult to accomplish with Idealists, who tend to think in broader, more global terms. For example, in response to a question about what they want to accomplish in therapy, they are likely to say something like, "I want to be happier," or, "I want to improve my relationships." It is up to the therapist to help the NF client specify more concrete goals, by asking questions like: "How exactly would you and your life look different if you were happier," "What particular relationship would you like to improve?" or, "How would someone who observed you and your mate be able to tell if your relationship was improved?" Therapists should not move on with Idealist clients, until tangible goals have been set with them.

A second way of assuring that sessions with Masqueraders are productive is by asking for specific examples whenever possible. These clients may gloss over sensitive issues by using lots of generalizations. Concrete examples enable therapists to clarify what is really bothering Idealist clients. For example, a client reports, "Relationships with women always make me feel depressed." In response to a request for a specific example of a time when he felt depressed because of a woman, that client might describe a recent interaction with his mother, who is verbally abusive with him. Without asking for a clear-cut example, chances are that the clinician would have assumed the client was talking about recent girlfriends rather than his mother.

A third way to circumvent the Grasshopper game is to firmly, gently, and consistently refocus the session to the topic at hand when clients try to change the subject. Sometimes it is necessary to do this over and over again with Masquerade players who repeatedly hop from sensitive issues to less-threatening ones. It may help to remember that this subject switching tactic is done unconsciously and inadvertently by NF clients, who only wish to protect themselves from the pain of rejection.

Fulfilling the Idealist's Basic Needs

Idealists play Masquerade when they fear that their needs for integrity, identity, and rapport with others cannot be met. The Masquerade game is one of deception, used to keep both the self and others from noticing where the NF has been inauthentic. It is a desperate attempt at sustaining relationships and avoiding the scorn of others. A Masquerade player is like the mother bird who flaps her wings and pretends to be injured in order to keep the hunter from spotting her young. These clients use their dramatic and captivating performances to attract attention, thus protecting their most vulnerable selves from being discovered. For example, a young ENFJ man who has been miserably unhappy in his marriage for years feels guilty about his desire to leave his wife. He knows that initiating a divorce would mean risking the rejection of his wife, family, and friends. Rather than expressing his true feelings, which he is ashamed of, the young man begins to fall asleep at inappropriate times and places. He cannot seem to stop himself from falling asleep during his favorite college classes, or at red lights while driving, or while waiting in line at fast-food restaurants. His game of Statue keeps everyone (including himself) from noticing what is really troubling him.

In order to stop the Masquerade game, it is essential to find ways of helping Idealist clients to be true to themselves. Usually, Masqueraders face a dilemma in which they cannot be true to themselves and true to others at the same time. If they maintain their standards of integrity, they risk earning the disapproval, displeasure, or disappointment of important people in their lives. Yet, if they behave in accordance with the expectations or desires of significant others, then they violate their own personal ethics. In this double-bind situation, it is no wonder that they turn to survival game playing. By employing Masquerade tactics, NF clients manage to either avoid behaving inauthentically, or to conceal their phoney behavior from themselves and everyone else.

For example, an NF high school girl must either lie on behalf of her boyfriend, who was caught selling marijuana at school, or risk losing her relationship with him. Days before the legal hearing at which she is to testify, she loses her voice, though physicians can find no medical reason why she cannot speak. Her survival game of Statue is designed to protect her from jeopardizing both her relationship with her boyfriend, and her personal integrity. As long as she cannot speak, she cannot lie in favor of her boyfriend; nor can she testify against him by telling the truth.

In order to meet their need for authenticity, Masquerade players often require assistance in resolving the ethical conflicts they face. Sometimes it is enough to help them clarify their options. At other times, it is necessary to help them find the courage to stand behind their principles and risk the rejection of others. The following case is an example of a twenty-four-year-old INFP who stopped playing the Statue variant of Masquerade when he began to act with integrity.

> Jeff came to me for therapy because he was experiencing frightening episodes daily during which he felt as if he was in a strange dream and nothing around him was real. Jeff said that these awful feelings could come on at any time—for example, while he was working in his office as a writer for a local magazine, or while he was out on a date. And nothing he tried seemed to make them stop. These episodes had gotten so bad that he had called in sick to work often in the past few weeks. He had also been curtailing his social activities.

> Jeff was willing to talk with me about his family, his work (which he claimed to enjoy very much), his interest in sports, and his male friends. I noticed that he mentioned that he had a girlfriend, but that he changed the subject whenever I asked him about her. With further gentle but persistent questioning, I was able to learn that Jeff actually had *two* intimate relationships—with an ESTJ school teacher, (Jane) and an ESFP dancer (Amanda). While Amanda knew about Jane, and didn't really care if Jeff had another relationship or not, Jane thought that she had a monogamous relationship with Jeff, and that the two of them would eventually marry. Jeff confessed that he felt *terribly* guilty about not being honest with Jane, but that he was fearful that he would hurt her deeply if she knew about Amanda. What's more, he was afraid that Jane would break up with him if she knew the truth. He claimed to admire Jane very much, and thought that he might want to marry her someday. But in the present, he was enjoying his relationship with the carefree, spontaneous, charming Amanda far too much to want to end it. He especially valued their exciting sexual encounters.

> Once Jeff had told me about his situation, he seemed visibly relieved to have gotten it all out. Next, I helped him

explore his options using Gestalt techniques. For example, I had the part of him that wanted to continue to lie to Jane dialogue with the part of him that wanted to tell Jane the truth. Eventually, Jeff concluded that he could not live with himself any more unless he was honest with Jane about his relationship with Amanda. Since he was not willing to end his liaison with Amanda, he felt that Jane had a right to know about it. He also decided that perhaps Jane wasn't the right woman for him, since they had never had too much fun together, especially in bed. He confessed that she was often critical of him, just like his mother had been when he was growing up. Using the empty chair, we rehearsed what Jeff would say to Jane about their relationship and the existence of the other woman.

Shortly after Jeff told Jane the truth and the two of them decided to end their association, his dreamlike episodes stopped occurring. When we terminated therapy, Jeff reported that he was enjoying his relationship with Amanda more than ever.

Idealists must have a sense of meaning and purpose in their lives. They feel best about themselves when they are making a valuable and unique contribution to humanity. Sometimes Masquerade players need help in finding ways of making a positive difference in the lives of others. Idealists thrive in occupations like teaching or counseling that enable them to foster individual growth. They may also find it very rewarding to participate in a social movement or "cause" that is in alignment with their most cherished values and strongest beliefs. An example might be a community group devoted to the eradication of poverty, prejudice, or pollution, or an organization aimed at protecting the rights of children or animals.

On a more intimate level, the Masquerade player may benefit by writing poetry, essays, or fiction, by tutoring illiterate adults or children, by writing and performing uplifting music, or by acting in a community theater production. In schools, peer-counseling opportunities are ideal for these clients. In short, anything that enables NF clients to *inspire* others is an appropriate way of helping them to meet their needs. This is in contrast to the SJ, who needs to be of *service* to others.

Usually, Idealists who are playing survival games are out of touch with themselves. Often, in an effort to be the *ideal* mate, child, student, or parent, they have lost sight of their *real* selves.* It is as if these NFs become so caught up in playing the roles that are expected of them, that they lose sight of their true identities. Piece by piece, they have disowned important parts of themselves that may not be acceptable to others. Eventually, they begin to feel apathetic and listless.

The problem here is not that the Idealist is playing roles—certainly all personalities play a variety of roles in their lives. The problem for NFs is that they try to fill their roles in accordance with other people's ideals rather than their own. For example, a woman might try to be the perfect wife, not according to her own values and beliefs, but according to those of her husband, mother, or mother-in-law. Although she might long to go to college to earn a bachelor's degree, and to take up painting as a hobby, she refrains from doing so because it is not in alignment with what others expect of her. Over time, she begins to wonder why she is just not happy.

For Idealists, apathy is a very painful feeling—since it means that their normal enthusiasm for life and empathy for others is gone. Usually, NFs who are playing Masquerade will report that they don't know what they feel—they just know that they aren't happy, and they don't understand why. Since Idealists tend to repress negative emotions—pushing them far out of consciousness—they really aren't aware of the anger, guilt, resentment, or sadness that is buried deep inside of them.** Typically, all they notice is the *absence* of good feelings. According to Keirsey, the apathy of the Idealist is different from the emptiness of the Artisan, who is devoid of impulses. It

---

* Carl Rogers described this process beautifully in his classic book, *Counseling and Psychotherapy* (1942).

** In contrast, Guardians are consciously aware of their negative emotions, though they try to deny to themselves that they are feeling whatever they are feeling. Thus, the SJ who feels resentment, says to him or herself, "I shouldn't feel that way—I must not feel that way—I don't really feel that way." The NF, however, simply buries the resentment from the start, so it remains out of consciousness.

is also unlike the depression of the SJ, who is filled up with sadness, or the tenseness of the NT.

Masquerade players need help in discovering their true identities. This means unearthing the buried treasures that lie within them—thoughts, feelings, and desires that have long been out of their awareness. It means discovering and activating their previously untapped potential. And ultimately, it means transcending their personalities (or egos) to identify with their greater selves. For it is in transcendence that NFs find the meaning of life that they are perpetually seeking. Idealists want to know themselves as spiritual, as well as physical beings; for them, self-realization is the process of becoming one with the soul.

To facilitate the process of self-actualization, NFs may profit from participation in groups, classes, workshops, seminars, and/or alternative means of healing (such as breathwork and bodywork). Idealist clients are also likely to find journal writing and the recording of their dreams a worthwhile and fulfilling experience. In addition, most Masquerade players love to read, and they will devour books which help them to better understand themselves and their relationships.

NF clients often enjoy listening to audio tapes for stimulating their personal growth. These tapes may be lectures offered by wise teachers, or they may be guided visualizations which assist clients in journeying deep within themselves for inner healing and the activation of their greatest potentials.[*] I have found that audio tapes are so effective with Masquerade players, that I create individualized, guided visualization tapes for these clients during therapy sessions in my office.[**]

---

[*] See the back of this book for information about *Bridges Across Time*—a recording of two guided visualizations that are examples of this kind of work.

[**] I make guided visualization tapes for all four types of clients. It is the Idealist clients, however, who are the most likely of all to play them regularly, and thus, to profit from them. Some Artisans, Guardians, and Rationals will also report that they find the tapes extremely helpful and enjoyable.

Doing Parts Work

Most Masquerade players have unconsciously disowned or rejected those parts of themselves that they find shameful or threatening (see Small, 1991).* The dissociated parts can be unacceptable thoughts, feelings, or desires, or they can be painful memories of past actions. These fragmented parts of the self may be repressed—as in the games of Forgetful, Martyr, or Statue—or they may be projected onto someone else, as in the game of Mind Reader. They may also be stored in the muscles, as in the game of Twitch. It is important to recognize that the NF client's parts (or subselves) being described here are *not* separate personalities. Rather, they are little pieces of the self that have been split off from the whole.

There are many ways of helping Masqueraders recover their missing pieces and become complete again; among the most effective are those methods that enable clients to have dialogues with or between different parts of themselves (see Landis, 1988). When therapists direct Masqueraders to split themselves into various pieces for the purpose of conducting therapeutic dialogues, they are actually employing the method of symptom prescription. Paradoxically, it is by instructing the dissociated NF to dissociate even more (under the therapist's direction) that integration is ultimately achieved.

Conversations between parts can take place in the client's imagination—with guided visualization techniques—or they may involve the use of an empty chair. By holding dialogues with or between their various subselves, Idealists can become aware of their buried thoughts, feelings, and desires. They can also resolve inner conflicts, find healthier ways of meeting their needs, release negative emotions, and uncover and activate powerful inner resources for creating positive changes in their lives.

Idealists are usually highly imaginative clients who are very comfortable with ambiguity. Hence, they are almost always willing to try things in therapy that will make other types

---

* While people of all four personalities can, and do, dissociate, it is the NF who does so to the greatest extreme.

balk. Not only will they participate willingly in Gestalt, role playing or guided visualization exercises requiring them to split themselves into pieces—they will do so with a sense of drama, flair, mystery, and adventure. Set the stage for Masquerade players, and they will create the rest, drawing from the richness of their own unconscious processes. What's more, since Idealists naturally seek (and find) meaning in everything that happens to them, they will automatically search for a way of construing their experience so that they may derive maximum therapeutic benefit from it.

Parts work is useful whenever clinicians suspect that Masqueraders face some sort of inner conflict or dilemma—whether conscious or just beyond the realm of the clients' conscious awareness. The conflicts may involve contradictory beliefs, desires, emotions, or behaviors. It is helpful to stage dialogues between those parts of the client that appear to be discrepant—for example, the head can converse with the heart, or the part of the client that wants to end a particular relationship can talk with the part of the client that wants to maintain it. Similarly, a client's fearful self can converse with his or her confident self, or the part of the client that wants to be physically healthy can talk to the part that is physically ill.

Counselors can utilize visualization methods for doing parts work by having Masqueraders close their eyes and get in touch with the part of themselves that feels, thinks or behaves in a certain way. To facilitate contact, it is often helpful to have clients focus on the way their body feels when they experience the emotions or behavior they want to change. When contact is made, some clients will see an image, others will feel the part's presence, still others will only hear things. Clients can imagine themselves talking with one particular subself, or they can visualize two or more parts of themselves having a dialogue.

Visualization is particularly effective for engaging more than two of the client's parts in a dialogue. For example, therapists can ask Masqueraders to imagine that an observer self is watching and listening while remaining detached and objective, as two other parts converse. At appropriate moments, this observant part of the client can be called upon to offer new perspectives on the situation being discussed. Still another example is to have clients use their imaginations to access a wise and loving inner advisor, who offers conflicting parts alternative solutions to current problems.

The Voice Dialogue Method is still another very powerful way of doing parts work with Masquerade players (Stone and Winkelman, 1989). This approach enables the therapist to hold conversations directly with the client's various subpersonalities.

Parts work is a great way to help Masqueraders get in touch with their disowned strengths. Often clients are more focused on their liabilities than on their assets. It can be very therapeutic to ask clients to be the part of themselves that is courageous, confident, secure, powerful, creative and/or wise, and to dialogue with the part of themselves that is fearful, lacking in confidence, insecure, weak, noncreative, and/or ignorant. Where clients balk and declare that there *is* no confident part of them, counselors can ask them to just *pretend* that it is there, and to imagine what it would be like if it did, indeed, exist. By pretending, Idealists can access and activate their hidden potentials.

While clients are playing the part of their insecure or fearful sub-selves, it is best to have them verbalize all of their greatest insecurities and most extreme fears. Usually, these feelings are the result of irrational or limiting beliefs involving absolutes that the client has long accepted as the truth (see Ellis, 1962). When clients are prompted to state those beliefs repeatedly out loud—using words like *never, always,* and *impossible*—often they become highly motivated to change their attitudes and behavior.

For example, I used the empty chair to do parts work with a forty-three-year-old INFJ named Diana, who had been severely physically, sexually, and emotionally abused as a child. Diana had always isolated herself from friendships—particularly with women. This position had also been doubly reinforced by Diana's mother (who violently beat her) with messages about how women could not be trusted. During one session, I asked the part of Diana that wanted to reach out and form new friend-ships, to interact with the insecure part of her that was hiding from people. What ensued was a very emotional dialogue between those two subselves. The isolationist part of Diana expressed her terror of letting people in and her intention to keep Diana safe, although the price of that safety was loneliness and the absence of love. With my prompting, this subself stated that she could *never* let Diana have any friends, because *no* woman could *ever* be trusted. She indicated that *no one* would want to be Diana's friend, anyhow. What's more, she declared that Diana absolutely could not handle getting rejected ever again, and that the only way to protect her from rejection was to keep her completely isolated from others.

In contrast, the part of Diana wanting friendships with women verbalized her anger, frustration, and grief over years of being deprived of the joy that only a close friendship can bring. She was able to accept and even love the insecure part of her that was trying so hard to keep her safe. However, she declared herself fully capable of finding at least a few trustworthy female friends, expressed her belief that she was both likable and lovable, and voiced confidence in her ability to handle whatever rejection might come her way. Almost immediately following that session Diana began to create new and satisfying friendships with women.

It is important to remind clients that all of their parts exist for the purpose of helping them in some way. When Idealists disown negative or conflicting aspects of themselves, those parts simply go underground and cause even greater distress. As Masqueraders acknowledge and even embrace their troublesome subselves, they are able to bring those fragments back up into the light and to integrate them. Hence, it is therapeutic for clients to recognize the positive intentions of even their most distressing parts and even to thank those subselves for trying to be helpful. Often it is as Masqueraders begin to love and accept *all* parts of themselves, that they are free to let go of their survival game playing.

In some cases, clients may use subself dialogues to arrange that the troublesome parts accomplish their objectives in new ways that are beneficial rather than detrimental. For example, an ENFP woman discovered that a part of her made certain that she was always late for everything, so that she would get lots of attention. Using an empty chair, the woman held a dialogue with that particular subself. After sincerely thanking it for its efforts to help her, the woman suggested new, more positive ways that this part could help her gain the attention of others—for example, by helping her dress in an attractive and tasteful way. Following this session, the woman reported that she was on-time far more often, and that she was receiving lots of compliments on her choice of outfits.

Rewriting Traumatic Scenes

Where a subself is feeling or behaving in ways that are not helpful to the client, it is often useful to trace its origins. Usually, parts that are causing clients problems in the present were created specifically to help clients survive traumatic or painful events in the past. Behaviors that were necessary for clients to survive an abusive childhood are often a source of problems in their adult relationships. By using the imagination to change the content and quality of early traumatic scenes, it is possible to reverse limiting patterns of behavior that were established during those episodes. By pretending to change the past, the Idealist's subselves are free to change in the present.

There are three ways to find out when a subself first entered the scene: (1) by asking the part when it was first created; (2) by asking clients to go back to the first time that they made a certain decision; or, (3) by asking clients to tune into and describe the uncomfortable feelings in their body associated with a present problem and to recall the first time that they felt the same feelings in their body. Each of these methods is most effective when clients have their eyes closed and they are deeply relaxed.

When Masqueraders are guided to rewrite original traumatic scenes using their imaginations, they experience transformations in their perspectives that enable them to change their behavior. Memories may be rewritten so that they happen the way clients would have liked for them to have occurred. If desired, the grown-up self of the present may be written into the new scenes, in order to effect a positive outcome. Painful memories may also be rewritten so that the client's original role is changed—for example, from that of victim to that of a powerful giant who fights off a potential abuser. After clients have drafted an alternative scene in their mind's eye, I often guide them in specifying the new decisions which they are able to make about themselves and their lives, and the new roles that the subself in question is able to play. The following case is an example of this process.

A thirty-five-year-old INFJ named Sharon had developed gynecological problems that had persisted for years and could neither be fully explained nor cured by her medical doctor. These physical symptoms caused Sharon enormous discomfort—and they also made sexual intercourse almost impossible for her. Now that she was in a new relationship with a man whom she really loved, Sharon was terrified that her physical problems would drive him away.

When I asked Sharon to close her eyes, relax, and imagine the part of her that kept her sick, she saw an insecure little girl who was sucking her thumb. The little girl told Sharon that she needed to be sick and weak, in order to make certain that Sharon was loved and cared for. Further exploration revealed that Sharon's mother had been seriously ill for six years of her childhood, and that Sharon watched her mother receiving an outpouring of love and attention from Sharon's father during that period. It became clear that in childhood, a part of Sharon had decided that a woman had to be sick and helpless in order to be loved and cared for by a man.

Next, as Sharon imagined that she was talking with the insecure little girl, she explained that the physical problems were now actually *preventing* her from receiving love and caring from a man, rather than the reverse. Sharon wrote new childhood memories in which her mother was healthy and strong and still loved and cared for by Sharon's father. Then, Sharon imagined that she and the girl wrote a new decision on an imaginary blackboard—that Sharon could be loved and cared for by a man by being healthy and strong. In addition, Sharon suggested new ways to the little girl that she could help

Sharon be more lovable—for example, by being kind, playful, imaginative, and curious.

Finally, I made a guided visualization tape for Sharon in which she rewrote the key scenes of her childhood and her early decisions, and she gave the insecure child within her lots of love and support. At the conclusion of the tape, I had Sharon travel one year into the future, where she found herself healthy, happy, and able to enjoy a fulfilling sex life with a loving and caring mate. When I saw Sharon several months later, she indicated that she had been listening to the tape daily, that the gynecological problem had greatly improved, and that she was able to enjoy regular intercourse with her partner.

Gestalt Dreamwork

Gestalt dreamwork can be another very effective method to use with Idealists, whereby the client has the opportunity to re-enact a dream, and to play the role of anyone or anything in it (Perls, 1969; Mahrer, 1989). The following case illustrates the use of this method in working with a thirty-three-year-old INFP who had been playing the Statue and Martyr variants of Masquerade.

Catherine decided to go to therapy because she wasn't happy, though she didn't understand why. In addition, for some time she had noticed that most of the left side of her body was numb. Although she was thirty-three years old, married, and the mother of two daughters, Catherine seemed more like a young girl than a woman in the way she presented herself. I learned that she had been raised in a very traditional, conservative, patriarchal culture, and that she had been separated from her family and sent to the United States from Latin America to live with relatives at the age of thirteen. Catherine married before she reached eighteen and had children right away. A bright and articulate woman, Catherine was proud that she had recently completed a B.A. and a master's degree in English Literature.

Catherine confessed that she had tried so hard to be the perfect daughter, wife, and mother for her whole life, that she didn't know who she was anymore. She was ashamed that she did not feel she had ever loved her husband, an ESTJ who ruled the household. She was terrified of divorcing him, for fear of what that would do to him and the children. And she wasn't sure that she was capable of living on her own—with or without the children.

Shortly after we began working together, Catherine told me about a recent disturbing dream in which she had encountered a teenage girl who was stuck in the middle of a frozen lake. We spent the next two and a half hours working on that dream, using Gestalt dreamwork. I had Catherine replay the dream as if it was happening right in the office, while tuning in to her emotions and the sensations in her body. Catherine played the role of herself and described how helpless, fearful, and shocked she felt seeing the girl. She felt sorry for her, and yet, she knew she alone couldn't safely rescue her. I had her imagine herself calling out to the girl and offering reassurance. Then, I had her play the role of the woman in her dream who ran to go get help. Finally, I had her play the role of the girl in the middle of the lake. Catherine stood stiffly in the middle of my office with her eyes closed and began to talk as if she were the teenage girl, about how it felt to be frozen and isolated. As she talked about how cold, lonely, paralyzed, and numb she was, she began to sob. She spoke of how it was to feel nothing—no hope, no love. She talked about how glad she was that Catherine had found her, and how she wished that she could be saved.

I had Catherine imagine that help finally arrived, and that the girl was safely transported to the land. Catherine imagined herself holding the girl, comforting her, and warming her with blankets. When Catherine awakened from her deep trance, she was shocked to learn that almost three hours had passed! We closed the session without much discussion of what had transpired.

Catherine returned two weeks later to report that she felt like a new person. The sensations had returned to the left side of her body, and she had begun to feel hopeful again. She had confronted her husband with her desire for a divorce, and he had moved out. She felt positively about the future, and confident in herself.

Catherine and I continued to work together for awhile, until she became established in her new life. Over time, she began to look and act more like a woman, rather than a girl. She chose to remain single for several years, rejecting more than one opportunity to marry again right away.

A part of Catherine was fixated in adolescence, frozen in time. The dreamwork enabled Catherine to reclaim and nurture her lost self, thus becoming whole again.

The Martyr Game

Catherine's attempt to be the perfect wife and mother is characteristic of the Idealist who is playing Martyr. Martyr players try to cover up deep-seated feelings of inadequacy by being as good as they can be. They will sacrifice their health, peace of mind, and well-being—suffering in silence—in an effort to earn the love and approval they so desperately seek. These clients live in constant fear that others will see through them and recognize them for the inadequate phonies they believe themselves to be. They hide behind their masks of perfection, hoping to avoid discovery and rejection.

In intimate relationships, Martyr players try so hard to be the person that they think their mate wants them to be, that they completely lose themselves. They consistently sacrifice their own needs in order to please their partner, who becomes the center of their world and the focus of their existence. They try to value what their mate values, want what their mate wants, believe what their mate believes, and even feel what their mate wants them to feel. And unlike the Guardian types playing Doormat, Martyr players don't usually complain about their sacrifices. In fact, these clients usually don't even know that they are forfeiting their identities, until the loss is almost complete. Typically, the first thing they notice is that they aren't happy—although they can't understand why not. Sometimes they will shock both their partners and themselves by exhibiting mini-explosions, during which their repressed feelings begin to leak out. Eventually, Martyr players come to the frightening realization that they don't know who they are anymore.

Martyr players need assistance in learning how to assert their own thoughts, feelings, and desires in a relationship. Usually, they are terrified of confronting the displeasure or disapproval of others—since they believe that they must be perfectly pleasing all of the time in order to be loved. They need help in establishing their own separate identities. The challenge for Martyr players is to learn how to have an intimate relationship without losing themselves.

Removing the Rose-Colored Glasses

Idealists are fond of wearing rose-colored glasses—particularly when it comes to viewing their mates. There are two ways that this causes problems for them. First of all, NFs can involve themselves in unhealthy relationships because their rose-colored glasses prevent them from seeing the negative aspects of another person. Somehow, Idealists manage to overlook the red flags that indicate trouble ahead at the beginning of a relationship. Through the rosy glow of their idealistic lenses, NFs can ignore the fact that a potential mate is an alcoholic, or that he or she is abusive. By the time reality hits, the Idealist is often in over his or her head.

Even where Idealists manage to involve themselves in relatively healthy relationships, the rose-colored glasses can be a problem. Inevitably, there comes a day when Idealists take the glasses off. Suddenly, the mate's human frailties are all too apparent; what's more, the relationship's problems are painfully visible. At this point, Idealists are prone to conclude that the solution lies in ending the relationship and going off in search of a more ideal partner. Too often, Idealists hold the false assumption that an ideal relationship is problem-free.

It is essential that Idealists learn to recognize and acknowledge those red flags that indicate potential danger when establishing a new relationship. In addition, it is important that NFs learn that there are no perfect relationships, and that even the best relationships have their ups and downs.

Stopping the Rescue Mission

Idealists are born rescuers. This means that they tend to sympathize with the underdog, and that they often get caught up with rescue operations, trying to save someone whom they perceive as a hopeless, helpless victim. The problem with this tendency is that it is often more harmful than beneficial to both the Idealist and the other person. For one thing, viewing someone as a helpless victim means seeing that person as powerless and incapable of solving his or her own problems; hence, the message inadvertently sent to the other person that he or she is inadequate or weak. For another thing, the Idealist is often engaged by the other types, who need a third player to complete their Victim-Rescuer-Persecutor triangle. Artisans are particularly good at engaging the Idealist in feeling sorry for them and in trying to rescue them from some big, bad, persecutor. The persecutor may be a parent, a teacher, a mate, an administrator, a boss, or even a whole school system. As long as the Idealist participates in this game, nothing will ever change. The Idealist wearing the rescuer hat is bound to feel not only frustrated but also increasingly responsible for trying to create change. It is only by refusing to view someone as a powerless victim that the NF can really be helpful to that person.

The following case is an example of the Victim-Persecutor-Rescuer roles that family members can end up playing with each other, and how changing those roles can alter the family dynamics in positive ways.

> Jill (an ENFP) came to therapy because she was upset over the way in which her husband, Ted (an ESTJ) was treating her son, Michael (a thirteen-year-old ESFP). I learned that Michael had been failing in school and in trouble with the law, and that most of Ted and Jill's fights were about him. It seemed that Ted often came down hard on his stepson, and that Jill would usually get furious with Ted and end up intervening on Michael's behalf. She was deeply concerned that Ted was damaging Michael's

self-esteem with his constant criticism. On the other hand, Ted felt that Jill was too easy on Michael, and that someone needed to teach the boy to be responsible.

Jill often shared secrets with Michael that were kept from Ted, and she was constantly trying to prevent the two of them from getting into disagreements. Most of the time, Michael and Ted communicated through Jill, rather than directly with each other.

I worked with both Ted and Jill to help them find a common ground in their parenting. While Ted learned to back off and stop many of the negative commercials for good behavior, Jill tried to step out of the way so that Ted and Michael could develop a relationship with each other. Both Ted and Jill began to set reasonable limits with Michael and to employ logical consequences when he went beyond the boundaries they established.

As Michael's behavior improved, Ted and Jill began to work on the problems in their marital relationship. Jill reported that she felt that Ted was too controlling regarding her time and money, and highly critical of her. (Her complaints about how Ted treated Michael were really about how he was treating her.) On the other hand, Ted felt overly burdened with their money problems and frustrated over Jill's spending patterns. After several conjoint sessions, things had just begun to get a little better between them when the family stopped coming to therapy. Ted and Jill continue to have their problems, but Michael seems to be doing fine.

Planting the Seeds of Suggestion

Idealists are the most suggestible of all of the types. They are the true believers—likely to take what the psychotherapist says to heart, and to make it a part of their reality. Clinicians can make therapeutic use of the Masquerade players' responsiveness to suggestion by planting lots of seeds about hidden potentials, personal growth, and metamorphosis in the rich, fertile soil of their subconscious minds.

There are many subtle ways of creating a positive expectancy for change in Idealists.* When offering suggestions, it is best to be vague about exactly what the positive changes might be—the goal is just to get the Idealist to anticipate change and to create a kind of self-fulfilling prophesy. In this way, clients will experience exactly those shifts that are best for them.

For example, at the end of a session, therapists can express curiosity regarding exactly what desired changes the client will experience *first*. Similarly, clinicians can suggest at the end of a therapy hour that the client be certain to take note of and remember all of the positive transformations that take place during the forthcoming week, so that they can be discussed during the next session. Still another option is for therapists to make mention of the positive results that someone just like the client experienced after doing the same kind of work on the same issues.

One of the best ways of utilizing the NFs' vivid imagination and impressionable nature is to direct them to meet their future self using guided visualization. The future self can be pictured as having successfully translated many of the Idealist's dreams into reality. He or she can be seen as enjoying rewarding work and loving, fulfilling relationships. In addition, the client's future self can embody any or all of the qualities that the client aspires to, including perfect health, radiant vitality, confidence, courage, joy, creativity, wisdom, and peace of mind. It is beneficial to ask clients to pretend to stand in the shoes of their future self and to feel what it is like to be this self who has accomplished their goals, and developed many of the inner qualities that they desire to possess. Finally, clients can be given the suggestion that their future self already exists within them, and that they can access the strengths of this wise and loving part of themselves whenever they wish.

---

* See the works of Dr. Milton Erickson for numerous examples of methods for creating positive expectancies.

The Power of Pretend

Idealists are like chameleons; they change themselves according to the needs of each situation. This character trait often bothers NFs, who are deeply concerned about behaving authentically. Idealists worry that they are being phoney when they find themselves changing so dramatically from one situation to the next. And they tend to wonder, "Who am I, really?"

The NF's natural ability to play different roles can be utilized therapeutically. When Masqueraders would like to behave in a certain way but can't, it is often helpful to assign them the task of pretending to be someone else. In effect, the NF client is asked to play a different role—to act "as if" he or she was another person—without telling anyone about the playacting. It is best if the clinician is intentionally vague about what this role playing would look like, so that clients are forced to access their own creativity. This is a powerful assignment, since one is not asking the Idealist to actually *be* different—just to *pretend* to be different. Of course, as clients start to behave differently, they end up changing the way they feel inside, too. For example, if a Masquerade player reveals that he hates himself, and that he absolutely can't like himself, a therapist might suggest that he pretend for a day or a week to be a person who likes himself. This would not mean that he stops hating himself—only that he acts as if he likes himself. He would simply be playing a role— like a part in a play—and making it as real as possible. Chances are, after two weeks of pretense, that the client would begin to shift some of his negatives feelings about himself into positive ones.

Using Symbols

According to Roberto Assagioli, who developed the theory and methods of Psychosynthesis, symbols are a way of bridging a client's conscious and unconscious processes—a means of providing integration (1965). Assagioli claims that by working with symbols, it is possible to create unconscious transformations in clients which then produce changes in external behavior. Symbols hold a special attraction for Idealists, who are naturally gifted in the use of metaphor and analogy. Hence, those methods which make use of symbols—particularly sandplay, guided visualizations, and passport metaphors—are excellent to use with Idealist clients.

Regardless of the method used, it is important that therapists refrain from interpreting symbols for clients. Even if clients ask for an interpretation, it is best if clinicians decline the invitation to offer one. Clients must have the opportunity to attach their own meanings to the symbols that emerge in the therapeutic process. These meanings might be conscious, or they might remain out of the client's conscious awareness. It is possible for symbols work to be done entirely at the unconscious level, and yet create dramatic, positive shifts in how the client feels, thinks, and behaves.

In sandplay, clients have the opportunity to make their own world by placing symbolic objects in relationship to each other on a tray of sand (see Kalff, 1980; Weinrib, 1983). Therapists accept the client's creation without judgement, evaluation or interpretation. Based on Jungian theory, this process enables clients to work through unconscious conflicts by representing them in physical form.

The passport metaphors discussed in chapter five on stopping the Complain game are ideal for seeding Masqueraders with transformational symbols. These may be lengthy stories[*] or just brief descriptions of powerful images that inspire listeners with hope and courage. For example, therapists might talk about a caterpillar who emerges from a cocoon as a beautiful butterfly, or they might describe courageous explorers who discover magnificent treasures buried deep under the ocean's floor.

---

[*] The Jungian analyst Clarissa Pinkola Estés, Ph.D. has produced several excellent tapes of myths and stories which are ideal for NF clients. Notable are: *Women Who Run With the Wolves*, on the wild-woman archetype, and *Warming the Stone Child*, on abandonment and the unmothered child. Contact: Sounds True Recordings, 1825 Pearl Street, Boulder, CO 80302. (303) 449-6229.

Often clients present symbols which may be utilized in guided visualizations. For example, Corey was a precocious eight-year-old ENFJ whose mother had died several years before after a long and painful illness. When Corey's dad remarried, he began to have nightmares and exhibited difficulty in accepting his new stepmom. During one session, Corey told me that whenever he looked up at the moon at night, he saw his mother waving at him. Utilizing that image, I put on relaxing music, and then asked Corey to close his eyes, take some deep breaths, and to imagine that he could travel up to the moon to visit his mother in a bubble of light. Corey reported that several angels flew him in the bubble right up to the moon. Once he arrived there, he had a joyful reunion with his mother. When he told his mother about his new stepmom, she gave Corey her blessings. Corey's adjustment to his new family situation improved considerably after that session.

Another approach is to encourage Masquerade players to come up with their own, spontaneous symbols during guided visualizations. It is the clinician's job to, first, suggest that the client look for a symbol to appear at appropriate moments and, then, to assist the client in making therapeutic use of the symbol—without ever analyzing it. This is illustrated in the following case.

> Victoria was a very bright, pretty, and enthusiastic forty-four-year-old ENFP who had always believed that she wasn't very intelligent, in spite of much evidence to the contrary. I learned that Victoria's mother had told her since she was a preschooler that she was too stupid to read or write well. In addition, she recalled that many of her teachers in the private church schools she attended through high school were quick to label her as dumb. Consequently, throughout her life she avoided reading and writing whenever possible.

> During one of our sessions, I put on some relaxing music and suggested to Victoria that she close her eyes and become deeply relaxed. Next, I told her that, unfortunately, something very precious—her belief in her own intelligence—had been stolen from her when she wasn't even aware of it. It belonged to her, and people had taken it without asking. I had her imagine that all of the people who had stolen that from her were lined up in an audito-

rium. She saw her mother and many of her teachers, standing in a row. Then, I told her that she was to *demand* that each of them return to her what they had stolen long ago. As they gave back what they had stolen, I asked Victoria to tell me what she saw. Victoria reported that each person held a huge, beautiful, and precious gem. There were enormous diamonds, rubies, emeralds, and pearls. She told me that she had a large golden bowl in which she collected all of the gemstones being returned to her.

Finally, I asked Victoria to put her gems back inside of her, where they belonged. She told me that they melted into a nectar, and that she drank the nectar from a golden chalice. I talked to her about all of the untapped potential within her that was awakening as she drank the nectar— particularly, the power of her mind to read, write, or do whatever she desired. I asked how it felt to be aware of her intelligence, once again, after all of these years. I suggested that she would notice many positive changes in how she would think, feel, and behave over the next few days. And then she came back—with a big smile on her face.

One month later, Victoria returned to say that she was feeling better and better about her intelligence. She mentioned that on several occasions, her mind was flooded with memories of times when she had done things that could be taken as evidence that she was very bright. She also indicated that she had been reading some nonfiction books, and that she had decided that she was not going to be "playing dumb" anymore.

Conclusion

This chapter has outlined some methods for assisting Idealists in stopping their game playing. There may be times when these techniques are also useful in working with the other three types. No doubt there are numerous other approaches not mentioned here which can also be effective in working with NFs.

In part three, there are additional cases which show how to use observational clues to identify Idealists and also how to work with Masquerade players who are experiencing difficulty in their relationships with the other types.

When Idealists stop playing Masquerade, they can become their most inspiring selves. NFs are adept at finding and developing the potential that lies within each of us. They are the motivating teachers, mystical healers, and charismatic leaders, who offer guidance to those who seek it. Idealists dedicate themselves to causes that expose and eradicate social evils and that spread a message of goodwill, peace, and love.

Idealists support family members in their personal growth. They see the good in everyone, and they naturally encourage each person to be his or her best self. NF's are empathic, unselfish, thoughtful, sincere, authentic, enthusiastic, and sensitive. They teach us how to love ourselves and others unconditionally. Idealists light the fire within us, and show us how to keep it burning brightly.

As Idealists give up their games, they throw away their disguises and express themselves honestly, without fear or shame. Healthy NFs are authentic, real, and true to their deepest selves. They have owned and embraced their dark side, thus becoming whole again. They have learned not to be quite so sensitive—not to take everything so seriously, nor to allow others to hurt them so easily. They trust and follow their inner guidance and believe in themselves. While their heads are in the clouds, their feet are planted firmly on the ground. These Idealists have found the courage to follow their own unique path in this lifetime—a path that affords them the opportunity to continue to grow spiritually, while working towards the fulfillment of their highest ideals.

PART III

THE CASES

Introduction

The eight case examples in this section provide an integration of the information presented in Parts One and Two of this book. Each case involves one or more individuals who are playing survival games. The cases include examples of all four games* and many of their variants. In some of the cases I worked exclusively with an individual, while in others a couple or an entire family is involved.

Following each case there is a discussion of the clients' personality types, the observational clues used to identify those types, and the survival games being played. In addition, there is a recounting of the primary interventions that I used and an explanation of my reasons for employing them.

For several reasons I intentionally selected cases which are mostly examples of brief therapy. First of all, I believe that a shorter case is more likely to hold a reader's interest than a longer one. Secondly, I also maintain that shorter cases provide better examples for those who are just learning the Keirseyan model. They offer convincing evidence of how knowledge of personality types can aid the therapist in understanding the problem and in designing and implementing an effective treatment strategy.

Certainly not all of the work I do is brief therapy. While the majority of clients I see require from six to twelve sessions to reach the goals that they set for themselves at the start of therapy, there are some who take less time, and others who take much longer. I have found that those adult clients who have been badly abused or neglected as children are most likely to be in need of longer-term therapy. Where I have worked with a person for over a year, there is usually a combination of sexual, physical, and/or emotional abuse in the individual's history.

---

* Though all four of the games are represented here, readers may note that there is a preponderance of cases involving Artisans who are playing Blackmail. Although I have had occasion to treat all four games, the majority of couples and families that I see end up coming to therapy because of a mate or child who is playing Blackmail.

In spite of my best efforts, not all of my psychotherapy clients benefit the way I would like them to. There are always a few people who see me once or twice and then decide that they would rather not continue our sessions. There are also those individuals, couples, and families who perpetuate their game playing after hours of therapy with me. Case #5, "The Solar System," is an example of one such family.

As mentioned in chapter three, I always use observational clues to identify client personalities and/or to confirm client test results on either the Myers-Briggs Type Indicator or the Keirsey Temperament Sorter. Even where I have administered a test, I never assume that the scores are correct before I check out the client's actual behavior to see if it is in alignment with the test results. This is especially necessary with clients who are playing survival games. In particular, Artisan clients who are playing Blackmail are prone to scoring as one of the other three temperament types.

Now and then I have difficulty in placing someone in one of the four temperament groups. This always gives me reason to pause and ask myself, "What does this person seem to need *the most?*" Certainly, everyone needs some freedom and excitement, responsibility and security, identity and integrity, and competence and achievement. Personality theory is just a way of identifying which of these values a person seems to place *first* in his or her life.

Sometimes clients reveal strong *primary* as well as *secondary* needs. For example, one woman seemed to have a very high need for freedom and excitement, but also a high need for identity and integrity. In this case, I concluded that I was working with an Artisan who had a well-developed Idealist side to her personality. Her Idealist nature might be seen as her secondary type. In my therapy with her, I tried to address the needs of both the Artisan and the Idealist. This approach proved highly successful.

Once I am fairly convinced of what someone's personality type is, I may discuss that information with the client, if I believe that it would be helpful. When I do tell clients about their personality types, I am always careful to present that information in a way that is positive and affirming. I stress that all personalities are good, and that each type has its unique strengths. I talk about how we seem to be born with certain *preferences* that determine our personalities.* Generally, these preferences appear to remain fairly constant throughout our lives, though our environment (physical, social, and economic) also plays a major role in determining the extent to which we act according to our natural preferences, and the manner in which we do so. I emphasize that we have all dimensions to our personalities, and that we are free to develop whatever aspects of ourselves that we desire. Yet, that does not change what comes most naturally to us.

In families, I encourage clients to use this model to better understand, respect, and appreciate the ways in which they differ from each other.** Where parents are labeling an Artisan child as "bad," I may talk at length about the many ways in which SPs are gifted, and the ways in which they usually employ these gifts to be successful in life.

Often, besides trying to determine my clients' personalities, I ask clients key questions about their significant others in order to hypothesize as to what their types might be. (See chapter three for information on identifying personalities.) This information can be particularly useful for helping clients resolve communicational difficulties where the others involved are unwilling or unable to attend joint counseling sessions. For example, in case #2, "Teaching the Boss," I am able to help a woman deal more effectively with her boss based upon my speculation as to the boss's personality type.

The following eight cases provide readers with an opportunity to practice: (1) recognizing clues for determining personality types; (2) identifying the four survival games and their vari-

---

* See the suggested readings on type and temperament for further elaboration on this issue.
** Often families include parents and children with diverse types. One cannot predict the children's personalities on the basis of the personalities of the parents.

ants; and, (3) designing effective interventions for stopping the games. Toward this end, readers are encouraged to stop and ask themselves the following questions when they appear in the case examples:

What are the clients' personality types and what is the evidence used to identify them?

What are the survival games being played and by whom?

What treatment interventions might be useful in stopping the survival game playing?

The answers to these questions are addressed in the discussion at the end of each case.

As is evident in these case examples, it is rare for me to see clients on a weekly basis. Most often, I prefer to schedule sessions two weeks apart and gradually stretch the time between sessions to around four to six weeks as clients prepare to terminate therapy. Sometimes I will see clients weekly for the first month and then move to an every-other-week basis. With couples, I may work with the individuals one week and the couple on the alternate week. Scheduling sessions every two or more weeks seems to work best for my clients, since it gives them ample time to process what has taken place during the previous session and to do their homework assignments.* It also defines our relationship as one in which I am somewhat like a personal consultant, but they remain responsible for creating the changes they desire in themselves and in their lives.

---

* Homework assignments are an integral part of my work. They are a means of getting clients to take little steps in the direction of shifting old patterns. In my experience, these little changes will usually snowball into bigger ones.

Case #1

LOWERING MOM'S BLOOD PRESSURE

The Phone Call:

Mrs. Martin called me reluctantly about her son, Ronnie. At sixteen, Ronnie was rebellious and out of control, and she was convinced that her only option was to have him committed to a psychiatric hospital. She had tried counseling before, and it had not worked. However, Mrs. Martin's had promised a friend that she would try counseling one more time before having Ronnie hospitalized. She told me that he had been apprehended by police for possession of alcohol at the beach the night before, and that in the morning she had overheard him making arrangements with a friend to purchase marijuana and smoke it before school. She feared that he was a drug addict. Mrs. Martin explained that when she had tried to discipline Ronnie, he had either become so violently out of control that he had destroyed parts of the house and its contents, or he had threatened to run away. According to her, he was belligerent, angry, and seriously disturbed, as evidenced by the frightening, bizarre pictures which he had drawn for the past few years. In addition, he had gotten worse since he broke up with his girlfriend a few weeks ago.

I emphasized that she was absolutely right in her conclusions that this was a very serious problem and that something needed to be done about it immediately. I convinced her to try therapy first, by stressing the high costs of hospitalization (she had no health insurance) and suggesting that it could still be a last alternative, if counseling wasn't effective.

Session One:

Mrs. Martin, a perky, slender woman, arrived for the first session dressed much like a flashy, fashionable teenager herself. Accompanying her were Ronnie and his fourteen-year-old sister, Susie. At sixteen, Ronnie was already towering over his mother and sister. He was well-groomed and wore his blond hair down to his shoulders. Since Mrs. Martin had divorced her second husband, their stepfather, several years before, there had been no man living in the house. Mrs. Martin told me that her children's father had disappeared when Ronnie was just three years old. Currently, Mrs. Martin had a boyfriend whom both Ronnie and Susie said they liked very much; however, with two husbands behind her, Mrs. Martin wasn't sure that she ever wanted to marry again. She definitely enjoyed the freedom that being single afforded her.

Both Susie and Ronnie were very quiet and polite during the session, smiling and appearing somewhat embarrassed to be talking with me. Each told me that their mother was a very hard worker, and that they were more on the lazy side themselves. Indeed, Mrs. Martin had her own outdoor landscaping business that required putting in long, exhausting days. In her spare time, she was painting their apartment one room at a time and doing various repair jobs. Apparently, Mrs. Martin never complained to anyone about her heavy schedule. She just did what she had to in order to support the three of them. Besides that, she said that she really liked her work and the fact that she could be her own boss.

The three family members seemed to agree that Ronnie was the troublemaker of the family, and therefore the source of most family difficulties. Not only did he refuse to do what his mother asked, he also harassed his sister and picked fights with her. While Ronnie admitted that he was the family "problem child," he also complained that his mother was always on his back. Ronnie resented that his mother frequently accused him of doing things that he used to do, but that he had stopped doing, like tearing up his room when he was in a rage. It made him mad that Susie almost never got into trouble, although she also did things she shouldn't, like drinking beer at parties, lying, and talking on the phone for hours at a time in spite of her mother's objections.

Mrs. Martin indicated that Ronnie's violent outbursts had begun when he was in junior high school, at the time his stepfather began abusing him. Everyone agreed that the stepfather was awful to Ronnie, calling him degrading names, telling him how stupid he was, and beating him up almost everyday. Much of this would occur when Mrs. Martin was out of the home. Once she found out what was going on, she kicked her husband out and filed for divorce.

I asked about the incident on the beach which had precipitated Mrs. Martin's call to me. Ronnie said that he was very embarrassed about it, because when the cops came, all of his friends took off and left him standing there with the open beer bottles. He said he had not been drinking, and Mrs. Martin confirmed that the police report indicated there was no alcohol in his blood. Ronnie claimed that he was not an alcoholic, and that he only drank a little, occasionally on weekends at parties. He admitted that he had smoked marijuana in the past, but he maintained that he was no longer doing so.

When I asked about school, I learned that Susie's grades were all Bs and Cs, and that Ronnie, whose grades were previously Ds and Fs, had recently raised his grades to Cs and a few Ds. Once again, Ronnie complained that his mother hadn't noticed his improvement, just like she hadn't noticed that he rarely had tantrums anymore, and that he no longer destroyed the house or its contents when he did have one.

I questioned Mrs. Martin about discipline. She indicated that she just yelled a lot or went into her room when things got too bad. She said that Ronnie had started to yell back at her, saying things like, "If you don't like my music, then leave." Ronnie was a member of a rock band, and he would often practice his electronic keyboard in their apartment with the speaker volume turned up full blast. It made her angry, but she became tired of yelling, so she would try to ignore it. Apparently, their apartment was a daily gathering place for a large group of teens. Ronnie and Susie said that most of their friends really liked to be around Mrs. Martin, because she was nice, friendly, and so much fun. Mrs. Martin did not object to the fact that most of them smoked during their visit, being a smoker herself, and often she truly enjoyed their company. But now and then she wanted some peace and quiet at home. Consequently, she had asked her kids not to invite so many friends over every day. When they didn't comply, Mrs. Martin's solution was again to retire to her bedroom. Mrs. Martin said she definitely didn't want to be a nag, and she didn't know what else to do, so she just kept quiet after a while. Similarly, when it came to chores around the house, Mrs. Martin had almost given up trying to get either Ronnie or Susie to help her. When she asked for their help and they didn't respond, she'd just do it herself.

What are the clients' personality types and what is the evidence used to identify them?

What are the survival games being played and by whom?

What treatment interventions might be useful in stopping the survival game playing?

First Session Interventions:

Early in the session I began to refer to Ronnie as "the man of the family" often and in a matter-of-fact way.

Toward the end of the first meeting, I emphasized the most recent problem, when Mrs. martin had to pick up her son at the police station. It was something that would certainly be hard for a mother to forget, unless Ronnie did something to repay his mom for the horrible ordeal that he had put her through. I asked

Ronnie what he would be willing to do for his mother to make up for the agony he caused her, and he suggested two weeks of laundry. Both Mrs. Martin and Ronnie seemed to like this idea very much, so we all agreed that Ronnie would start the next day.

Finally, I asked Ronnie to show any piece of completed homework to his mother at least every other day, and for his mother to say something positive about it. Mrs. Martin was instructed to avoid criticizing the homework in any way. She was only to say that it looked good, or that she was so pleased that he was doing his homework, or that she was proud of him, or whatever positive words she felt like using. Once again, both Mrs. Martin and Ronnie readily agreed to this assignment.

Session Two:

From the second session on, I met with only Ronnie and Mrs. Martin. At the start of each session I saw both of them to get a general report on how things had been going, and to check on whether or not they completed their assignments. After seeing each of them alone, the three of us met again for the last few minutes of the meeting to wrap things up. The second session lasted two hours, and the other five were one hour each.

Since I had seen them one week before, Ronnie had faithfully shown his mother his homework every night, and she had made only positive comments about it. Ronnie indicated that he liked this, and his mother said she was willing to continue, so I asked them to keep it up.

Ronnie had not done the laundry, using the excuse that he had "forgotten." I emphasized how important it was, and sternly reminded him that he had agreed to do it. We decided that he would begin when he got home from the session, and Mrs. Martin promised that she would not remind him.

Ronnie had thrown one tantrum in response to his mother's complaints about his keyboard playing. Though he had not damaged anything, he had yelled and screamed at his mother for getting on his back.

During my time alone with Ronnie, the first thing I did was ask him to draw a picture of everyone in his family doing something. As I handed him a large piece of construction paper and some colored marking pens, he smiled and said "I'm an artist, you know." He proceeded to sketch rather quickly.

Ronnie positioned himself and his sister at the top of the page, doing things they enjoyed. Ronnie was playing his keyboard, and his sister was talking on the phone. Ronnie's mother was at the bottom of the page, situated well beneath her children. She resembled a witch, and was sweeping with a broom. I asked Ronnie's permission to show that drawing to his mother, and he said it would be okay.

Next I asked Ronnie to draw anything he wanted. He drew a human body with a very detailed, ugly, monkey's head. The figure looked like an ugly, stupid monster. In response to a request that he tell me about his picture, Ronnie said that the guy in it was now dead, but that when he was alive, he had no self-confidence, and thought of himself as awfully stupid.

With additional questioning, I learned that Ronnie didn't like school very much, and found it difficult. He confided in me that recently his girlfriend had dropped him for another guy. Though he had to admit that she had never treated him very nicely, he missed her a lot. He felt shy around girls and didn't know how to find a new girlfriend since all of his girlfriends had always made the first move. He wanted to graduate from high school, and then work as a diesel mechanic. He loved art, and thought it was the one thing he could do well. He had worked at a few part-time jobs, but currently wasn't working and didn't want to.

I asked Ronnie to think of a friend who seemed to know how to meet girls, and then suggested that he watch that friend as much as he could, to notice what he did and said when he was around girls. I also gave Ronnie some paper and asked if he would draw five pictures for me of how he was feeling at various times during the next two weeks.

When I spoke with Mrs. Martin alone she appeared very nervous, as if she was concerned that I might blame her for Ronnie's problems. After getting a report on how the week had gone (she and Ronnie had gotten into more arguments about the keyboard playing), I told her I wanted to share some of my observations with her. I began by commending her on what a great job she had done in raising two kids practically all by herself. Her children were well groomed, polite, intelligent, and kind, and this was clearly a reflection of her good parenting. It was apparent that she was a very devoted mother and that she put a lot of time and energy into doing a good job with her children. I assured her that this showed, and that it was impressive to see how hard she was willing to work in order to make ends meet and to give Ronnie and Susie all that she could.

I said that I did have one concern, however, and that it involved *her*. I told her it appeared that *she* was the one who was getting the short end of the stick—that she was an *abused mother*. As evidence of that, I showed her Ronnie's drawing, and pointed out that she was doing all the work, and was the lowly servant, while the kids played and stomped all over her. Mrs. Martin seemed surprised to hear this, and anxious for me to continue. I explained that she seemed to have little say in her own household about what went on, and that she endured noise, a house full of teenagers, and all of the housework in spite of the fact that she had worked hard all day long and absolutely deserved some peace and quiet and a little help now and then. Mrs. Martin shook her head in avid agreement, and asked what she should do.

I told Mrs. Martin that she was too easy on her kids—she needed to *stop* talking so much and letting them abuse her and *start* taking action. She responded with, "You mean, I need to start pulling in the reins!" I instructed Mrs. Martin in how to "pull in the reins," by asking her to name the two things that Ronnie or Susie did that bothered her most. She said it was Ronnie's loud keyboard playing all day and all night, and the constant flow of teenage visitors to the house. At my request, Mrs. Martin specified reasonable hours of keyboard play without headphones for Ronnie, and she decided that he could play anytime if he wore his headphones. I suggested that if Ronnie played without headphones one minute past the time that she had specified, that she should say nothing, but simply take his keyboard and lock it up in her car for twenty-four hours and then give it back. Since this was not punishment, she was to be nice to him and talk about anything but the keyboard. I cautioned her not to say anything to him when she gave the keyboard back, either—no "I told you so's," or "You'd better be good," or "This will teach you your lesson!"

Mrs. Martin decided that it was reasonable to permit friends to visit Tuesdays, Thursdays, and Saturdays. If her children's friends arrived on one of the other days, she would expect Susie or Ronnie to explain that they would need to leave and why. In the event that Ronnie or Susie did not comply, then they could have no friends over for the rest of the week.

The last request I made of Mrs. Martin was to ask for her help in helping Ronnie to feel good about himself. I emphasized that she was the most important person in his life, and her opinion of him mattered more than anyone else's. At my request, she readily agreed to spend time alone with him twice a week (something they never did anymore) doing something fun—going to the beach for a walk, having dinner, or whatever. She also agreed to make three positive comments a day to Ronnie about what he was doing that was good. I gave her examples of how she might comment on things that he *did* well, rather than just saying that he was a good kid, or whatever. For example, she might say that he did a great job in washing the dishes, or in playing a particular song on his keyboard.

At the end of the session, I told Ronnie (in his mother's presence) about the instructions I had given his mother regarding new house rules and their enforcement. I told him that I wanted him to be sure to play his keyboard without using headphones at times when he was not supposed to, in order to give his mother practice in doing what I had instructed her to do (locking his keyboard in the car until the next day). Ronnie brought up the issue of his bedroom door (his mother had removed it months ago when he had bashed a hole in it during a fit of anger), and noted that if it was put back in place, he wouldn't bother anyone when he played the keyboard. I told him that we could not discuss his door and what could be done about it until he fulfilled his agreement to do two weeks of laundry. Ronnie grinned, and said okay.

Session Three:

Both Mrs. Martin and Ronnie smiled as they told me how they had done most of their assignments. Ronnie had handled two weeks of laundry with no reminders. A few days after the second session, Ronnie had played his keyboard without headphones during off hours. Mrs. Martin had locked up the keyboard in her car without comment for twenty-four hours. Since then he had abided by her rules regarding his music. Ronnie had not thrown any tantrums during the past two weeks. Though both kids had objected, Mrs. Martin had also successfully enforced her rules regarding house visitors.

I complimented Mrs. Martin for doing a good job of pulling in the reins, and thanked Ronnie for giving his mom a chance to practice her new skills. Ronnie had shown his mother his completed homework almost every day, and she had responded according to my instructions, with positive comments. Also, they had spent time alone together walking on the beach and having dinner. They agreed to continue to spend time alone together doing fun things at least twice a week.

During our private meeting, Ronnie and I discussed what he had seen his friend doing when he flirted with the girls. Ronnie gave me the five pictures he had drawn, all of various monkey/monsters with human bodies, one with two heads. He said that his mom had been on his back a lot during the past few weeks, and that his sister was mad because his mom had started to get on her, too. He objected that she had taken his keyboard away when he had talked on the phone too long. We discussed Ronnie's door. He agreed to do all of the work necessary to fix the hole in it, paint it, and hang it, if his mother would permit him to do so.

Mrs. Martin reported during our time together that she felt comfortable pulling in the reins, and that, in fact, she had also decided that she was going to start spending time doing things *she* liked to do on the weekends, instead of always catering to her children's desires. I said I thought her idea was great, and that a hardworking mom like herself deserved a little time off to have some fun. She said that her doctor had told her to relax more, because her blood pressure had been dangerously high for the past few months, but that until now, she had not followed his recommendations.

Mrs. Martin had noticed many positive things that Ronnie had done during the past two weeks. She said that he seemed to like it when she would comment on them, and she agreed to continue with that program. She emphasized that Ronnie still did not help out enough around the house, and that she was starting to get after both Ronnie and Susie more about doing their share.

Mrs. Martin said that the keyboard playing had been fine since the time she took Ronnie's keyboard away. In fact, that method had worked so well that she had recently locked his keyboard in her car when he had been on the telephone too long. I explained that it would be best if she took away the privilege that Ronnie or Susie had abused. Hence, if either of them abused the privilege of using the phone, then they would lose the chance to use the phone for the next day. Similarly, the keyboard would be taken away for a day when Ronnie abused the privilege of playing it. Mrs. Martin said she understood.

When Ronnie, Mrs. Martin and I regrouped at the end of the session, I told Ronnie that I had a serious concern, and that I was going to have to ask for his assistance. I explained that his mother's blood pressure was dangerously high, and that the consequences of high blood pressure can be a heart attack, or even death. I confessed that I had tried to lower his mother's blood pressure, but that I had failed. Her medical doctor had failed, too. Since he was the man of the family, I thought that he was the logical one to turn to for help. Would he be willing to take charge of his mother's blood pressure to see to it that it was lowered? It would require making certain that she got plenty of rest, and that nothing happened to get her upset, since when people are upset, their blood pressure tends to go up.

Ronnie nodded vigorously, and affirmed his willingness to help. I told him I was grateful, because I was very worried about his mother. Mrs. Martin agreed that if Ronnie was willing to try to lower her blood pressure, then she was most certainly willing to help him put a door on his bedroom. Any final plans about the door would be made during the next session.

Finally, I told Mrs. Martin that since yelling or nagging can raise her blood pressure, I wanted her to just ask Susie or Ronnie once to do what she wanted. If they did not comply, I wanted her to make a list, and bring it to our next meeting in one week.

Session Four:

Ronnie walked into my office for the fourth session looking like a changed person. He held his head up high and stood up straight. He looked me into the eye, spoke more loudly and confidently, and smiled broadly.

I began by asking whether, as the man of the family, Ronnie had been able to do anything about his mother's blood pressure. Mrs. Martin was all smiles as she said that, indeed, her blood pressure was lower than it had been for the entire past year. I immediately turned to Ronnie, and commended him for being able to do what no one else could. Mrs. Martin went on to explain that Ronnie had completed all of his chores before she had even asked him to. Furthermore, he had gotten along well with his sister, and he had convinced her to behave also. Ronnie had applied for work at five different stores, and he thought that one place would probably hire him. In addition, he had told his mother several times how much he appreciated her and loved her. They had been getting along better than ever.

I brought up the topic of Ronnie's door, and we arranged that Ronnie and Mrs. Martin would fix it and paint it on the following weekend, and hang it a few days after that.

When I met with Ronnie individually, he told me that he had a new girlfriend, and that they were spending lots of time together. He was delighted with her, and pleased with himself for making the first move necessary to meet her.

While alone with Mrs. Martin, I complimented her for doing an excellent job in raising her son's self-esteem. I indicated that Ronnie really seemed to be feeling better about himself, and that she obviously had a great deal to do with his improvement. I reminded her to continue telling him what she saw him doing that was good and arranging times when they could be alone together. I added that it was also important that she avoid talking about Ronnie's past misbehavior, since it would detract from the positive effects of all of the good work that she was doing.

Session Five:

At our next session, one month later, Mrs. Martin and Ronnie indicated that they were doing well. Mrs. Martin's blood pressure was still down, so I commended Ronnie again for his excellent work as the man of the family. Mom and son were getting along very well, and Mrs. Martin had continued to pull in the reins and take more time for herself.

Mrs. Martin brought up the subject of Ronnie's most recent report card, which was Bs, Cs, a D in English, and an F in physical science. Mrs. Martin was disappointed, and said that maybe she should punish Ronnie for his low grades. Ronnie said that he was surprised by the low grades, and that he had done all his work. The teachers' comments indicated that his attendance and homework were good, but that his grades in the two classes were low due to poor test performance. Ronnie indicated that he felt stupid when it came to tests, and that he just knew when he was taking a test that he probably wouldn't pass it.

After much discussion, Mrs. Martin said that she preferred to let Ronnie take charge of his own school and that he had done a good job so far in raising his grades, so she knew that he could do so now if he wanted to. I agreed that Ronnie's grades should be Ronnie's business. Mrs. Martin would not talk to him about his grades; however, she would continue to make positive comments when he showed her his homework.

I asked Ronnie if he wanted my help in raising his grades, and he said yes. I suggested that we use guided visualization, explaining that I had been able to help lots of people improve their test scores with that method. We sent Mrs. Martin out of the room, and after putting on some relaxing background music, I turned on the tape recorder. First, I had Ronnie close his eyes and breathe deeply, while I introduced various relaxing imagery which incorporated the use of all of his senses. Next, I introduced various metaphors which emphasized the transition from boyhood into manhood, leaving the past behind and growing in confidence and self-assurance. I talked a lot about art and music, since he could relate to those subjects. Finally, I instructed Ronnie to imagine himself before, during, and after a test, as he would like to be feeling, thinking and behaving. Ronnie's final assignment was to listen to the tape once a day for a month, and then whenever he felt like he wanted to after that.

Follow-up Call:

When I called her six months later, Mrs. Martin told me on the phone that she and her family were doing just fine. She said Ronnie never "blew up" at her anymore when she asked him to do things. Perhaps, she added, "that's because he's growing up!" Ronnie was working part time after school, and he was going to be working full time in the summer. What's more, his grades had improved. Mrs. Martin's blood pressure was down, and she had broken up with her boyfriend because he had been making too many demands on her.

CASE DISCUSSION

Mrs. Martin is an ISFP, or Player/Composer-type Artisan, as is evidenced by her dress, her choice of occupation, her lifestyle, and her style of parenting. Like many Artisans, Mrs. Martin dresses in a way that is fashionable, flashy, a little on the wild side, and designed to attract attention. She has been married two times, and now enjoys being single. It is the Artisan who is more likely than other types to marry and divorce often, and also to cherish the freedom of the single life. Mrs. Martin labors long and hard in her landscaping business, which enables her to be creative with her hands. SPs are not strangers to hard work; they often enjoy working with their hands, and they often prefer to be their own bosses rather than working for someone else. It is significant that Mrs. Martin doesn't complain about her exhausting schedule or her high blood pressure, as Artisans are unlikely to complain about fatigue, aches, or pains. Note that a Guardian-type person in the same situation would probably complain often, and loudly. Like many SP parents, Mrs. Martin enjoys fraternizing with her children's friends, and she is a very tolerant parent.

In accordance with her ISFP nature, Mrs. Martin is quiet, warm, gentle, and kind. ISFPs don't often tell other people what to do; their motto is "live and let live." Mrs. Martin demonstrates this quality when she retires to her bedroom in response to her teenagers' troublesome behavior, rather than directing them to quiet down.

Ronnie reveals his Artisan (SP) nature in his love of drawing and playing music on his keyboard. Artisans are often talented in art and music, and they will spend endless hours engaged in these activities. It is especially significant that Ronnie reacted to his stepfather's abuse by throwing violent tantrums and destroying his room, since it is the Artisans who are most likely of all four temperaments to respond to parental abuse by abusing themselves, another person, or someone's property. When Ronnie says that he hates school, he echoes a large number of Artisans who report that they dislike school. They find it boring, and lacking

in the hands-on experience and practical emphasis they crave.[*]
Ronnie's hairstyle—down to his shoulders—is characteristic of
the Artisan, who often dresses in a way that attracts attention
and defies society's conventions.

Ronnie may be seen as an ESFP, or Player/Performer-type of
Artisan because he enjoys socializing, partying, and performing.
He doesn't usually give other people directives—"Do this!" or
"Do that!"—the way STP types of Artisans do. (Although he
does tell his mother to leave the room if she doesn't like his
music.) And he is more gregarious and assertive than the ISFPs.

When Ronnie has tantrums, or abuses alcohol or drugs, he is
playing the Artisan game of *Blackmail*—specifically, the
Outrage, *Delinquency*, and *Binge* variants. Ronnie started
playing these games when his stepfather abused him (the stepfather was also playing Blackmail). Ronnie's tantrums, destruc-
tion of his room, and substance abuse are the ways he gets even
for his stepfather's abuse, and later, for his mother's getting on
his back about things. Remember, in the Blackmail game, the
player impulsively does something exciting that also provides a
means of getting even. Furthermore, there is an implicit threat
that the Blackmail player will take away or destroy something
the other values, if the other doesn't do what the Blackmail
player wants. Ronnie's mother fears that Ronnie will have a
tantrum and hurt her or her house if she doesn't do what he
wants. While these game tactics are clearly a way for Ronnie to
control his relationship with his mother, they are also a way
for Ronnie to mask his low self-esteem and self-confidence.
According to Keirsey, SPs get their feeling of self-esteem (pride)
from being socially powerful, and their feeling of self-confidence
by being impressive to others.

Often when children or adolescents are employing survival game
tactics, their parents are as well. In this case, Mrs. Martin is
exhibiting the *Shocking* variant of the *Blackmail* game when
she allows her children to demean and abuse her. Shocking
players permit themselves to be stepped on and taken advantage
of by others.

---

[*] This is why Artisans make up the bulk of the high school dropouts.

My interventions with Ronnie and his mother were designed to take over the game of Blackmail, while also building Ronnie's feelings of self-esteem and self-confidence. To stop Ronnie's Blackmail game I used two methods that are often effective for that purpose—*restitution* and *deprivation*. With restitution, Ronnie is given the opportunity to do something good to make up for having done something bad. Hence, Ronnie agreed do the laundry to make up for the pain and anguish he caused his mother when caught by the police on the beach. The deprivation method was employed when Mrs. Martin was instructed to remove whatever privilege Ronnie abused for a specified period of time. I advised Mrs. Martin to avoid the use of commericals, since Artisan children and adolescents typically respond to parental efforts to convince them to behave by doing the very opposite.

To motivate Mrs. Martin to employ deprivation, I relied on the wonderful metaphor that she offered me—that of "pulling in the reins." This metaphor was ideal for use with an SP, since it is action-oriented and so engaging to the senses. Had Mrs. Martin been a Guardian-type parent, it would probably have been more effective to emphasize that it is her *responsibility* to teach Ronnie to be accountable by setting clear limits and imposing consequences when he oversteps them.

As another way of altering the communication patterns between parent and child, Mrs. Martin was instructed to replace her negative comments to Ronnie with positive ones. Rather than just telling her what *not* to say, Mrs. Martin was given specific instructions regarding what she *was* to say to Ronnie—that is, encouraging comments about good things she noticed Ronnie doing. By having Mrs. Martin say positive things when viewing Ronnie's homework, it was hoped that she would begin to acknowledge the progress that he had been making on his own at school.

While instructing his mother in the use of deprivation, Ronnie was given the prescriptive assignment to misbehave in order to test his mother and to give her a chance to practice the new methods she was learning. In addition, a variety of methods were used to try to build Ronnie's self-confidence and self-esteem.

In order to help Ronnie play a more powerful (and positive) role in the family and feel and be more impressive, I began to refer to him often as "the man of the family." Furthermore, I put him in charge of lowering his mother's blood pressure. When giving this assignment, I was careful to *ask* for his assistance, while emphasizing the importance of the task and confessing that others, including myself, had failed in our efforts on his mother's behalf. This, in particular, gave him a positive and very impressive role to play in the family drama.

My final intervention was to use guided visualization to build Ronnie's confidence in his ability to perform well on tests. As is my usual practice, Ronnie was given an audio tape of the twenty-minute session that he was instructed to listen to daily. Through repeated exposure, audio tapes provide a wonderful method by which to increase the power and effectiveness of guided visualization.

Case #2

TEACHING
THE
BOSS

Session One:

Diane, an attractive, gregarious, effervescent woman in her thirties, explained that she had come to see me because she was having a horrible time dealing with her boss, Nadine. Although she loved everything else about her job working with human relations and staff development in a large corporation, things had gotten so bad with her boss that she was thinking about quitting. Diane told me how she had tried her very hardest to please Nadine over the past two years, but that Nadine did nothing but find fault with her. She noticed that Nadine kept a careful watch on her, anxious to catch her doing something wrong. Nadine found errors in every memo, every letter, and every report that Diane wrote. Diane dreaded playing her message log each day, since it was usually full of "nastygrams" from Nadine accusing her of having fouled up one thing or another—often things that Diane could not possibly have done. At staff meetings, Nadine made fun of her in front of the other employees. Diane was constantly on edge at work, waiting for the next bomb to fall. Each meeting in Nadine's office was like marching into hell. Nadine attacked her with one question after another, and Diane ended up in tears, feeling helpless, utterly frustrated, and defenseless. When Diane tried to tell Nadine about her feelings, Nadine would dismiss them as completely irrational. That very morning, Nadine had told Diane that she was "surrounded by incompetent people," and Diane had burst into tears, convinced that Nadine was really talking about *her*.

Diane hated the way she felt around Nadine, noting that there had been more than a few other people in her past who had made her feel the same way. Confessing that she had never learned to deal with people like Nadine, Diane explained that she had come to see me to solve this problem once and for all. Though the idea of quitting her job was tempting to her, Diane felt that she would be better off if she stuck it out and learned some new ways of behaving instead. Besides, everything else about her job was entirely satisfying. The office she managed was harmonious, the people warm and friendly, and the work gave her an opportunity to be creative and to really make a positive difference in the lives of others. She loved working with small groups, helping individuals to develop to their fullest potential. She felt that she had grown a lot at this job, and that she could continue to develop herself by remaining in her current position. If only she could stop letting Nadine get to her so easily.

Immediately after tearfully spilling out these feelings, Diane began to defend Nadine, confessing that she truly felt sorry for her. Diane told me that nobody in the company liked Nadine. Apparently Nadine had almost no social life away from work. According to Diane, Nadine was well respected in the company for her brilliant ideas and her efficiently run department, but her impersonal treatment of others had earned her an unfortunate reputation as "the Ice Woman." Diane felt awful when she heard people calling Nadine names, for she knew it would hurt Nadine's feelings if she ever found out. Diane assured me that she liked Nadine and would love to help her. She saw Nadine as someone who was desperately in need of a friend. Diane confessed that she felt guilty complaining about Nadine and making her sound like a bad person. She assured me that Nadine was *not* a bad person, just a perfectionist and very difficult to work for.

When I questioned Diane about her past formal evaluations from Nadine, she indicated that they were always in the excellent range. This had always shocked Diane, since Nadine *never* told her she was doing a good job, and always pointed out her many errors.

As for her own employees, Diane said that they would do anything for her and she for them. Diane cared a lot about her employees and often bent the rules for individual cases. Her job, she said, was to bring out the very best in each individual. And, indeed, her employees outperformed the other departments time and time again. Still, Nadine complained to Diane that she would rescue her employees from tight spots rather than allowing them to accept the logical consequences of their own actions.

Though Diane was warm, personal, and a natural complementer with everyone else on the job, she was distant and private with Nadine. Nadine had voiced her disapproval when Diane had become pregnant soon after Nadine hired her. Diane admitted that she felt guilty for having let Nadine down. While pregnant, Diane had never missed a day on the job, in spite of severe morning sickness. Since her son's birth, Diane never talked about him to Nadine, since she didn't want to remind Nadine of her betrayal. In fact, Diane never mentioned her husband, either. It was as if, when she was around her boss, Diane pretended to be single.

I asked Diane to think of a recent episode with Nadine which she had found upsetting, and then I instructed her to show me exactly who said what by pretending that Nadine was seated in an empty chair across from her. Diane demonstrated how she had gone into Nadine's office that morning to give her a report, and to get her okay on an important change in a current project. After playing herself, I had Diane switch roles and show me how Nadine responded to her. Then I had Diane play herself again to respond to Nadine, and so on.

In watching Diane's role-playing sequence, I noticed that she approached Nadine as a little girl might approach a parent. She spoke with hesitation, and seemed to be sending the message, "Here are the facts. Now please tell me what I should do." Nadine responded consistently with, "I would like you to think for yourself! What do *you* think you should do? You tell me!" To which Diane would respond, "Well, I'm not sure. Perhaps you can tell me what you would like me to do."

What is the client's personality type and what is the evidence used to identify it?

What are the survival games being played and by whom?

What treatment interventions might be useful in stopping the survival game playing?

First Session Interventions:

After viewing Diane's role-playing sequence, I offered some observations about how she was coming across to Nadine. It seemed to me that she sounded and looked like a scared little girl going in to ask for Mommie's advice and permission. I noted that *never* in the course of the dialogue did she voice an opinion of her own. It appeared that the message she was sending was: "I'm not able to decide this for myself—please tell me what to do." I asked Diane if that is the message she wanted to send, and she said no, absolutely not.

Next I talked about personality types, explaining that Diane was an Idealist, while Nadine was a Rational. I told Diane that there are certain things that Rationals do and don't do that frequently bother Idealists, and vice versa. I pointed out that during the roleplay, it was very clear that Nadine wanted Diane to *think for herself*. It is common for NTs, who are managers, to expect this of their employees. I told Diane that if she wanted Nadine to respect her, she needed to demonstrate to her that she could think for herself. Of course, I emphasized that she was already thinking for herself all day long, every day on the job. It's just that she had not been *communicating* to Nadine in a way that gave her that impression.

I suggested that Diane go to Nadine with her mind already made up about something and tell Nadine, "This is what the problem is, and this is what I have decided to do about it." She should be ready to provide the complete rationale that led to her solution, but was only to reveal it if Nadine asked for it. Diane recalled that whenever she had approached Nadine in the manner I was describing, Nadine had responded very favorably.

I asked Diane to replay the scene she had acted out earlier, only this time, to approach Nadine by describing a current departmental problem and then outlining the solution that she had decided upon. In spite of my detailed instructions, Diane reverted to her previous behavior. Next, I demonstrated this alternative way of talking to Nadine. Then, as she practiced several more times, I offered Diane feedback on her performance by pointing out what she was doing right and what she could still do better. Finally, I gave her the assignment of approaching Nadine once a week in the way we had practiced. She readily agreed.

I explained to Diane that Rationals are simply not the natural appreciators that Idealists are. Many NTs, like Nadine, assume that if they told you once five years ago that you are doing a great job, then they needn't say it ever again. In fact, they feel silly repeating themselves. Giving compliments is embarrassing to most Rationals. I stressed that Diane would probably never get from Nadine the words of praise that she was looking for. But that didn't mean she wasn't doing a fine job from Nadine's perspective. What's more, I stressed that NTs often say things that are meant *impersonally*, and that NFs are prone to taking everything *personally*. Hence, chances are that Diane was getting her feelings hurt when Nadine wasn't even talking about her.

I told Diane that Nadine will always point out her errors, since that is what NTs do best. I explained that when Rationals take the time to point out one's errors, they are saying that the work is good enough to be criticized. I emphasized that it was a good thing that she made ample errors, since without them, Nadine would probably feel that she was of no use to Diane. I suggested that she make at least three intentional errors every week on written work that Nadine would see. In that way, she could be certain that Nadine would have something to correct. If Nadine pointed out the errors, then Diane was to act defensively, so as not to let on that the errors were intentional. Diane reluctantly agreed to this second assignment.

I asked Diane if she realized why Nadine had hired her. She said that she often wondered about that, since Nadine seemed so displeased with her. I told her that the reason was very clear to me when I looked at their two personality types. Nadine had hired her so that she could learn from Diane. I explained to Diane that as an Idealist, she knows more about how to get along harmoniously with others, how to appreciate others, and how to inspire others to do their best, than any other type of person. I told her that Nadine had much to learn from her, and that Nadine knew that better than anyone else. I asked if she had noticed Nadine observing her when she was interacting with her employees. She said that Nadine did that all the time. I said that she was an excellent role model for Nadine. When I questioned Diane about what she had taught Nadine so far, Diane named a few ways that she had recently noticed Nadine copying her. I commended Diane on her excellent modeling and teaching. I requested that Diane identify those things that she would still like to teach Nadine, and she listed the following: how to be nicer to her secretary, how to be more pleasant when meeting strangers, and how to loosen up and play every now and then. I commended Diane on her list, and I suggested that she choose a different lesson for Nadine every week. She was to do her best to teach Nadine that lesson without, of course, revealing to Nadine or anyone else what she was up to. Diane said it sounded like it actually could be a lot of fun.

Finally, I suggested that in order to teach Nadine how to be more personal with people, Diane was going to have to be more personal with her. I asked Diane to stop acting like she was single and to start showing pictures of her husband and son to Nadine on a regular basis. Although she anticipated that it would be hard, Diane was willing to try.

Session Two:

When Diane arrived three weeks later for our second session, she was all smiles. She said that she had done all of her assignments, and that she was feeling much better around Nadine. According to Diane, things were greatly improved. There had been no more nastygrams on her message machine. She had not cried around Nadine, nor even been close to tears. Every time she had approached Nadine and told her what she intended to do to solve a departmental problem, Nadine had simply said, "Okay." Diane felt more confident and more in control when interacting with Nadine. Throughout the day she had ceased to fear that Nadine might jump on her about something she had or had not done.

As I had assigned, Diane had shown Nadine pictures of her son and talked to her about her husband. In response, Nadine had begun to show Diane pictures of her nephew, and to talk about her relationship with her boyfriend. Diane told me that she had begun to treat Nadine in the same positive way that she did her own employees. She had let Nadine know that she empathized with her (Nadine faced a lot of pressure in her position at the top), and she had found several opportunities to let Nadine know what she appreciated about her leadership.

Diane had made at least three intentional errors every week. She told me that she let her secretary in on the little game, and they had many good laughs about it. Both were surprised to discover that most of the time, Nadine did not even catch the errors they had made on purpose. In fact, since Diane had gone to Nadine and told her how much she appreciated her numerous corrections, much of Diane's work started coming back to her with hardly any red marks on it at all.

Diane told me that until our first session, she had never realized how much she could teach Nadine, nor how much Nadine watched her in order to copy her. In accordance with my instructions, she had chosen a different lesson for Nadine every week, and she reported that her student was progressing nicely. Diane wanted to continue with this program, and I urged her to do so.

When I asked her what she thought she still needed to work on, she indicated that there were times when she still felt like Nadine was attacking her with a barrage of questions, and her tendency was to feel scared and to immediately try to defend herself. She wanted to respond differently, but she didn't know how. I asked her to show me exactly how Nadine would question her, and then, taking Nadine's role myself, I had her demonstrate how she would typically respond.

At my inquiry, Diane said it never occurred to her to respond to Nadine's questions with a question of her own. In a role play, I had Diane pretend she was Nadine firing rapid questions at me about the numbers on a report. I responded to her by asking "Could you tell me more about what you'd like to know regarding this report, so that I can be sure to dig up all of the information you are after and get back to you with it?" After I had modeled the desired behavior, I pretended I was Nadine and let Diane practice responding to my questions with a question. After each role-play sequence, I gave her feedback and encouraged her to try it again. When she seemed comfortable with the way of responding to Nadine, I assigned her the task of trying it out once a day with her boss.

Next we discussed Nadine's competitive, "me versus the rest of you" mentality. I recommended to Diane that she begin to speak to Nadine about "our team" as often as possible, so that it was apparent that they were on the same side.

The last thing I did was to assign Diane a day-long relapse. I said that I was concerned that she might be changing too much, too fast, and that a day of relapse would ease my fears. I explained that it was normal for people to have relapses when they change. I said that since she might not automatically have a relapse, I felt it would be best if she planned to have one. During her day of relapse, she was to return to her old way of responding to Nadine, and that if she could end up in tears, that would be even better. She seemed puzzled, but agreed to do as I had assigned.

Session Three:

Diane reported that things couldn't be better between her and Nadine. She had done every one of her assignments, and she was pleased with the way that she had been responding to Nadine. It was still difficult for her to respond to a question with a question, but she was improving daily. The day of relapse was very hard to do, but she had complied with my instructions, though she just couldn't take it all seriously enough to end up in tears. Since she had been speaking of "our team," Nadine had begun to talk the same way to her. Nadine seemed happier at work, and she was sharing increasingly more of her personal life with Diane. For the first time, Diane had also refused to work several weekends, in favor of spending time at home with her husband and son.

We practiced some more of the skills Diane had been learning using role playing and decided that we need not schedule any more appointments. I suggested to Diane that she call me if she decided that she could benefit from another session.

Follow-up:

When I heard from Diane a year later, she was doing very well in her personal and professional life. Much to her delight, she was pregnant with her second child.

CASE DISCUSSION

As an Idealist, Diane's primary focus is on developing herself and others. Her job as a human relations consultant and staff development trainer enables her to use her special gifts to assist people in their growth and to help them work together harmoniously. It is no surprise that she loves her work, since it is perfect for someone of her type. Diane is warm, friendly, personal and kind. She is most concerned about the *people* of the organization, rather than rules, results or procedures. In fact, Diane's willingness to consistently bend rules for individual cases is a strong indicator that she is an NF, as opposed to an SJ, who would be much more likely to insist that rules be followed without exception.

Still another clue that Diane is an Idealist, is the manner in which she readily puts herself in her boss's shoes and senses Nadine's loneliness and pain. Note that once Diane told me what bothered her about Nadine, she immediately reversed her position and began to defend her boss. I have noticed that it is the NF who is most likely to do this during counseling interviews. NFs have an exceptional ability to truly empathize with the other—even if the other is an adversary. They are also prone to side with the person who is the object of ridicule or abuse—although that person may be driving them crazy.

Diane's effervescence is especially typical of the ENFP, or Advocate/Revealer-type of Idealist, who appear to bubble over with enthusiasm. As a Perceptive-type, she is reluctant to give directives, and she is likely to offer information instead. Her Extroversion is apparent in her ease in talking with strangers and her tendency to become revitalized by interacting with others.

Nadine is a typical Rational manager who is impersonal, efficient, and far more likely to verbalize criticism than praise. As an NT leader, she wants her employees to think for themselves and to face the logical consequences of their actions. She is a perfectionist who expects a great deal from her employees. Those who do not know her well judge her (unfairly) as cold and uncaring. There is not enough information in the case to determine which of the four types of Rationals Nadine might be.

Diane is playing the *Mind Reader* and *Martyr* variants of the *Masquerade* game. Diane is constantly monitoring Nadine's reactions to her. She projects many of her self-doubts and insecurities onto Nadine by deciding that Nadine is always watching her and judging her as incompetent or stupid, and by concluding that Nadine just doesn't like her. In her efforts to earn Nadine's approval and validation, Diane employs Martyr tactics when she sacrifices her real identity—as the mother of a newborn infant—and tries to pretend that she is single and childless around her boss.

Nadine counters Diane's Masquerade game with her own game of *Robot*. When Nadine rapid-fires questions at Diane, she is playing the NT game of *That's Illogical*. It appears that Nadine is also playing *Super-Intellectual*, by presenting a cold and distant exterior, and *Nitpick*, with her excessive focus on every little detail that Diane puts in front of her. Chances are that these games are Nadine's way of keeping her distance in social situations where she feels inadequate.

To stop Diane's Masquerade game, I utilized type theory to place Nadine's behavior in a new light. Diane was encouraged to view Nadine's actions as a function of her personality, and not as a result of anything that Diane did or didn't do. Diane was also able to learn some new ways of communicating that would be more acceptable to her NT boss—for example, she began presenting her own recommendations to Nadine and backing them up with appropriate evidence, rather than approaching Nadine seeking advice or permission. In order to help her to overcome her fear of making mistakes around Nadine, I prescribed that Diane make three intentional errors per week.

Nadine's watchful behavior was reframed as evidence that she wanted to learn from Diane, as opposed to an indication that she was trying to find fault with her. I suggested to Diane that she think of herself as Nadine's teacher by using herself as a role model so that Nadine could learn more about human relations. In this way, I utilized Diane's natural desire to develop people to shift the role she played with Nadine from that of a helpless, inadequate child to that of a capable and competent mentor.

I asked Diane to show Nadine pictures of her husband and son, and to talk about them now and then, as a way of teaching Nadine to be more personal. Naturally, my other motive here was to stop Diane's pretense and to help her be more herself around her boss.

Since Diane reported changing so rapidly, I prescribed a one day relapse. This was to make certain that if she did slide backwards, it could be construed as a positive sign, rather than a negative one. When clients change fast, it is not uncommon for them to regress a little or a lot after the second or third session. By prescribing a relapse, I want to help clients avoid feeling discouraged and hopeless should they find themselves once again employing those game tactics that they thought they had abandoned for good.

Case #3

MY PUPPY

Session One:

The Taylors initiated family therapy at the recommendation of their son's first grade teacher in order to stop Matthew's almost daily biting of other children on the school playground. At the first session, Mr. and Mrs. Taylor indicated that although their primary goal was to get Matthew to stop biting, they also wanted to stop his frequent episodes of bed-wetting and soiling his pants. One of the first things that they told me about Matthew (with him present) was that he did poorly in school because he had "attention deficit disorder with hyperactivity" like his twenty-year-old stepbrother, who was Mr. Taylor's son by a previous marriage. Matthew, a good-looking boy who was rather tall for his age, appeared very alert, though he fidgeted a lot in his chair. As I asked Matthew questions while his parents were in the room, I noticed that he talked like a three-year-old, in incomplete sentences with a very limited vocabulary for a child his age.

I spoke briefly with Mr. and Mrs. Taylor without Matthew present, to ask them what they did when their son bit someone at school. Mrs. Taylor explained that she would take from thirty to sixty minutes right after school to explain to him why he shouldn't bite people. This lecture was delivered while sitting on Matthew's bed with her arm around him. Mrs. Taylor believed that Matthew bit other children because he was "slow" and didn't know any better. Hence, she followed each biting incident with still another attempt to teach him right from wrong. Mrs. Taylor confessed that she was very worried about her son's biting, and terribly embarrassed by the frequent calls she received from Matthew's teacher. She just didn't know how to help Matthew understand that biting was wrong.

Mr. Taylor said that he was busy working most of the time and that he didn't see much of Matthew, so he just let his wife handle it. He explained that he worked long hours at the trucking business that they owned, where there was always another crisis to be handled. Mr. Taylor told me that he liked his work because it was challenging, he enjoyed working on mechanical equipment, and there was never a dull moment. He was a high school dropout out who had joined the army in search of adventure. He left the military after a few years and then borrowed some money and started up his business, which had since become a very profitable enterprise.

Apparently, the Taylors spent little time together doing fun things as a couple or as a family. Mrs. Taylor complained that her husband was always exhausted when he got home after a long day, and he usually fell asleep in front of the TV set. She repeatedly told him how much this bothered her, but she got the impression that he just "tuned her out." On weekends, he would watch sports on TV, go fishing, or go to the horse races. Mrs. Taylor told me that she loved being a mother and a homemaker, and that she enjoyed keeping the books for the family business during the hours that Matthew was in school. A warm, sociable woman, Mrs. Taylor also participated in the parent-teacher association at Matthew's school; she was room-mother for his class, and she was very involved in the social affairs and the community service activities at her church.

Up until this point in the session, Mrs. Taylor had done almost all of the talking, while Mr. Taylor sat and nodded quietly. However, when I asked the Taylors to name something that Matthew could do well, Mr. Taylor came to life and began to tell me about how Matthew excelled at sports and loved to compete. He said that Matthew was only six, and yet he played touch football with eight and ten-year-old boys, and he could throw a ball, catch, and run as well as most of them. Mr. Taylor told me

MY PUPPY / 193

that he and Matthew enjoyed spending time together watching sporting events on television, and that Matthew had memorized all of the names and numbers of the Ram's football team. Mr. Taylor claimed that Matthew could even follow a tennis match on TV, since he understood the rules of the game and the means of scoring, although he had never played the game.

In addition to sports, Matthew's parents reported that he also enjoyed constructing things. They had watched him spending hours alone building miniature towns out of hundreds of Legos.

Next, I met with Matthew alone. As he told me about his school and his friends, the first thing I noticed was that his speech had altered dramatically since his parents had left the room. He was using complete sentences and a vocabulary appropriate for a child much older than six.

What are the clients' personality types and what is the evidence used to identify them?

What are the survival games being played and by whom?

What treatment interventions might be useful in stopping the survival game playing?

First Session Interventions:

After we became a little better acquainted, I leaned slightly towards Matthew, and I told him that I wanted to tell him a story about my puppy. He nodded, and his eyes seemed to open wide. With much enthusiasm and animation, I began by describing my puppy in detail: his cute little wagging tail, his long, soft, floppy ears, his wet black nose that wants to sniff everything. I told him that my puppy could do many wonderful things—that he could run faster than the other puppies, catch a ball in his mouth, and that all the other puppies on the playground loved to play with him, because he was so good at all kinds of sports. Matthew seemed captivated with my story, and he even leaned forward in his chair. At one point, he interrupted me to ask "Where does your puppy go to school?" "Los Angeles," I responded, matter-of-factly (knowing that Matthew lived in that city). "Oh," he said, as if that satisfied him. I went on describing my puppy's great popularity, skillfulness, and success on the playground until Matthew suddenly burst out with, "Let me tell you about *my* puppy!" I said that I would *love* to hear about his puppy. He went on, "*My* puppy did all of his math problems and he took home a math paper with a star on it and his mother was really proud of him!" I ooohed and aaahed, and he continued, "He did more math problems than any of the other puppies! And he did all of his other schoolwork, too. And my puppy's teacher told him that he was the best one on the school playground, and his mother was really proud of him for that." I listened with great interest and delight, as Matthew went on and on about the great things his puppy did at school, and how proud that made his puppy's mother.

When Matthew finished telling me about his puppy, I had his parents rejoin us, and I said, "I have noticed that whenever you bite someone, Matthew, you get to spend lots of time with your mother. I think you have found a *great* way of keeping your mother very busy with you!" When Mrs. Taylor saw Matthew break out in a big smile, she looked at me, and said, "Not any more. From now on, if he bites anyone, then he'll have to spend an hour *alone* in his room after school." I asked if, besides giving Matthew the time alone in his room, both parents would be willing to try an experiment in which they didn't even *talk* to Matthew about his biting. I cautioned that it wouldn't be easy, and explained that if he tried to bring it up, they would just have to change the subject. Both parents readily agreed to our experiment. Then I told Matthew that I wanted him to test them by trying to bring up the subject to see what they would do.

Finally, I enlisted Mr. Taylor's help in helping Matthew. I explained that Matthew needed lots of practice in playing nicely rather than biting, and I asked Mr. Taylor if he would be willing to play an indoor or outdoor game with Matthew every other day. Mr. Taylor readily agreed to this request.

Session Two:

When I saw the Taylor family a week later, they reported that Matthew had come home three days in a row with a happy face on the back of his hand, indicating that he was one of the best children on the playground. He had not bitten anyone since our previous session. And, for the first time all year, he had brought home math papers with stars on them for his excellent work. What's more, though it had hardly been addressed during our first session, there had been no episodes of bed-wetting or soiling his pants. Both parents had kept their agreement to avoid talking with Matthew about his biting. And Mr. Taylor had played games with Matthew on three alternate days.

With Matthew present, I spent the first half of the second session talking to the Taylors about their son's personality type. I had spoken to Matthew's teacher since our first session, and he had confirmed my suspicions that Matthew was an Artisan child. Matthew's teacher indicated that he was very bright and that he did not appear to have any kind of learning disability. The astute teacher told me that Matthew became easily bored with routine, repetitive tasks, and that he seemed to enjoy learning in a hands-on way. In the classroom he was impulsive, impatient, and full of energy.

I told the Taylors that Matthew seemed to be an Artisan child, and I explained that this type of child is often mislabeled as attention deficit disordered or hyperactive because they are not likely to respond well to a traditional, routine classroom environment. I talked about the SP's need for action, freedom, and excitement, and the SP's unique talents and strengths. I mentioned the names of famous Artisans who have been world leaders, Olympic gold medalists, gifted musicians, and courageous war heroes. I also discussed the challenges involved in parenting Artisan children. I emphasized how SP children are natural gamblers, prone to testing the limits, whatever those limits might be.

I told Mr. and Mrs. Taylor that it appeared to me that Matthew was a particularly bright Artisan child. As evidence of that, I mentioned his remarkable ability to recall the names and numbers of the Ram's football team, and his ability to follow a tennis match on TV.

During this time, Matthew interrupted me once to ask if I could have his parents leave so we could talk some more about our puppies. So, following the discussion of Matthew's personality type, I asked Mr. and Mrs. Taylor to leave the room. Immediately, Matthew launched into a discussion of his puppy's most recent exploits. As before, I listened intently and responded enthusiastically.

Towards the end of the session, I told Mr. and Mrs. Taylor in private that they shouldn't be surprised if Matthew bit again in the next week or so, since people often get worse again before they get better once and for all. Finally, I suggested that they read *Please Understand Me*, and I got their commitment to continue to follow through on the assignments of the previous week.

Session Three:

During the next week, Matthew did, indeed, have two more biting episodes at school, and one more episode of soiling his pants at home. His parents had said nothing to Matthew about his biting, and they had sent him to his room for one hour after school following each episode.

Both of Matthew's parents had read *Please Understand Me*, and they told me that they could see that Matthew was, indeed, an Artisan child. They had also begun to notice that Matthew was much more capable than they had originally thought he was.

Matthew's father had continued playing with him around three times per week. I asked that the entire family to go on an afternoon outing together sometime in the next two weeks. I also asked Mr. and Mrs. Taylor to go out on a date without Matthew before our next session.

Session Four:

Two weeks later, the Taylors returned to report that there had been no more episodes of biting at school. What's more, Matthew had not been wetting the bed or soiling his pants during that time, either. The three of them had enjoyed an afternoon together at the zoo. In addition, Mr. and Mrs. Taylor had gone out to dinner without Matthew for the first time in over a year. I encouraged them to continue to have dates, and also to have family outings on a regular basis.

During our fourth session, I noticed that Matthew had begun to speak around his parents like a bright six-year-old rather than a three-year-old. I did not comment about this, and neither did his parents.

Follow-Up:

I saw the Taylors only two more times spaced over a six-week period. Matthew did not bite again, and he also completely stopped soiling and wetting his pants. A phone call several months later indicated that all was going well for Matthew and his parents.

CASE DISCUSSION

Much of Matthew's behavior is characteristic of the Artisan child. He is impulsive and action-oriented. He enjoys learning in a hands-on way. He loves competition and contests. He becomes easily bored with written tasks in the classroom, and yet he will spend uninterrupted hours captured by an activity that fascinates him, like building. He is keenly aware of concrete details in his world—for example, the names and numbers of the Ram's football players. Matthew's exceptional athletic skills are also characteristic of the SP; although any type of child can be gifted in athletics, it is the SP who is most likely to shine in this area.

I suspect that Matthew is an ISTP, or Operator/Instrumentor-type of Artisan. It is not surprising that Matthew is already interested in construction, since that is a field in which ISTPs excel. As an Introvert, he takes longer to warm up to people, and he enjoys spending long hours playing alone. Matthew also appears to be directive rather than informative. An example of this is when he says to me, "Let me tell you about *my* puppy," in a rather forceful manner. His biting is also characteristic of the Thinking-type Artisan, who is more likely than the Feeling-type Artisan to employ those Blackmail tactics that hurt others.

Matthew's mother is an ESFJ, or Conservator/Protector-type of Guardian. As an ESFJ, Mrs. Taylor is warm, sociable, friendly, and nurturing. True to her Guardian nature, she is a traditionalist who gives of herself freely to her family, home, business, church, and community. She enjoys doing bookkeeping—a task that demands the SJ's patience, accuracy, and extreme attention to detail.

In contrast, Mr. Taylor appears to be an ISTP, just like his son. It is the Artisan who is most likely to drop out of high school and join the military in search of adventure. It is also the Artisan who is most likely to risk borrowing money to start his own entrepreneurial venture. Mr. Taylor likes his business because it enables him to use his mechanical expertise and it provides him with the excitement and challenge of handling crises. He is typical of Artisan men in his love of sporting events, fishing, and horse racing. While other types—especially the SJs—also may enjoy watching sporting events and fishing, it is the Artisans who are most attracted to the thrill of betting on horses. As an Operator/Instrumentor-type of Artisan, Mr. Taylor is quiet, impersonal, and a loner. He becomes visibly excited only when discussing Matthew's athletic prowess—an obvious source of pride for him.

Matthew's biting, as well as his bed-wetting and soiling of his pants are indicators that he is employing the *Outrage* and *Shocking* variants of the *Blackmail* game.* I used a variety of methods to stop Matthew's game-playing. It was obvious that Mrs. Taylor's attempted solution for stopping Matthew's biting was actually maintaining the problem. Every time she sat on his bed and talked to him about why he shouldn't bite, she made it more likely that he would bite again. Fortunately, Mrs. Taylor decided to respond differently to Matthew's biting by sending him to his room for an hour alone. This use of *deprivation* was not designed to punish Matthew—rather, it was meant to remove the privilege of being around his mother and his friends every time he employed his Blackmail tactic. In conjunction with the use of deprivation, I also asked Mr. and Mrs. Taylor to stop talking with Matthew about his biting. This *moratorium* was designed to insure that all lectures, advice, and reminders about biting would cease. These verbal attempts to get him to change his ways must stop in order for deprivation to be effective.

Using a *passport* metaphor, I communicated to Matthew that it was both possible and okay for him to behave differently by telling him a story about a puppy who is admired for his skillfulness on the school playground. I selected this metaphor because of Matthew's exceptional coordination, his love of sports, and, of course, his habit of biting.

One way in which Matthew's game playing was helpful to his family was that it got his Mr. Taylor more involved with his wife and his son. Hence, one of my goals was to make certain that Mr. Taylor was spending more time with Matthew and Mrs.

---

* Bedwetting and soiling one's pants are not exclusively demonstrated by Artisan children, although Artisans are the most likely to use these problems as a means of playing Blackmail with significant others.

Taylor, so that Matthew's game tactics would no longer be necessary. Towards that end, I asked Mr. Taylor to play games with Matthew every other day, so that Matthew could learn how to play nicely. I also assigned Mr. and Mrs. Taylor the task of going out on dates together and I encouraged the three of them to go on regular family outings.

My most important intervention was to perform a "labelectomy" on Matthew. Unfortunately, because they do not fit in well in the traditional classroom, Artisan children like Matthew are the most likely to be labeled as *defective* by their parents, teachers, and/or counselors. This label communicates to the child that he or she is not expected to do as well as the other children in school. Children may not always behave in the way that their parents and teachers *want* them to, but they almost always do what those adults *expect* of them. This is evident even in Matthew's tendency to speak like a three-year-old around his parents, and in his bed-wetting and soiling, since both are typical behaviors of very young children.

To perform a "labelectomy," I chose to substitute a positive label—*Artisan*—for the Taylor's negative label—*attention deficit disordered with hyperactivity*. With the new label I assigned to Matthew, his behavior was reframed as normal rather than abnormal, and he was suddenly viewed as capable rather than incapable. As his parents raised their expectations of him in accordance with their new frame of reference, Matthew's behavior changed as well

Case #4

THE
VULCAN

Session One:

Daniel, a handsome nineteen-year-old with an athletic build
and a very serious expression on his face, arrived at his first
counseling session weighted down with a massive pile of papers
that he handed to me. He explained that the pile consisted of
philosophical essays and creative drawings that he had produced while in high school and that he wanted me to review, so
that I might better understand him. In response to my question
regarding what he wanted to accomplish in our sessions, Daniel
told me that he was lonely, and that he didn't seem to know how
to get along with people very well. He said that he had only one
male friend, and that he didn't have a clue as to how to go about
finding a girlfriend. According to Daniel, people acted like they
just didn't like him very much. They seemed bored whenever he
would talk about things that interested him.

I learned that Daniel had moved from the Midwest to
California by himself shortly after graduating from high
school. He had already completed twenty units of college work
in an accelerated program during his senior year, and he was
currently waiting to fulfill residency requirements so that he
could attend a California university. Daniel told me he wanted
to be a Renaissance man. He planned to study philosophy and
engineering in college, so that he could be both a philosopher
and an inventor, and also write books on those subjects.

For fun, Daniel mostly would play with his computer or read. He devoured books on a wide range of subjects, but he especially enjoyed philosophical works.

Daniel was the youngest in a family of twelve children. He had always felt different from everyone else in his family—like the black sheep. Daniel's parents were down-to-earth, practical people who had no use for his constant reading or his excessive interest in theories. His father thought it was fine for him to go to college, as long as he studied something reasonable—like business. His mother had never forgiven him for rejecting her religion, in spite of his attempts to explain to her that it was not in alignment with his personal ideology. Daniel had never felt accepted or acknowledged by his family when he was just being himself. He told me that it seemed as if the most important parts of him were invisible to his parents, no matter what he said or did.

Daniel had recently read *Please Understand Me*, and he indicated that it had already made a world of difference for him. He had come to me for therapy because he had hoped to learn more about the different personality types and how to get along with them. He wanted people to like him. He wanted friends. And he wanted to feel more at ease when interacting with others. Daniel reported that he was often highly critical of himself in social situations. Frequently, when trying to have a conversation with someone, he would be so busy putting himself down (in his head) that he would end up going blank and saying nothing at all.

In addition, Daniel said that he that he really longed to be more spontaneous, free, and playful, like an SP. He believed that there was an SP inside of him who just wasn't able to come out most of the time.

What is the client's personality type and what is the evidence used to identify it?

What are the survival games being played and by whom?

What treatment interventions might be useful in stopping the survival game playing?

First Session Interventions:

I told Daniel that I thought he could benefit from learning the technology of social interaction, and his eyes lit up. I began by teaching him how to smile, and how to offer verbal reinforcement (compliments) to others. We practiced these techniques, using role playing, until he seemed comfortable. I assigned him the task of smiling and offering verbal reinforcement twice during the next week.

I explained to Daniel that during the high school years, while NFs, SJs, and SPs are refining their *social* skills, NTs (especially the Introverted ones) are more likely to be focusing their energy on utilizing their *academic* skills. It is not uncommon for INTs to decide to put some time and attention into acquiring the tools of social interaction during their late teens or early twenties.

Next, I suggested to Daniel that one of the keys to being a competent conversationalist was the ability to discuss those topics that each type was likely to find most interesting. I asked him to reread *Please Understand Me,* so that he might identify those topics that would be most likely to capture the interest of each temperament.

In order to acquire additional social interaction tools, I also asked Daniel to read Manuel Smith's book, *When I Say No, I*

Feel Guilty (1985). During future sessions we would rehearse some of the methods described in that book.

The final assignment I gave Daniel was to notice his negative self-talk in one social situation and to write down exactly what he says to himself.

Session Two:

Daniel returned with a chart of the four temperaments, and a listing of those topics that he thought would be of particular interest to each. We discussed his chart, and I commended him on a job well done. We talked about the difference between abstract people (Intuitive-types) and concrete people (Sensing-types), and the things they often preferred to talk about. Daniel realized that when he launched into a discussion of some complicated geophysical theory at the beginning of a conversation with someone, chances are he would lose that person's interest, unless that person happened to be another NT. We rehearsed conversations about such concrete topics as food, shelter, recreation, and transportation, until Daniel felt comfortable talking about those subjects.

Daniel had practiced smiling and offering verbal reinforcement, and he was already getting more positive reactions from strangers and co-workers alike. He had also read *When I Say No, I Feel Guilty,* and he had begun to practice asking open-ended questions. We used more role playing to rehearse some of the other methods described in the book, like how to listen for and offer "free information" in the course of a conversation. Free information is the extra, personal information that people disclose about themselves while conversing. As homework, I asked Daniel to practice having at least one conversation using the new tools he had learned.

Daniel had also written down the critical comments that he made in his head during one social encounter. Much to his surprise, these were the same negative messages that he had received from his father for most of his life.

I introduced the Transactional Analysis model to Daniel, and we talked about the critical parent inside of him that mimicked his own father and that seemed to be keeping his child ego state locked up inside of him. Using an empty chair, I had him pretend that his critical parent and child ego states were interacting with each other. Then, I had him pretend that his adult ego state could step in and intervene in defense of his child. I equated Daniel's child ego state with the SP inside of him that he wanted to bring out. As homework, I suggested that Daniel do an experiment for one day which would involve letting his inner child do anything he wanted to do. This would require that he was free all day to be spontaneous and to have fun. He was to note the results of the experiment so that we could discuss them during our next session.

Session Three:

Daniel came back three weeks later looking more relaxed and happy. He reported having had several lengthy conversations with SJs and SPs that seemed to go very well. He also reported that his experiment with letting his child out had been so much fun that he had chosen to repeat it for about three days a week. As a result of his newfound spontaneity, he had made several new acquaintances—both male and female, and he was feeling fairly comfortable when talking with them. He told me that it seemed as if they really liked him. He was definitely beginning to feel more socially competent.

In keeping with his training in the technology of social interaction, I taught Daniel how to use active listening. With a little practice and coaching, he caught on very quickly. He agreed to try it out at least once a week, to develop additional expertise.

Since he had planned a trip home for the holidays, we spent the rest of the session working on Daniel's relationship with his family in general and his father in particular, who seemed to fit the description of the ESTJ. Using the Gestalt empty chair exercise and guided visualization, Daniel was able to tell his father how he had always longed for his approval, and how much it hurt never to receive it.

I explained to Daniel that, as a Rational-type person, he was very much like Mr. Spock on Star Trek. That meant he was actually half human and half Vulcan. I emphasized that most humans would not understand him fully because of this—not even his family members, as he well knew. At best they would recognize that he was different. What's more, his Vulcan side was something very precious, to be shared fully with only very special people who would genuinely appreciate it. Daniel nodded in agreement with my analogy. I assigned Daniel the task of seeing the movie *Star Trek IV*, in which Mr. Spock wears a hat to cover up his Vulcan ears while he is wandering around San Francisco.

Session Four:

When I saw Daniel four weeks later he reported that his trip home had been very successful and satisfying. Daniel told me that his conversations with his mother and father were the best that they had ever been. He was able to be assertive with his father about his future plans, and for the first time his father did not try to oppose his decisions. He was also able to comfortably talk to his parents about topics that were important to them. What's more, Daniel was able to accept that his parents loved him the best they could, and that they just weren't able to give him the acknowledgment for his Vulcan nature that he had wanted from them for so long. Thus, he had let go of trying to obtain that validation from them. I commented that it was all a part of becoming a man and of being one's own person. Daniel just grinned.

Session Five:

By our fifth and final session, Daniel was able to report that he had several new male friends whom he really liked, and that he had a terrific girlfriend, too. He was allowing his spontaneous, playful self to emerge more and more. He was confident in his ability to handle social situations. He was proud to be half Vulcan. And more and more, he was finding people who recognized and appreciated his Vulcan nature, too.

CASE DISCUSSION

Daniel's interest in philosophy, engineering, and inventing are characteristic of the Rational-type person. So is his desire to be a Renaissance man—that is, someone who is knowledgeable and capable in many diverse fields. After all, it is the NT who places such a high value on acquiring competencies. Two additional clues that Daniel is a Rational-type are that he prefers reading theoretical material and that he is particularly fond of computers. Though all types may enjoy using a computer for work or just to play games, it is the Rational who is most likely to devote leisure hours to mastering a computer's software capabilities.

Of the four kinds of Rationals, Daniel is probably an INTP, or the Engineer/Designer. I base this on two observations. First, he is particularly interested in designing, as opposed to planning and organizing, which would point more to the INTJ. Second, he appears to be more of an informative person than a directive one. There is no question that he is an Introvert, given his solitary nature and lack of social awareness. I have noted that of all of the types, it is the INT who is most likely to be deficient in social skills.

Daniel is playing the *Super-Intellectual, Haunted,* a n d *Blanking Out* variants of the *Robot* game primarily due to his feelings of incompetence and failure when it comes to interpersonal relations. It appears that Daniel decides to seek therapy when he no longer has his schoolwork to use as a way to preoccupy himself and to build his sense of self-esteem. Suddenly, his inadequacy in social situations is painfully obvious to him. To protect himself, he immediately brings up highly technical subjects in conversations with others, as a way of maintaining his distance and bolstering his feelings of inferiority. What's more, he appears cold, unapproachable, and aloof. He is haunted by negative self-judgement that distracts him during social encounters, and he is prone to going blank when he tries to think of something to say.

In speaking to Daniel's temperament, I offered to help him acquire the tools associated with the *technology* of social interaction. I spoke of *verbal reinforcement*, rather than strokes or warm fuzzies. And I gave him the assignment to *experiment* with allowing his child ego state to emerge. All of these terms were meant to appeal to Daniel's scientific NT nature.

Much of my work with Daniel involved teaching him how to converse with people. I did lots of coaching in my office, and I gave him an abundance of positive feedback on his performances. In addition, I encouraged him to use two models—personality types, and Transactional Analysis—in order to better understand himself and others.

Finally, I used the Vulcan analogy to reframe Daniel's experience of being rejected by his family and others. It offered Daniel a new way of viewing himself in social situations, while also suggesting that he has incredible Vulcan capabilities within him to be utilized whenever he wishes.

Case #5

The Phone Call:

Mrs. Blake called me out of desperation to ask if I could possibly help her two stepdaughters. She reported that Courtney, the six-year-old, was stuttering, soiling her underwear and hiding it, wetting her bed four times a night, and lying. Lauren, the seven-year-old, had been stuttering and wetting her bed on occasion, but she was not having nearly as many difficulties as her younger sister. She went on to explain that these problems, no doubt, had been caused by the girls' visits every other weekend and one evening per week with their biological mother, Denise. As evidence of that, Mrs. Blake pointed out that the girls were always much worse when they came back from Denise's house. According to Mrs. Blake, Courtney was so troubled by her visits with Denise that recently she had refused to have anything to do with her. I scheduled a session with both girls, and one with Mr. and Mrs. Blake for the following day.

Session One:

Courtney and Lauren arrived for the first session immaculately groomed and dressed like beautiful little dolls. While Courtney was quiet and shy, watching my every move carefully with her big, serious, blue eyes, Lauren was outgoing and very verbal.

Lauren immediately began wandering around my office, touching everything she could get her hands on. Laughing easily, she picked up the toys that she found and asked if it was okay if she played with them. Courtney followed her sister around the room and just looked, without touching anything or speaking much. When Courtney did speak, she expressed herself clearly and succinctly.

Eventually, I sat both girls down at a small table and asked them each to draw a picture of their family, with everyone doing something. Courtney approached the task slowly and carefully, attending to each and every detail of the picture, while Lauren plunged in, grabbing as many colored pens as she could hold and splashing color across the page. Each time that Courtney selected a new colored pen to use, Lauren would announce that she needed that particular color—"*right now!*" Courtney would say nothing and continue using the pen, until she was completely finished with it. Then she would silently hand it over to Lauren and select another color for herself. As she drew, Courtney seemed very anxious to get everything just right. Lauren was done with her family drawing and two more pictures before Courtney had finished the first one. Yet, Courtney did not seem concerned about taking too long—she just continued to draw at her own pace. Lauren's second and third pictures were covered with rainbows, butterflies, and flowers. She dedicated both of them to me and asked me to spell *Eve* for her so she could write my name on the drawings, surrounded by several hearts.

While waiting for Courtney to finish, Lauren asked me if I had any tape. When I gave her some, she promptly went over to an office window and hung her three pictures in the center of it. Afterwards, she sat down and grinned broadly at me. Eventually Courtney finished and went to hang her picture on the window, too.

Both Courtney and Lauren had drawn their father (Mr. Blake), stepmother (Mrs. Blake), and themselves lined up across the page, with no one touching. Courtney drew herself and her stepmom standing side-by-side. In the picture Courtney was holding a flower, and her stepmom was holding a can for watering flowers. Lauren was on Courtney's other side, standing under a tree, and Mr. Blake was situated on the other side of Mrs. Blake, reading the newspaper. Lauren had drawn everybody dancing. She was next to her father and Courtney, with her stepmother on the other side of Mr. Blake. No one in Lauren's picture had arms or hands.

Next I asked the girls to draw a picture of Denise, their biological mother. Courtney indicated that she didn't want to draw "Denise," (as the girls called her), but at my urging, she complied. She drew a picture of a woman with her hair standing straight up, standing next to an empty grocery cart. Courtney began to stutter as she explained that Denise didn't have enough money for groceries, and that she felt sorry for her. She told me that she was also mad at Denise for lying to her, and that she didn't want to see Denise anymore. When I asked her about the lying, Courtney explained that Denise was often late in picking her up and in dropping her off. She had told the girls for a long time that she would buy them their own beds and she had not done so. She would also promise to take them places and never would do it.

Lauren drew Denise floating in the middle of the page with a black broom, and explained that Denise was sweeping. Lauren told me that she liked Denise just fine, but that it was bad that Denise "plays favorites—whatever that means."

I asked the girls what they called Denise when they were around her. They said that they called her "Mom," because she told them that it hurt her feelings when they called her "Denise." They were also careful to call Mrs. Blake by her first name—Joanne—when they were in Denise's presence. But they never called her that to her face, because she wouldn't like it. The girls confessed that it was very hard for them to be around both of their Moms at the same time, because they didn't know what to call them.

I spent a few minutes talking alone with each of the girls and I asked them to tell me more about themselves and their families. During this time I also asked them specific questions to try to determine if either of them had ever been physically or sexually abused. Nothing the girls said made me suspicious that they had been victims of such mistreatment. They explained to me that they knew the difference between good touching and bad touching, and that their mom had always told them that they should tell her immediately if anyone ever touched them the wrong way.

Both sisters reported that they loved their "mom" (Mrs. Blake) very much. While Lauren claimed to get along well with her dad, Courtney revealed with much stuttering that she was afraid of him, because he yelled at her a lot. She said that when she wet the bed or soiled her panties, he would scream if he found out. When she hid her soiled panties under her bed and her mom and dad discovered them there, then they washed her mouth out with soap for lying because she told them she didn't know why she did it.

I asked six-year-old Courtney to tell me one thing that she had always wanted to do. Courtney smiled and said that she wished that she could ride a horse up to the top of a very high mountain, while doing math problems in her head. Courtney explained that this was because she enjoyed doing math problems, and although she was already good at doing them, she wanted to be even better.

At the end of the session, both girls said they would like to come back again.

Session Two:

Mr. and Mrs. Blake, an attractive couple in their early thirties, spent the first half of our initial session complaining nonstop about Mr. Blake's ex-wife, Denise. Both of them seemed to be enraged as they told me about how Denise would almost always arrive two to three hours later than she was supposed to in order to pick up her daughters for the weekend. According to them, she would never feed them the right foods and she would bring them home dirty and hungry and several hours later than she said that she would. She also failed to enforce proper rules with them—for example, she would let them eat whatever they wanted and go to sleep when they wanted. What's more, her child support payments were invariably late—sometimes she would fall two or three months behind in making them. When they tried to tell Denise what she should do differently, Denise would end up saying something that would make Mr. Blake so angry, that he would blowup. At that point, Denise would storm off, and nothing would ever get resolved. Mr. and Mrs. Blake told me that they hated Denise, and that they had often thought about taking the girls and moving away somewhere so that they would not have to deal with her anymore. They were sure that Denise was causing Courtney's problems, since Courtney always got worse when she returned from a visit with her.

I discovered that Mr. and Mrs. Blake constantly voiced their complaints about Denise to the girls. When Courtney and Lauren returned from Denise's house, the first thing Mrs. Blake did was to make them strip and jump into the shower, where they were to scrub themselves clean. Next, Mr. and Mrs. Blake would grill Courtney and Lauren relentlessly about what they were fed, where they went, and what they did. After that, they would criticize everything that Denise said or did to the girls for the next week or two. They told the girls often that Denise was a liar, that she was dirty, irresponsible, cheap, and lazy, because they "wanted to be honest with their daughters."

I learned through questioning that Mr. and Mrs. Blake had married when Lauren was four and a half and Courtney was three years old, after Mr. Blake and Denise had been divorced for several years. Denise had not wanted custody of the children when she left the marriage, so they had always lived with their father. Mr. Blake was employed full time for the telephone company as a line foreman, and Mrs. Blake worked part time while the girls were in school as a bookkeeper/clerk at the local school district office.

Mrs. Blake loved being a mother more than anything else in the world. She was completely devoted to her stepdaughters—making most of their clothes, cooking wholesome foods, and trying hard to meet their every need. She was particularly grateful that her husband and stepdaughters had come into her life, since surgery in her early twenties had left her unable to have children.

Mr. and Mrs. Blake said that their relationship was a very good one—they almost never argued or fought and they shared the same relatively conservative opinions on almost everything. Both liked to spend weekends fixing up their house or going on family outings. And both agreed that their lives would be just about perfect, if it wasn't for Denise.

I asked Mr. and Mrs. Blake to tell me more about Courtney and her recent problems. They told me that she was a serious child— a perfectionist who was always asking questions about why things are the way they are. While Lauren was fun-loving and free-spirited, Courtney seemed more reserved and concerned about her performance in any activity. Mrs. Blake told me that she suspected that Lauren was going to have a lot more fun in life than Courtney, but that Courtney would probably excel academically. While both girls got good grades, Courtney was already the better student—reading at a level far beyond her six years.

Mr. and Mrs. Blake told me that Courtney's lying bothered them more than anything. They wondered if she had inherited the tendency to lie from her biological mother, since she physically resembled Denise so closely. When Courtney wet her bed, or soiled her pants and hid her panties, they just wanted her to be honest and tell them *why* she did it. Thus, they would punish her when she said, "I don't know." They also expected Courtney and Lauren to be clean, responsible, and to mind their manners.

Mr. Blake often yelled at Courtney for her stuttering, since he thought she just needed to slow down. Dinnertime was a particularly stressful experience in the house, since Mr. Blake was usually yelling at the girls to clean their plates, while Mrs. Blake was reminding them every few minutes to mind their manners.

What are the clients' personality types and what is the evidence used to identify them?

What are the survival games being played and by whom?

What treatment interventions might be useful in stopping the survival game playing?

Second Session Interventions:

The first thing I did was to let Mr. and Mrs. Blake know all of the ways in which they were doing a wonderful job as parents. I emphasized that they were giving the girls a secure and comfortable home, that they presented a united front with the girls as a couple, and that it was obvious that they truly loved the girls and wanted what was best for them. I commended Mr. Blake for finding such a generous and devoted woman to be his children's stepmother. And I told Mrs. Blake that both of her daughters appeared to love and appreciate her tremendously. Courtney seemed to feel that Mrs. Blake was her main source of nurturing, as evidenced by her picture of Mrs. Blake watering her flower. In fact, both girls viewed Mrs. Blake as the primary maternal figure in their lives.

Next, I told the Blakes that it appeared to me that Courtney was like a precious doll who was falling apart at the seams, and that I was deeply concerned about her. I indicated that if drastic and immediate steps were not taken to "mend" her, then we could anticipate her getting progressively worse. I emphasized that it was not too late to do something, but that I would definitely need their help in order to repair her splitting seams. I explained that they were actually the ones who were capable of mending her—not me. In particular, I told Mr. Blake that he was the one person who had always been there for his daughters, and so he was clearly the most important person in their lives. As a result, he was the one with the greatest ability to help Courtney to mend. I talked about the role of a father in a girl's life—how a good relationship with her father can have a positive impact on a woman's relationships with men for the rest of her life.

The Blakes listened with great concern and then responded by asking me if I thought that Denise was to blame for the fact that Courtney was falling apart at the seams. I responded by emphasizing that no one could ever know for sure who or what is to blame—but that, fortunately, we didn't have to know in order to help Courtney.

At that point, Mrs. Blake asked me, "Shouldn't we stop saying bad things about Denise in front of the girls?" Shortly thereafter, Mr. Blake told me, "I scream too much—I think I have to stop it." Finally, Mrs. Blake said to me, "I am terribly jealous of Denise—can you help me to deal with that?"

After some discussion, the couple decided to stop saying bad things about Denise in front of the girls, and Mr. Blake decided he would make an extra effort to restrain himself from yelling at his daughters. Mrs. Blake and I planned to have an individual session in order to address her jealousy of Denise.

Next, I outlined a "mending program" for Courtney and suggested that they use the same program for Lauren, so that she could benefit, too. This program would require that each parent spend one-half hour of quality time alone with one of the girls each evening just doing something enjoyable. Every other night, they would switch, so that Courtney would meet with Mrs. Blake one night, and Mr. Blake on the next, and so on. It would also require that they say three positive things to each child daily about her behavior. One further requirement was that Mr. and Mrs. Blake were to keep notes on the frequency of Courtney's bed-wetting, soiling, and stuttering, without saying or doing anything about those behaviors. Finally, it would be necessary that Mr. and Mrs. Blake make dinnertime a peaceful and pleasant experience for the entire family. This might mean putting less emphasis on manners and cleaning one's plate, and more emphasis on friendly conversation and family togetherness.

At the close of the session, I talked about the sacrifices that this mending program demanded and the importance of being dependable and responsible in following through with all of its components. When I asked if they were willing to help, Mr. and Mrs. Blake readily agreed to follow the mending program as diligently as possible.

Session Three:

One week later I met again with Mr. and Mrs. Blake, who reported that the mending program was going well. Courtney had not been wetting her bed or soiling her pants since our last session, although she had still been stuttering occasionally. Dinnertimes had been more pleasant, and the girls had actually consumed more of their meals than before. Mr. and Mrs. Blake were dutifully spending quality time daily with their daughters and making positive comments on their behavior. Mr. Blake had screamed at the girls considerably less, and both parents tried hard not to say bad things about Denise, though they had slipped up several times.

Once again, Mr. and Mrs. Blake tried to get me to pin the blame for Courtney's problems on Denise, and once again I declined to discuss the issue of blame. Instead, I took out a large piece of paper and I drew a circle on the center of the page. I labeled that circle as the sun and then I drew four planets circling around it. I named two of the planets "Courtney" and "Lauren," and the other two Mr. and Mrs. Blake. Then I asked the Blakes to tell me who they thought was the sun in their family's lives. I reminded them that the sun is the center of the solar system and that all planets revolve around it. Simultaneously, they both said, "We have made Denise the sun in our solar system." I told them they were right about that and wrote "Denise" in the circle representing the sun. I said that it appeared to me that most of their family's conversations, moods, and actions were all determined by what Denise did or didn't do. I emphasized that it made the girls feel insecure and unstable to have Denise as the sun, rather than Mr. and Mrs. Blake, because they could not depend on Denise the way that they could depend on their father and stepmother. I stressed that Denise needed to be a part of the girl's solar system, since she was their biological mother. But that she should be Pluto, not the sun.

The Blake's had become visibly excited by now, as they assured me that they didn't mean to make her the sun, and they wanted her to be Pluto. That's why they wanted to move away. I advised them that the way to make her Pluto was not to move away; rather, it was to stop making such a big deal about what she did or didn't do. Certainly, the girls should have the chance to see Denise and to enjoy their time with her. But their time with Mr. and Mrs. Blake should not be spent with Denise as the focus, unless they wanted Denise to remain the sun in their solar system.

Mr. and Mrs. Blake asked me to be more specific about how to shift Denise's place in their solar system. For example, they asked what they should do when Denise arrived three hours late to pick up the girls for the weekend. I suggested that if Denise did not show up within forty-five minutes of when she said she would to pick up the girls, then the four of them could leave the house, rather than staying there to wait for her. But they should not make a big deal about it with the girls.

Toward the end of the session, Mrs. Blake told me that Lauren and Courtney were supposed to spend the next weekend with Denise, but that Courtney had said that she didn't want to go. Mrs. Blake wasn't sure if it was best to force Courtney go, or to just let her stay home. I recommended that she let Courtney make the decision as to whether or not she went to Denise's at this time. I explained that I planned to schedule a session alone with Denise as soon as possible, in order to explain the situation to her and to elicit her cooperation. I also scheduled some individual sessions with Courtney and one with Mrs. Blake.

Session Four:

I met individually with Courtney for session four. She emphasized once again that she didn't want to see Denise anymore, because Denise lied to her. We spent the session playing with puppets, drawing, and doing mutual-story-telling. I noted that her stuttering was decreasing in my presence.

Session Five:

In session five I met with Denise, a very beautiful young woman in her midtwenties. Denise cried throughout the session as she told me that she was being systematically erased out of her daughters' lives and that she had allowed this to happen. She told me that she was poor and that she just couldn't compete with the Blakes for what they could provide for her daughters. She told me that she had struggled with various awful jobs and destructive relationships over the past few years, and that she had made some bad choices for herself. When things got tough, her solution had been just to walk out the door. At present she was barely able to afford to pay for her rent, food, and bills. On the positive side, she had been attending school part time to learn to be a manicurist, and she knew that she would be able to increase her income considerably when she graduated.

In the meantime, Denise told me that she was trying her best to be a good Mom to her girls, but that she felt totally inadequate compared to Mrs. Blake. Although she liked Mrs. Blake, and truly appreciated all that she was willing and able to do for Lauren and Courtney, she also felt bad inside—like she had no place in her daughters' lives now. She confessed that she felt even worse because she had shared these feelings often with the girls and had even cried on the girls' shoulders about how abandoned and neglected she felt.

I told Denise that Courtney had indicated that she never wanted to see her again. I emphasized that I wanted Denise to have good relationships with both of her daughters, because I truly thought that is what would be best for the girls and for her. However, I could not change the way the girls felt about her—only she could do that.

For the remainder of the session, we talked about the things that Denise might do in order to improve her relationships with the girls. Denise said that she knew that if she tried harder to cooperate with the Blakes, then that would make it easier on her daughters. She told me that Mr. and Mrs. Blake were both hung up on all kinds of rules that just didn't matter to her at all. She admitted that she did things that she knew would annoy and irritate them just because they had treated her like dirt for so long.

In the end, Denise agreed that she would be more careful about staying up-to-date with her child support payments, and that she would try hard to be on time in picking the girls up and dropping them off. She also decided that she would refrain from talking about adult matters with the girls or pouring out her hurt feelings to them about a difficult situation. She said, too, that she would try only to make promises to the girls that she could keep.

Denise said that what she really wanted to do was to have fun with her daughters, but she had not done so because it seemed too childish and not grown-up enough. I encouraged Denise to have as much fun with her daughters as she possibly could. I told her that she could be like a coach to them—teaching them various sports (since she was very gifted in athletics) and introducing them to a variety of ways to enjoy life. She gleefully reported that she was going to start by teaching them how to build and fly kites. I indicated that I would speak with Courtney about spending time with her, but that we might have to start with just a few hours, and work toward a full weekend. Denise agreed to see me again in two weeks.

Session Six:

My next step was to meet alone with Mrs. Blake. Though she began the session complaining once again about how awful Denise was, she eventually was able to admit that she was terribly jealous of her. She told me that she feared that Mr. Blake still secretly loved Denise, since it had been Denise who had ended their brief marriage. Denise was sexy, smart, and lots of fun. Another fear that Mrs. Blake harbored was that the girls would prefer to live with Denise when they got older, since she would be so easy on them. They would end up getting pregnant, or getting into drugs, because she wouldn't enforce proper rules with them.

I used Gestalt exercises to work with Mrs. Blake on her self-esteem. I accused her of underestimating the love that Mr. Blake and the girls had for her, as well as her importance in their lives. I also told Mrs. Blake that the more she tried to keep the girls away from Denise, the more likely it became that they would resent her for doing so when they got older. Thus, by creating distance between them and Denise in the present, she could be making it even more likely that they would want to live with her in the future.

I emphasized that the key to dealing effectively with the girls in their teenage years would be to establish trust and good communication with them in the present. I also stressed that the girls would only profit from improving the relationship between Denise and Mr. and Mrs. Blake. We decided to work on communication and trust in a future session with Mr. Blake present.

Sessions Seven and Eight:

For the next two sessions I met alone with Courtney and she agreed to spend a Saturday afternoon with Denise, just to see how it would go.

She reported afterward that it was fun, and that Denise didn't lie to her. So I said, "Oh, so Denise isn't lying to you anymore." Courtney immediately corrected me, with the comment, "No, I didn't say that. I said that she didn't seem to lie to me this past weekend!" Courtney agreed to begin to have regular visitations with Denise once again.

During one session Courtney told me that another problem she had was that she would forget what she was going to say just before she said it. This would happen right in the middle of a sentence, when she would not be able to think of the next word that she wanted to use. She told me that it really bothered her when this happened.

Sessions Nine and Ten:

I had two more sessions with Mr. and Mrs. Blake, in which they reported that Courtney had not wet the bed or soiled her panties for quite some time. Her stuttering was almost gone, too. I cautioned them that it was not yet time to stop the mending program. They agreed to continue. Both told me that they had tried hard not to make Denise the sun anymore, and that it was getting easier and easier.

Mrs. Blake told me that she was feeling more secure in her relationship with the girls and her husband and far less threatened by Denise. She had even had several friendly telephone conversations with her and invited her into the house on one occasion for a brief visit. Denise had been prompt in picking the girls up and bringing them home and she had paid all of the back child support money that she had owed. Mr. Blake said that as a result, he had been able to carry on "civil" conversations with Denise for the first time since their divorce. When Mrs. Blake told him that she feared that he still loved Denise, he flatly denied it, and said that he felt more anger toward her than anything.

I addressed the issue of what the Blakes called "lying" during one of the sessions. I pointed out that it was not helpful for them to ask the girls "why" they did something wrong, since chances are the girls truly did not know the answer to that question. Even adults do not know why they do what they do a good deal of the time. Hence, the girls were not lying when they responded, "I don't know." I encouraged the Blakes to read *Positive Discipline*, by Jane Nelson (1981), in order to get more ideas about how to deal effectively but nonpunitively with misbehavior.

I also talked to the Blakes about their own personality types, as well as Denise's. I tried to encourage them to use information about their different personalities to better understand and communicate with Denise.

During the next session, we worked on how they could communicate in ways that would build trust between them and their daughters. I taught them to use active listening, and also to employ "I" statements. They had the chance to practice, using role playing. In addition to practicing these new skills with the girls, I suggested that they read *How to Talk So Kids Will Listen, and Listen So Kids Will Talk,* by Faber and Mazlisch (1980) as homework.

Session Eleven:

Once again, I met with Denise, who reported great improvement in her dealings with the girls and with Mr. and Mrs. Blake. We worked some more on her issues with Mr. Blake and I encouraged her to continue to teach the girls how to have more fun.

I explained personality types theory to Denise, emphasizing how she was different from the Blakes and how she could use that information to better understand their behavior and improve her relationship with them. Denise told me that she had thought that she had to be a serious, duty-bound, rule-oriented person (an SJ) in order to be a mother to her daughters. It was a relief to her to learn that she could be herself and still contribute something valuable to their lives.

I addressed the issue of what the girls call her, and she told me that she knew that they called her Denise when they were with the Blakes. She cried as she let me know how much that hurt her. I listened with empathy for her position. Then I told her how difficult this was for her daughters, since they were the ones in the middle. After much discussion, she agreed to let the girls call her Denise all of the time if they wanted to. We planned to raise this issue at the next session, which would be with Denise and the Blakes.

Session Twelve:

I began the next session by saying that my primary reason for being there was to help Courtney and Lauren. I told Denise and the Blakes that when I began working with them, they were cooperating at about a ten on a one-to-one-hundred point cooperation scale. I commended them for moving up the scale to their present position of about sixty. I confessed that I didn't know if any of them were capable of going any higher than that, while emphasizing that the higher they were on the scale, the more they would be helping their daughters. I also stressed that sixty was not terrible, if that was the best they could do. It just wasn't as good for the girls as it might be.

All three of them responded by assuring me that they were willing and able to cooperate even more than they had been recently. I reiterated that it sounded great, but that I wasn't so sure if that was possible with them.

Next, I gave each of them a chance to air their thoughts and feelings about their relationships with each other and with the girls. Toward the end of the session, I raised the issue of what each of them was willing and able to do to cooperate more fully with each other. Denise and Mrs. Blake talked about what the girls called them, and each volunteered to have the girls call the other one "Mom." In the end, they decided to have the girls call Denise by her first name, and Mrs. Blake would be "Mom" to them.

The Blakes and Denise worked out many additional ways in which they could cooperate better with each other. They even decided to attend one of their daughter's soccer games together and to sit with each other in the bleachers.

Follow-up:

I had only a couple of additional sessions with the Blakes and Denise before I had to leave the area for an extended period of time. When I left, all seemed to be going pretty smoothly. Courtney and Lauren were doing well, and Courtney's survival games had completely stopped. Mr. and Mrs. Blake chose to terminate therapy, rather than to continue working with another therapist during my absence. They were concerned about the cost of therapy, and they also felt that the problems that brought them to therapy had been resolved.

Six months later, when I was back in town, I received a call from Mrs. Blake to set up another session for her and her husband. They came in filled with rage about Denise, fed up, and blaming her for Courtney's newest problems.

It seems that Courtney was back to stuttering and bed-wetting, and that she had also refused to do her homework, so her grades had fallen. When her teacher and parents asked her about her homework, they claimed that she had "lied." I learned that Mr. Blake was screaming again, and that Mrs. Blake had given her daughters a two page list of "rules" that included the amount of time that they were to spend doing homework, how often they were to eat, brush their teeth, and bathe, and how long they were to sit on the toilet each day—while reading a book. Courtney told me in private that it was actually her sister who lied to their parents about completing all of the items on the two page list each day. But it was Courtney who got in trouble when she refused to do many of the items listed, and she could not tell her parents the reasons for her refusal.

I saw Mr. and Mrs. Blake and Courtney in two family sessions and I met once individually with Courtney when the Blakes called me and said that therapy was not working, that it cost too much money, and they would not be returning. They told me that Denise was the *real* problem, and that they had decided to move after all.

CASE DISCUSSION

Courtney, the six-year-old labeled patient in this case, is an INTP personality type, an Engineer/Designer. She is a quiet and serious child, a perfectionist who asks a lot of "why" questions and speaks with clarity and precision. She longs to ride a horse up a high mountain while doing math problems in her head, in order to continually improve her performance. As an INTP, Courtney is more inclined to give information than directives to others. In all the time that I worked with her, I never heard her tell anyone what to do.

Our exchange about Denise not lying to her during a visit was a particularly strong clue that she is a Rational-type person. Courtney is quick to correct my global comment that Denise isn't lying to her anymore by adding several qualifiers. She points out that *it didn't appear to her* that Denise had lied *on that last visit*. It is typical of NTs to speak in a manner that is conditional and to use lots of qualifiers. Unlike the NFs who generalize, NTs are very careful to say exactly what they mean and to mean exactly what they say—even at the age of six.

Courtney's older sister, Lauren, is an ESFP, or Player/Performer-type of Artisan. She is outspoken, warm, friendly, and impulsive. She is not afraid to investigate the contents of my office by touching everything, and she proudly displays her colorful artwork on my window by affixing it there herself with tape.

Both Mr. and Mrs. Blake appear to be Guardians. While Mrs. Blake is the ESTJ, or Monitor/Supervisor, Mr. Blake is the ISTJ, or Monitor/Inspector. As SJs, the Blakes are devoted to home and family and deeply concerned about raising their children right. They are both conservative people, who value cleanliness, good-manners, honesty, and productivity. I believe that Mr. and Mrs. Blake are STJs, because they both appear to be highly directive in their communication patterns. Their jobs—as a telephone company line foreman and as a a bookkeeper/clerk at a school district—represent the kinds of work that Thinking-type Guardians find particularly satisfying. Both work for large, conservative institutions, and focus on numbers and things, as opposed to people. As Monitor-types, they are careful to keep track of everything that Denise says and does, and they also attempt to control a large number of their childrens' actions. While Mrs. Blake appears to be more outgoing, Mr. Blake is more quiet and reserved with people he doesn't know.

Denise is the fun-loving, outgoing ESFP, or Player/Performer, like her oldest daughter. True to her Artisan nature, Denise is less concerned about rules and regulations and more concerned about having fun. She is impulsive in the way that she deals with her jobs and her relationships. Currently, she is studying to be a manicurist—a job that ESFPs often find satisfying because of the action, artistry, and ability to interact with customers and co-workers. As an ESFP, Denise is quick to show her feelings, and she is informative rather than directive in her relationships.

Practically everyone in this family is playing survival games, although Courtney's *Robot* game is what brings them to counseling. When she stutters or forgets the words that she wants to use next in a sentence, then she is exhibiting the *Blanking Out* variant. Courtney's soiling of her pants and bed-wetting are not exclusive to the Robot game. These may be demonstrated by children of all four types—but often for different reasons. In Courtney's case, I believe that she is tired of being the pawn in the survival games that her father, mother, and stepmother are playing. Courtney is in a no-win situation—a double-bind—and she has no choice but to play games in order to defend herself. Her main dilemma is that she can be affectionate and close to all three of her parents at the same time. In order to love Denise, she must reject her father and stepmother, while to love her father and stepmother, she must reject Denise. Until the adults in her life get along with each other, she is in a position of needing to protect them from each other. It is interesting that she and her sister chose sides—each taking care of one of their mothers. Here the children must take care of their parents' feelings, rather than the reverse.

Still other reasons for Courtney's use of survival tactics are her father's and stepmother's attempts to control so much of what she says and does. Her Robot game may be seen as a means of preserving what little autonomy she has.

It is interesting to note that Lauren, the SP, was not as devastated by the tense situation between the adults in her life as Courtney was. Although Lauren mimicked her sister with occasional stuttering and bed-wetting, her games were not as self-destructive as those of her sister. According to Courtney, however, Lauren was lying to her stepmother about having completed all of the items on the rules list. While Courtney simply refused outright to do all that her stepmother was demanding of her, Lauren played the *Delinquency* game in order to get Mrs. Blake off of her back.

Mrs. Blake is playing the *Nag* variant of the *Complain* game in her interactions with Denise, and also at times with Courtney and Lauren. Mr. Blake's *Nag* game is similar, except that he frequently escalates his complaints to the point of screaming. Both Mr. and Mrs. Blake are also playing *Poor Me.* Denise is playing *Blackmail*—specifically, the *Delinquency* variant—when she shows up late and fails to make her child support payments for months at a time. Her tendency to present herself as a hopeless victim is characteristic of *Shocking* players.

In my interventions with this family, I began by telling the Blakes what they were doing right as parents, because I sensed that they were feeling insecure and fearful that I would label them as "bad" parents. Interestingly, once I commended the Blakes on their parental strengths, they told me three things that they needed to work on—not asking so many questions about Denise, not being so jealous of Denise (for Mrs. Blake), and not screaming so much (for Mr. Blake). Up until that point, they had only been focused on the ways in which Denise needed to change.

The issue of blame came up several times during my work with the Blakes, and each time I side-stepped it by explaining that I didn't know who or what was to blame, and that fortunately, I didn't have to know in order to help Courtney.

My next intervention was to get the Blakes to stop screaming, punishing, and over-controlling their daughters—and to start having more positive interactions with them. To do so, I used the *cancellation* metaphor of a doll that was falling apart at the seams and the related metaphor of mending the doll. I emphasized the seriousness of Courtney's problems in order to elicit the Blake's cooperation. I also used Guardian-type language as I outlined the "mending program" by talking about responsibilities, sacrifices, requirements, and necessities.

To motivate the Blakes to stop putting so much emphasis on Denise's behavior with the girls, I used the solar system metaphor. This *cancellation* metaphor was an effective way of getting them to stop grilling the girls after their visits with Denise and criticizing her every action. I also encouraged the Blakes to stop using Nagging tactics with Denise and to start using *deprivation* with her.

In later sessions I introduced active listening and "I" statements to the Blakes, and I tried to get them to stop asking "why" questions and then labeling the answer "I don't know" as a lie. I also worked with Mrs. Blake on overcoming her jealousy of Denise and tried to make her feel more secure regarding the important place that she had in her stepdaughters' lives.

I encouraged Denise to have fun with her daughters and to coach them in acquiring new skills, since that role was a comfortable one for her. I also discouraged her from laying guilt trips on the girls by emphasizing that her tears only pushed the girls away from her.

Finally, in my session with Denise and the Blakes together, I used the metaphor of a "cooperation scale" as a means of utilizing the competition between them in a therapeutic way.

In most cases, I find that the changes that couples and families make in therapy are maintained and even strengthened as time goes on. Usually, I have noticed that if I can get clients to take little steps in a different direction, then they will continue along that new path, even building momentum as they proceed. Hence, I was quite surprised to discover upon my return that the Blakes had completely reverted back to their old games, and even escalated them.

Why did this family's game playing resume within months after our work together? And why was I unable to stop their game playing the second time around? I can only speculate as to the answers to these questions.

I believe that a part of the problem was that Mr. and Mrs. Blake are almost identical in their personalities. Each personality type has its blind spots. Since both Mr. and Mrs. Blake are STJ types, they have a tendency to reinforce each others' limited perspective of their situation. Hence, when I departed, they immediately reverted back to their previous attitudes and behaviors, and there was no one around to present an alternative viewpoint.

Perhaps the relapse could have been avoided if I had not had to leave when I did. I now believe that I should have been more insistent that the Blakes continue therapy with someone else in my absence; chances are it could have made a positive difference. Then again, maybe the Blake's decision to distance themselves from Denise was the only viable solution for this stepfamily.

Case #6

YOUR
HUSBAND OR
YOUR SON?

Session One:

A woman in her early forties came to therapy because she was feeling very depressed and crying all the time. Margaret's husband, Stan, had walked out on her and her four children (two of them from a previous marriage) one year ago. Since that time she had tried everything to get him back, with no success. Margaret told me in a soft, gentle voice that she wanted to do the "right thing," but since she just couldn't decide what the "right thing" would be, she had come to me for advice. Divorce, she said, was out of the question, as she just couldn't live without Stan and his financial support. Furthermore, she felt obligated to continue to try to repair their troubled marriage as long as there was the slightest chance that she might succeed at it. This was her second marriage, and this husband was remarkably similar to her first one. Margaret explained sheepishly that she could not help worrying that if she got divorced a second time, she might regret it later on.

Since Stan had taken off unexpectedly a year before with all of their money, Margaret had managed to support herself and her four children on the small amount she earned as a clerk at a discount department store. She enjoyed her work—especially the opportunity it provided for her to associate with supportive co-workers, and to serve familiar, friendly customers. Margaret's friends at the job are very important to her. She indicated a willingness to extend help to them at any time, should they be in need.

Margaret complained that Stan had never been responsible when it came to paying their bills, and that since he had left she had lent him thousands of dollars. In fact, the day before our first session Margaret had lent him three thousand dollars. To date, he had never repaid any of these loans.

What is the client's personality type and what is the evidence used to identify it?

What are the survival games being played and by whom?

What treatment interventions might be useful in stopping the survival game playing?

First Session Interventions:

My first step in treatment also provided a means of collecting additional information. I asked Margaret to imagine that Stan was seated in an empty chair and to tell him how she was feeling. She began by expressing bitter resentment regarding his treatment of her and the children. She accused him of mistreating all of them with his angry outbursts, of calling them degrading names, kicking them around, and making life miserable for them whenever he was at home. She cried as she recounted how much the children had suffered because of his attacks. Next she told him that she resented how he was always so jealous of any attention she paid to the children. She added that her children would always be the most important thing in the world to her, and that she felt guilty for having allowed him to treat them so badly. Following that, she told him how much he had hurt her by leaving without saying a word, and how she couldn't believe that someone who said he loved her could treat her that way. She told him how rejected she felt, because he had refused to make love to her for the past year. She said that she had done her best to continue to cook for him and do his laundry when he did come around, but that he had given her nothing in return. Lastly, she told Stan how devastated she was that he had been living with another woman for the past six months. She begged him to come back to her. When I had Margaret change chairs and pretend to be her husband responding to her, "Stan" (in the empty chair) said that while he had no intention of ever living with her again, he had no intention of filing for divorce, either. He assured her that he intended to stay married to her, though he would never live with her again. And as for the other woman, well, they were "just good friends."

After having Margaret change chairs and play Stan, I had her return to her own chair and respond to him in the empty chair with her feelings. Eventually, in the course of this exercise, I prompted her to say to Stan, "I will never leave you, regardless of how badly you treat me," and "I am yours forever, "and "I could never live without you."

Once the role playing exercise was completed, I told Margaret that it was not difficult to see what was going on, and what she needed to do. Having sparked her curiosity, I explained that her husband was clearly more like a son to her, rather than a husband, and that she was clearly more like his mother, rather than his wife. As evidence of this I mentioned his sibling rivalry, his insistence upon having all of her attention, his irresponsibility, the absence of sexual relations between them, and his demands that she take care of him. Margaret readily agreed and even recalled a few more things he had done which were more typical of a son than a husband. I then commended her in her willingness to be such a good mother to him, for example, by seeing to it that all of his bills were paid.

At this point, she appeared agitated, and interrupted me to ask in a loud, demanding voice, "What should I do about this? Should I divorce him?"

"Absolutely not," I responded firmly.

"Why not?" she questioned in an angry tone.

"Because he needs a mother, and without you, I would worry that he wouldn't make it on his own. Stan's never been without a mother, and it would be traumatic for him to suddenly find himself without one now. For your husband's sake, I recommend that you continue to take care of him."

At his point, Margaret began to argue vehemently that she didn't want a son, she wanted a husband, and that furthermore, she could care less if Stan had a hard time making it without her. While maintaining my serious facial expression and tone of voice, I continued to caution her not to do anything that would be too hard on her husband/son. I emphasized that he needed a mother, and that she had been perfect for the job.

Since our hour together was almost over, I gave Margaret two assignments. First, I told her to continue mothering her husband, since it would be too traumatic for him if she was to do otherwise. Second, I asked her to read the book *Women Who Love Too Much*, by Robin Norwood (1985).

Session Two:

A smiling Margaret returned two weeks later to report that she was no longer depressed; rather, she felt great. She told me that in spite of my assignment, she had filed for divorce on the Monday after our Friday session. Furthermore, she had demanded that Stan return the three thousand dollars she had lent him the day before, and he had complied by sending back most of the money. Margaret reported that she had found the book *Women Who Love Too Much* both interesting and helpful; she was particularly surprised at how closely she resembled the women described in its pages. She told me she was determined to find herself a mate, not a son, and that she was making plans to move to another part of the country where she had friends and she had always wanted to live. After the second session, Margaret did move. I recommended that she seek counseling in her new town, so that she might learn to make different choices in her relationships with men.

CASE DISCUSSION

Margaret is a Guardian-type person, more specifically a Conservator/Provider-type of Guardian, or ISFJ. As a Guardian, Margaret's life focus is on providing for others, both her family and her customers at work. She is loyal and responsible in doing her duty. Rather than trying to develop or inspire others, like the Idealist, Margaret's emphasis is on serving them and caring for their basic needs, which is characteristic of the Guardian. She enjoys her work very much, and her job is the kind of routine, service-oriented work that often appeals to SJs. Like all Guardian-type personalities, Margaret is a traditionalist who is bound by conventions and whose primary focus is on doing the "right" thing.

As an ISFJ, Margaret is an unselfish giver and a warm, nurturing person. She enjoys caring for others and is the first to offer a hand to a friend in need. Above all, she is a responsible and devoted mother and wife, willing to sacrifice her needs for the needs of her family. Characteristic of the Provider is Margaret's tendency to go along with another's program rather than to assert her own needs and wants.

Margaret's husband, Stan, is an Artisan (SP), probably an Operator/Promoter-type, or ESTP, as is evidenced by his impulsive and freewheeling lifestyle. Further evidence of Stan's temperament is the expert manner in which he plays the Artisan game of *Blackmail*. His act of leaving Margaret and the three kids without warning and with no money was a *Delinquency* tactic. His angry, aggressive outbursts and his extortion of money and services from Margaret, even while living with another woman, are indicative of the *Outrage* and *Con Artist* variants of Blackmail.

While Stan's Blackmail game might not be effective with another Artisan or a Rational, the Provider Guardian plays right into his hands. After all, she gets her self-esteem from belonging—from membership—and her self-confidence by being of service. Stan's implicit threat of breaking off the relationship hits her right where she is most vulnerable. Margaret plays into his Blackmail scheme by trying to be even more responsible, an even better provider to him. And when that doesn't work, she, too, begins to play a desperate game designed to hold on to what little self-esteem, self-confidence, and self-respect she has left and to gain some control over her relationship with Stan.

Margaret is playing the *Depressed, Poor Me,* and *Worried* variants of the *Complain* game. Rather than expressing the bitter resentment she feels towards Stan and thereby risk losing the relationship, Margaret holds it all inside. Note that in addition to her sadness and tears, she also expresses lots of unfounded worries; for example, she is worried that she cannot provide independently for herself and her children, though she has been doing just that for one year, while also supporting her husband.

If Margaret's husband was of another temperament, perhaps an Idealist or another Guardian, chances are that her Complain game would have entangled him as she would like. But the Promoter is too shrewd to fall into the Provider's homespun web. His response is just to ignore her complaints, and to make himself scarce.

It is tempting when treating someone like Margaret to fall into the trap of doing what the layman does by giving advice. But this is typically a deadend, since SJ clients will usually respond to advice with the game of "yes, but..." It is also tempting to try to give a client like Margaret insight as to why she is doing what she is doing, with hopes that it will help her to change. But unfortunately, I have seen over and over again that insight does not usually lead to a change in behavior.

So, instead of telling Margaret to get a divorce or helping her to uncover the reasons why she hangs on to Stan, I attempted to make her more uncomfortable with the status quo. By increasing the amount of tension that Margaret felt, I hoped she would make a decision to let go of her husband and move on with her life. Toward this end, I used a Gestalt exercise, a cancellation metaphor, and then a behavioral prescription.

First, I had Margaret talk to her husband in the empty chair, while I prompted her to exaggerate her position ("I will never leave you no matter how terribly you mistreat me") and to voice it several times. Then I instructed her to pretend that she was her husband responding to her, so that she had the chance to experience her husband's perspective of her and the situation.

Next I told Margaret that her husband is actually her son, and I commended her for being a good mother to him. What's more, I encouraged her to continue to take care of Stan, since he obviously needed a mother like her. This *cancellation* metaphor was designed to present Margaret with an indelible image of herself being seen in an undesirable way. Note that the mother-son metaphor was particularly appropriate for Margaret, because as a Guardian she wants more than anything to be *conventional* and to appear that way to others. A mother-son relationship with her husband just isn't in accordance with her idea of the way things are supposed to be.

I often assign Robin Norwood's *Women Who Love Too Much* to Guardian women, since that book mostly tells their story, and they usually find it helpful.

I recommended that Margaret seek additional counseling, because she has established a pattern of mothering her husbands and making them her sons, and she does not wish to repeat it in her next relationship. This mother-son (or father-daughter) arrangement is especially common for two kinds of Guardians— Protectors (ESFJs) and Providers (ISFJs). I have noticed that when they were raised in alcoholic families, these people are particularly prone to marrying substance abusers who play the Blackmail game and behave like rebellious little boys or girls.

Case #7

ROCKING
THE
BOAT

Session One:

Judith, her new husband, Sam, and her sixteen-year-old daughter, Chris, came to therapy because they were constantly fighting with each other. According to Judith and Sam, Chris was disobedient, rude, out-of-control, irresponsible, and unappreciative. Recently, she had taken the family car without permission and stayed out practically all night long. She refused to do her chores and her bedroom and bathroom looked like a disaster area. She would yell and scream at her mother and stepfather when they tried to talk to her, often calling them obscene names before stomping out of the room and slamming the door. Recently she had screamed at her stepfather that she hated him, and that she wished he was dead.

I learned that Judith and Chris had been living alone since Chris was three years old, when her father left town. Since that time, Chris had not received so much as a birthday card from her father, in spite of her efforts to keep in contact with him. Judith had worked hard as a waitress to support herself and her only child, since she could not count on receiving child support. A charming, friendly, fun-loving woman, Judith said that she liked her work because it was fun to banter with all of her regular customers. She told me she liked being busy, so that she never got bored.

Judith told me that before she had married Sam, Chris had always been well behaved. In fact, Judith had hardly ever had to discipline Chris. Mostly, she just let Chris do whatever she wanted. Judith, an optimistic person, had a lot of confidence in her daughter, and didn't ever worry about her. Chris had always been independent and responsible, even at an early age. In many ways, mother and daughter had been more like sisters than parent and child. They enjoyed traveling together to unusual places, and doing exciting things, like downhill skiing and back-packing.

A slender, pretty, girl, Chris excelled in sports, and she hoped to win an athletic scholarship to a university someday. Chris told me that she planned to major in physical education and to eventually become a high school P.E. teacher. She had always been a good student, with As and Bs in all of her classes. She was popular, vivacious, gregarious, and liked to laugh. She had starred in several school plays, and she enjoyed performing in the band. Lately, much of her free time was spent participating in outings with her church teen group.

Before Sam, Judith had been in a five-year relationship with Bill, a carpenter. Though Bill had not lived with them, Chris and Judith had spent lots of fun times together with him at the beach and at his mountain cabin. It came as a complete surprise to both Chris and Judith when Bill announced one day that he was moving to Hawaii—alone. Shortly after that breakup, Judith met Sam. Sam moved in two months later, and just a few months after that, he and Judith were married.

Sam was a very quiet, kind, yet stern, probation officer who had a grown daughter and son from a previous marriage. As a strict disciplinarian, he believed that children should be respectful and follow the rules. Sam thought that Judith was far too lenient with her daughter. He had tried to help her lay down the law and get Chris under control. With each of Chris's transgressions, he had established even more stringent rules, tried to punish Chris for her wrongdoing, and he had also given her numerous lectures about how she should be more responsible and obedient. Sam told me that he wanted very much to have a positive relationship with Chris. He hoped to be someone she could talk to and trust. He wanted to buy her nice things and to do fun things together as a family. But so far, she had rejected every attempt he had made to get her to accept him.

When I asked Chris to give me her side of the story, she explained that Sam had moved into their house before she even knew him. Since his arrival, he had tried to boss her around like he was her father—even though she had just met him. She hated his lectures. What's more, her mother practically ignored her, except to blow up at her about things and to side with Sam all of the time. Since Sam's arrival, Chris claimed that her mother had completely changed. Suddenly, she was making rules about everything and trying to be really strict. Chris said that she thought her mother had become totally unfair now that Sam was around.

What are the clients' personality types and what is the evidence used to identify them?

What are the survival games being played and by whom?

What treatment interventions might be useful in stopping the survival game playing?

First Session Interventions:

I began by telling the three of them that it is completely normal for stepfamilies to be experiencing the kinds of problems that they were describing. I asked them to imagine what happens to a small boat with only two people in it, when a third steps on board. It is natural for the boat to rock back and forth for a while, until everyone manages to get situated so that the boat is balanced once again. It's not anyone's fault, and it is absolutely to be expected.

I made certain that each family member had the opportunity to tell the other two directly how he or she felt about what was going on. Then I sent Chris out of the room for a few minutes. In Sam's presence, I commended Judith on the fine job that she had done in raising her daughter. Chris was successful in school, athletics, music, and drama. She was ambitious. She did not appear to be involved in drugs or gangs. And she was attractive and popular. She was the kind of daughter that most parents would be very proud of.

Next, I told Judith and Sam that it appeared that Chris's belligerence was a way of protecting her mother from getting hurt again. In Chris's experience, men who said they loved her and Judith had always ended up leaving. If she could break up her mother's relationship with Sam right from the start, then she could spare her mother the eventual agony of losing a long-term relationship. Judith said that it hadn't occurred to her that Chris was actually trying to help her.

Sam confessed that he had felt terribly rejected by Chris. I emphasized that Chris would probably find it difficult to trust *any* man, given her experiences with her father and her mother's boyfriend. Sam reaffirmed his willingness to be patient and to do whatever was necessary to establish a good relationship with Chris.

I asked Judith and Sam to name the one thing that Chris did that bothered them the most. They agreed that they were most upset that she was getting home so late, even when they asked her not to. We talked about what a reasonable curfew would be, and they settled on 12:30 on the weekends, and 9:00 on school nights. I suggested that if Chris got home later than she was supposed to, she should then lose the privilege of going out for the next two nights. I told them that this method was only effective, however, if parents refrained from giving any reminders, advice, warnings, or lectures. They said that they were desperate, and that they would try anything.

I talked for a few minutes alone with Chris and encouraged her to share more of her feelings about her home situation. She voiced her anger and her hurt over the changes in the way her mother treated her and her resentment of Sam's intrusion in her world.

With all three of them present at the end of the session, I told Chris that I had advised her parents to specify a curfew, and that they had come up with 12:30 on weekends and 9:00 on weekdays. I asked what she thought of that, and she said it seemed reasonable to her. We agreed that it could be changed to accommodate special events if she asked ahead of time. I explained that if she got home one minute after curfew, regardless of the excuse, then she would lose the privilege of going out for the next two nights. I encouraged her to go ahead and stay out later than she was supposed to, in order to give her parents practice in doing what they said they were going to do. I suggested that she violate curfew when she didn't really want to go out for the next two nights, anyway. Finally, I reminded Judith and Sam that they had promised to stop all lectures, advice, or reminders about what time Chris was to come home.

Since Chris and Sam had never spent time alone together, I assigned them the task of having one fun outing together. Chris reluctantly agreed to participate. I also asked Judith and Chris to to do something together that they would both enjoy. We arranged to meet again in two weeks.

Session Two:

Since Sam was sick, Judith and Chris came without him to the second session. Each reported that things had been considerably improved during the past two weeks. Chris had only violated curfew once, and Judith and Sam had honored their agreement to enforce the consequence of not going out for two nights, without giving Chris any lectures, advice, or reminders. Chris said she liked this arrangement, since they were not bugging her about it, and she could always choose to be late, if she really wanted to be.

For their outing, Sam and Chris had gone to dinner and a movie together. Chris reported that she enjoyed it more than she had expected to. Chris was also delighted that she and her mother had spent a whole day together—shopping and having lunch— just like it used to be. Things had begun to calm down at home. Everyone seemed to be making more of an effort to get along.

244 / SURVIVAL GAMES PERSONALITIES PLAY

I spent the majority of the second session working alone with Judith. I told her that she seemed to be right in the middle in the tug-of-war between her daughter and her husband, and she agreed. She was constantly intervening, usually on Sam's behalf, to try to get Chris and Sam to get along with each other. When Chris was rebellious or disrespectful to Sam, Judith was afraid that Sam would think that she was a bad parent. Since Sam had a college education, he worked with teenagers, and he had raised two children already, she tended to trust his judgements about parenting more than her own.

I introduced the notion of personality types to Judith, explaining that both she and Chris were Artisans, while Sam was a Guardian. Judith agreed with my assessment, as I described the typical behavior of Artisans and Guardians. I reiterated to Judith my impression that she had done a wonderful job in raising her daughter, and I suggested that her expertise in parenting Chris was due in part to their similarities in personality. Since Chris is very much like herself, no doubt Judith is aware of what will be the most effective approach in parenting her. Then I talked about the difficulties that Guardian parents can have with their Artisan children, since they often don't understand each other.

I emphasized that because she knew Chris better than anyone, and she and Chris were so much alike, Judith needed to be the expert in the family on parenting her daughter. Although Sam's participation was important, I encouraged Judith to trust her own judgments regarding what was best for Chris. I reminded her that she had been a very effective parent before Sam had entered the picture.

Finally, I told Judith that if she wanted Sam and Chris to have a good relationship with each other, then she needed to get out of the middle. This would mean that she would not intervene to try to settle their disagreements, and she would not let them use her as a way of communicating with one other. If they had anything to say to each other, it was best if she encouraged them to say it directly. And if they got into it with each other, it would be best if she just left the room. Judith confessed that she would be relieved to give up the role of referee between Sam and Chris.

During the remainder of the session, I gave Judith and Chris the opportunity to communicate their feelings to each other. Chris let her mother know that she was angry and hurt because she felt that her mother had rejected her when she fell in love with Sam. Judith apologized to her daughter and assured her that she loved her very much. She promised to make the time that they would spend together a priority. Judith also told Chris how much it hurt her when Chris was mean and disrespectful to Sam. Chris agreed to try to be more civil to her stepfather.

At the close of the session I asked that Chris continue to have weekly outings with Sam and with her mother. Judith said she would explain the assignment to Sam, and that she anticipated that he would be willing to cooperate.

Sessions Three and Four:

I arranged to work exclusively with Chris for the third and fourth sessions. Using visualization and Gestalt exercises, she dealt with her relationships with her father and Bill, her mother's ex-boyfriend. With my prompting, Chris expressed the hurt and anger that she was feeling towards each of them. We also looked at the decisions that she had made about herself, men, and relationships, based upon her experiences with Bill and her dad. Chris realized that she had decided that she is unlovable, that all men will say they love you and then leave you, and that men are not to be trusted.

Using visualization, Chris was able to go back to the time when she had formulated those limiting beliefs, and to change the old decisions that she had made. Working with her inner child, she told herself that she was lovable, that some men could be trusted, and that she had nothing to do with her dad's or Bill's departures. Lastly, I assigned her the task of writing letters to both Bill and her dad—letters that she would keep to herself, for the purpose of putting her feelings down on paper.

Session Five:

All three family members attended the fifth session to report that things were going much more smoothly at home. As Judith had refrained from getting in the middle when Chris and Sam had a disagreement, daughter and stepdad had begun to get along better and better. They had enjoyed their outings together and were willing to continue them. Judith had begun to assert herself more with Sam on parenting issues, and Chris felt that she was being treated more fairly. Chris was more polite and respectful to Sam, and she was doing her chores. Sam had curtailed many of his lectures to her on good behavior. Everyone liked the arrangement regarding Chris's curfew and reported that it was working fine.

Follow-up Session:

At a final follow-up session six weeks later I noted that the family members' relationships had continued to improve, and that therapy could be terminated.

CASE DISCUSSION

Chris, an ESFP, has found many positive ways of meeting her needs for action, excitement, and looking impressive. Her involvement in sports, drama, band, and church group activities, are particularly suited for her Player/Performer-nature. Chris is outgoing, friendly, popular, and she laughs easily. These characteristics, as well as her personal warmth and sensitivity, are further evidence that she is the ESFP type of Artisan. Chris definitely has the potential to excel in her desired career—that of a physical education teacher—which she is also likely to find very satisfying.

Chris's mother, Judith, is the same personality type as her daughter. Her fraternal parenting style is typical of the SP parent, as is her tendency to allow Chris lots of independence. An optimist who lives in the moment, Judith is not inclined to worry about her daughter. She enjoys sharing exciting adventures with Chris, like backpacking, downhill skiing, and traveling to interesting places. Judith seems to be an ESFP, because she is gregarious, charming, and radiates warmth. She likes her work, since it puts her in contact with lots of interesting people, and the constant action keeps her from getting bored.

Not surprisingly, Judith was attracted to her opposite—the quiet, serious ISTJ. As a Guardian, Sam is very concerned about rules and regulations. A traditionalist, he favors a strict authoritarian parenting style in which he maintains a great deal of control. He is deeply concerned about being a responsible stepfather, and he uses lectures, advice, and punishment in his efforts to stop his stepdaughter's rebellious behavior. As a Monitor/Inspector-type of Guardian, Sam is not especially comfortable expressing emotions, and he looks forward to buying things for his stepdaughter and doing fun things with her as a means of conveying his caring for her. Sam's job as a probation officer meets his needs to belong to a large organization and to work through the justice system in order to be of service to his community.

Since Sam is an ISTJ, he is a directive-type person who is comfortable telling people what to do. When he married Judith, he began to direct her parenting efforts, and as an ESFP informative-type, she let him. Anxious to please Sam and to make a good impression on him, Judith abandoned her style of parenting and attempted to do the things that Sam said she should be doing.

This might not have been so disastrous, had the teenager in question been a Guardian or even an Idealist. But, as an Artisan, Chris reacts strongly to the new restrictions on her freedom and independence. To protect herself from even greater losses, she begins to employ *Blackmail* tactics—specifically, the *Outrage* and *Delinquency* variants. In response, Judith and Sam begin to use even more of their attempted solutions—lectures, punishment, and more stringent rules—as a way of trying to get Chris to change her ways. This makes Chris rebel even more.

To stop this escalating cycle, I tried to get Judith and Sam to stop their lecturing and punishing and to start employing the model of *deprivation*. Since Chris's parents were most upset about her violation of curfew, we set up consequences that the parents were to enforce each time she came home late. I was careful to emphasize to Chris that she had a choice—to come home on time or to be late and face the consequences. I also made certain that I prescribed that Chris overstep the limits, ostensibly to give her parents practice in restricting her.

I felt that the use of deprivation would satisfy Sam's need to have some control over Chris's behavior—while it would also de-escalate the power struggle that he and his stepdaughter were engaged in. I knew the use of logical consequences would provide the kind of structure that would appeal to Sam, and that it was likely to satisfy his need to be a responsible parent. It would also permit Sam and Judith to present a united front to Chris on the issue of her curfew.

In another intervention, I tried to strengthen Judith's position in the parental dyad by complementing her on the fine job she had done in raising Chris. During the second session, I took this one step further by pointing out to Judith that she and Chris were both SPs, and that she, therefore, would have a keen awareness of what kind of parenting approaches would be effective with her daughter.

During the first session, I was also able to reframe Chris's rebellious behavior as a way of trying to help her mother by protecting her from getting hurt. I used this to get her parents to see her as *scared* rather than *bad*.

The last thing I did with the family was to arrange for Judith to stop refereeing between Chris and Sam and trying to help them to get along with each other. Her well-meaning attempts were only keeping them at a distance from each other. At my request, Judith agreed to keep out of the middle between Chris and Sam. I also arranged for Chris to spend time alone with her mother so that she would not feel so neglected and jealous of Sam. In addition, Chris and Sam were asked to spend time together in order to get to know each other better.

In working alone with Chris, I used Gestalt and visualization exercises in order to release her emotions and rewrite limiting decisions she had made about men and relationships. These new attitudes, along with the changes in her parents' behavior, enabled her to accept Sam over time. By the follow-up session, she confessed to me that she was starting to like him "a lot."

Case #8

PHONEY CLUES

Session One:

An attractive professional woman in her early thirties made the decision to seek counseling after she and her husband of eight years had a terrible fight in which they exchanged physical blows. Melissa told me that there had been only one previous episode of physical violence, and that had occurred during the first year of her marriage. She knew that she and her husband, Richard, had many problems which had been getting increasingly worse. But when Richard began to punch her, and when she found herself punching him back, she decided that things had gone too far.

We spent the first session addressing Melissa's options. She told me that she loved her husband very much and that she did not want to separate from him or divorce him, but that she was unwilling to raise their two children in a violent household. She decided to write her husband a letter to let him know that she would agree to stay together only if they attended marriage counseling in order to resolve their disagreements. What's more, she wished to make it clear that if he ever struck her again, then she would leave him for good.

Melissa agreed to return the next week. Either she would bring Richard with her, or she would come by herself if he refused to participate in marital counseling.

Session Two:

Though he was reluctant, Richard accompanied Melissa to the next session. He told me that he was willing to attend marriage counseling so that Melissa wouldn't leave him, but that he didn't really want to be there and he didn't believe it was necessary. Yes, he had been the first to strike a blow during their most recent argument, but he had already promised her that he would never do that again. As far as he was concerned, the problem had been handled.

With questioning, I learned that Richard held an M.B.A. and that he worked long hours at an intense, high-pressure job in the entertainment industry. Though he liked his work a great deal, he needed lots of time to unwind in the evenings and on the weekends. In particular, Richard found that playing softball, volleyball, and basketball on the local sports teams was a great way for him to kick back and have some fun while meeting his need for socializing with his buddies. It was not unusual for him to play team sports six days a week, during his spare time. This meant he would be gone four evenings a week, plus all day Saturday and Sunday.

Melissa was also very busy in her career as an English instructor at the local community college. She loved her job, because it enabled her to inspire her students, foster in them an appreciation of fine literature, develop their writing potential, and encourage them to question the meaning of their existence. When she wasn't at work, her five-year-old son and two-year-old daughter took up the remainder of her time and attention. Often the three of them would go to watch Richard play his games in the evenings and on Saturday and Sunday afternoons. Melissa rarely had time to herself, but when she did, she enjoyed writing poetry and reading a variety of books—both fiction and nonfiction. She also enjoyed attending personal-growth seminars and classes.

I asked Melissa and Richard to tell me what they were arguing about when he hit her and she slugged him back. Richard told me that Melissa had refused to have sex with him for the past few months, and that she had been accusing him of having an affair with another woman. He had tried his hardest to convince her that this wasn't the case, but she continued to find new evidence that he was cheating on her. Richard swore to me (both in Melissa's presence and during a brief meeting I had alone with him) that he had never been unfaithful to his wife and that he had no desire to stray. He loved his wife and children very much and he just wasn't interested in anyone else. Yes, he would talk with the women at work, but it was completely innocent.

Melissa complained that Richard was just too friendly with other women and she was sure that he was having an affair. She had seen him put his arm around the women he worked with and flirt with them, and she knew exactly what was on his mind.

Melissa explained that she had stopped having sex with Richard, because she felt that sex was all he wanted from her. Every time they made love, she felt violated and used—like a prostitute. Although she had occasionally experienced orgasms, most of the time she just went numb from the neck down. In their marriage, their sex life had never been any different and she was tired of it. Melissa confessed that she avoided physical contact, except with her children. She was not inclined to give Richard hugs or kisses and she resisted his efforts to cuddle with her.

Both Melissa and Richard were able to agree that they wanted to improve the quality and quantity of their physical intimacy. In addition, they both felt that they were unable to communicate about their problems in a way that was helpful. Whenever they tried to talk about issues like sex, either Melissa would withdraw into a shell, saying nothing at all, or Richard would blow up. Hence, nothing ever got resolved.

Melissa also complained that Richard was never emotionally intimate with her. Whenever she tried to talk with him about deep, meaningful issues, it seemed like he would change the subject or fall asleep. Richard defended himself, saying that he tried to be intimate by making love, but she never wanted to. He just couldn't seem to please her.

What are the clients' personality types and what is the evidence used to identify them?

What are the survival games being played and by whom?

What treatment interventions might be useful in stopping the survival game playing?

Second Session Interventions:

The first issue I addressed was the physical violence that had occurred two weeks before. I emphasized to Richard that since hitting his wife was against the law, he could be arrested for doing so. I made certain that he understood that Melissa planned to end the marriage should he ever lay a hand on her again.

Next, I asked Melissa and Richard if they would be willing to arrange their lives so that they would have more time alone together. Richard said that Melissa was always complaining about how much he was gone, and that he would be willing to reduce his team sports playing in half from six days a week to just three. He said that he would play just two weeknights and on Saturday afternoons.

I asked Melissa to tell Richard some of the ways that he could share more of the responsibilities for the children. She mentioned feeding them, getting them ready for bed, and reading them bedtime stories. Melissa and Richard were able to agree on certain tasks Richard would handle on a daily basis and others that they could alternate between them.

Since they had not been out together in a long time, I told Richard and Melissa that I wanted them to have a date before our next meeting. They were to do their best to make this evening a special and enjoyable one for both of them. I also suggested that Melissa and Richard read the book *Getting the Love You Want*, by Harville Hendrix (1988).

I asked Melissa if she would be willing to schedule several individual sessions with me to work on some of the sexual issues that she had raised, in addition to coming to couples counseling with Richard. She readily agreed.

Session Three:

Both Richard and Melissa reported one week later that they had done most everything that they had agreed to do. Richard had only played his team sports on two evenings and Saturday afternoon, and he had been more involved in caring for their children. He and Melissa had enjoyed their date very much and they were willing to continue going out alone to have fun together at least once a week. They had begun reading Hendrix's book.

We spent most of the session talking about what both Melissa and Richard felt was acceptable behavior for each of them with the opposite sex. Richard believed that it was okay for him to hug, kiss, and flirt with women friends at social events, and that it was fine for him to go out to lunch alone with them, but that none of the same was acceptable for Melissa to do with men. Melissa argued that this was a double standard and that it was important for the same rules to apply to both of them. After much discussion, the two of them were able to agree on some mutual boundaries that permitted friendly flirting but ruled out physical contact and intimate lunch dates.

Since Melissa was still seeking evidence to prove that Richard was cheating on her, I ended the session by suggesting that perhaps Melissa needed extra practice in watching and interpreting Richard's actions more carefully. Toward that end, I asked Richard to make sure to present Melissa with five phoney clues which would make it appear that he had been dishonest with her, where he had actually been honest. Melissa's task was to see if she could identify the five phoney clues that Richard left her. At the next couples session, we would see how well Melissa had done in recognizing the phoney clues for what they really were.

Session Four:

During the next session I met individually with Melissa and I had the opportunity to delve more deeply into her past. I learned that both of Melissa's parents were alcoholics who divorced when she was very young. She spent much of her youth taking care of her mother, who was drunk most of the time. Melissa's family was very poor and she was rejected by the other children at school. Her childhood was lonely, sad, and filled with chaos. Most of the time she felt invisible and unloved. Worst of all, Melissa had been sexually abused by an uncle, and Melissa's mother had done nothing when Melissa had told her about it except to warn Melissa not to tell anyone, for fear of causing trouble in the family.

Melissa told me that she had survived her horrendous childhood by withdrawing and pulling inside, putting a protective layer of armor around herself, remaining isolated, and becoming extremely self-reliant. Though it had served her well, that pattern was now keeping her from enjoying physical and emotional intimacy with others. She wanted to take the armor off, learn to express and accept physical affection, and let more love in. She was determined not to pass her problems and limitations on to her children.

I asked Melissa to put her protective armor in an empty chair and to have a dialogue with it. She thanked it for all of the help it had given her, but also expressed her desire to be free of it so that she could be more capable of loving and of being loved. Reversing roles, she was able to pretend to be her armor and to verbalize all of her fears about suddenly removing the protection. With my prompting, her protective-armor self told the rest of her that she was *never* taking the armor off, under any circumstances. After all, *no one* could be trusted! Without the armor, she would surely get badly hurt. Switching chairs again, Melissa addressed her fears and indicated that she wanted to learn to trust people—especially her husband and closest friends. She agreed that it might not be safe to remove the armor in every situation, but that she would like to be able to take it off sometimes, so that she would not feel so lonely and estranged from others. She talked about how much it hurt her now to be wearing the armor—how much joy she was missing because of it.

When she finished the Gestalt exercise, I told Melissa that it seemed like she was a beautiful flower that was encased in a glass dome. The flower could never feel the warmth of the sun directly on its petals. Nor could it drink in rainwater that splashed on its dark green leaves, or bend gently in the softest wind. Yet, the flower was afraid that it could not survive without the protection of the glass. As I spoke, she just nodded her head and cried.

I suggested to Melissa that one way of helping herself would be to find the lonely, vulnerable, and frightened part of her inside, and to offer it love and protection. Melissa told me that she would be willing to do that, if I could show her how. I put on some soothing background music and used deep breathing and guided imagery to help her to become relaxed. Next, I directed her to go back to one of the earliest times when she felt lonely, vulnerable, and scared. Melissa cried when she saw herself as a very unhappy four-year-old who felt invisible and unloved in her family. I had Melissa pretend that her adult self entered the scene with the four-year-old, and that the two of them became acquainted. Eventually, Melissa was able to imagine herself holding the little girl in her lap and sending her lots of love through a golden cord that connected their two hearts. I asked Melissa to tell her child self out loud that she was precious, and that adult Melissa would always be there from now on to take care of her. At my prompting, she also told little Melissa that all of her thoughts, feelings, and desires were okay, and that she deserved to be happy.

At the close of the session, I asked Melissa if she would be willing to spend one hour alone with her inner child during the coming two weeks, doing anything the child wanted to do. She indicated agreement with a nod and a smile. I also asked her to go back to keeping the journal that she had been neglecting for the past few years.

Session Five:

Both Melissa and Richard reported at the start of the session that Melissa had not done her homework. Apparently, although Richard had carefully left five phoney clues for Melissa to find, she told me "I just stopped looking out of the corner of my eye." Melissa reported that she was tired of checking up on Richard, and that she was just going to have to trust that he was being faithful to her. She wasn't going to look for clues, even if I insisted on it.

Richard had continued to honor his agreement to limit his sports to only three days a week and to become more involved in caring for his children. Both Richard and Melissa had enjoyed their weekly dates immensely. And they were continuing their reading of *Getting the Love You Want*.

During most of session five, I worked with Richard and Melissa on their communication patterns. Richard voiced the complaint that he had backed away from participating in child care, because Melissa was always criticizing his parenting skills. Often in the presence of the children, she would reprimand him for something he did or said to them, as if he, too, was a child. Melissa told me that she had studied child development extensively, and that she was quick to tell Richard when he was doing something that might diminish the children's self-esteem and self-confidence. Richard confessed that he loved to get down on the floor and play with his kids, but that her negative comments only made him avoid doing so.

Conversely, Melissa resented the way that Richard was always telling her that she should lose weight and also pressuring her to have sex with him. These comments made her feel hurt and angry, and actually had the opposite effect of what Richard intended. Melissa would intentionally eat more, exercise less, and avoid sexual encounters.

I pointed out to Richard and Melissa that each of them was resentful when the other addressed him or her like a critical parent. Critical parent messages are easily identified because they usually begin with "Don't," "You'd better not," "You should," or

"You shouldn't." I indicated that their critical parent messages were actually activating the rebellious child in each other. This meant that the behavior they wanted to change in the other person actually became more pronounced.

I talked about alternative ways of communicating their thoughts, feelings, and desires to one another. I coached them in communicating from their nurturing parent and adult ego states using "I" statements, instead of "You" statements. I also taught them how to respond to each others' "I" messages using active listening.

After extensive practice, I assigned Melissa and Richard the task of practicing using "I" messages and active listening. Three times in the next week, each was to spend ten minutes talking about anything he or she wished, and ten minutes listening to the other. They were to use the kitchen timer to be sure that each had ten full minutes to talk.

I also asked them to compliment each other at least once a day. And lastly, I directed each of them to withdraw twenty one dollar bills from their bank account. Every time they addressed their mate using a critical parent message, they were to pay the other one dollar. When they returned in two weeks, we would see how much money they had given away, and how much they had received from their spouse.

Session Six:

Session six was another individual session with Melissa, who had followed through on her assignment to spend time with her inner child by taking a long walk on the beach. She had also been keeping a journal again and reported that she found it "deeply satisfying."

Since Melissa indicated to me that she was ready to begin dealing with the sexual abuse that her uncle had inflicted upon her, we made that the focus of our session. Melissa told me that although she had already been through several years of therapy to work on the sexual abuse, she had never been able to get rid of the shameful, hurtful, and angry feelings inside of her by just talking about it. I suggested that, rather than just talking about it, I could guide her through some visualization exercises that would enable her to heal the wounded little girl inside of her. Melissa said that she was open to whatever might help her to feel better.

After putting on some relaxing music, I instructed Melissa to breath deeply and to direct her attention to her body. Next, I had her recall how she felt when her husband tried to make love with her and to tell me where she experienced those feelings in her body. Melissa reported that she felt tightness, numbness, and tension in her pelvic area, and that she felt a void—like a hole—in her heart. When I asked her to label those feelings in one word, she said that she felt "violated."

I asked Melissa to stay with that feeling of being violated in her body and to trace it back to the *first time* that she felt the same way. She quickly located the scene when she was eleven in which her uncle climbed into her bed with the intention of molesting her. I instructed her to freeze that scene before he touched her and to imagine that her adult self appeared to rescue her. I also told her to pretend that both her child and her adult self were suddenly twelve feet tall.

Next, I had Melissa's adult self intervene on behalf of the child. She screamed at her uncle to stop and pretended that she was hitting him, while beating on a pillow in my office. When she was finished dealing with him, I asked her to imagine that her mother entered the room. I encouraged Melissa's adult self to tell her mother how angry and hurt she felt because her mother did not protect little Melissa. At the end of the scene, I had grown-up Melissa take the child away to a safe place.

Once they were alone in a private sanctuary, I directed Melissa to nurture and reassure her inner child and to promise that she would protect her from now on. Then, I had adult Melissa begin reparenting her child self. I asked Melissa to pretend that she could see a blackboard on which her old decisions about men and relationships were written down. On the blackboard were the following sentences: There is no one that I can trust; Sex is nothing more than a man violating a woman; Men are self-serving and they don't really care about my feelings; and, I have to keep everyone at a distance in order to remain safe. Together, Melissa's adult and child selves erased these decisions and wrote down new sentences to replace them. These included: It is okay for me to trust and be close to certain special people; and, Sex can be joyful and satisfying with someone I love.

Finally, I had Melissa put her child self in her heart, where she would be safe and surrounded by love, and I instructed her to awaken. She told me that she felt exhausted, relieved, and peaceful inside. At the close of the session, I asked her to write a letter to her child self for homework to explain the difference between violation and intimacy. I also asked her to write letters to her mother and her uncle to get her feelings about the abuse down on paper. These letters were not intended for the mail— they were for her to dispose of later on in the manner that she chose.

Session Seven:

Again I met with Melissa alone for the next session. She reported that she had been feeling especially peaceful inside since the last session. Melissa read the letters to her mother and uncle aloud and then decided that she was going to burn them when she got home.

After she read me the letter that she had written to her inner child, I instructed her to have a dialogue between her adult self and her child self using the empty chair method. Adult Melissa told the child that it was okay for her to recapture the side of herself that her uncle had stolen from her. The child responded by saying that she was afraid of being used and hurt again, and that she wanted proof that what her adult self said was really true. Adult Melissa reassured the child that there was a big difference between being abused by her uncle and making love with Richard.

I spent the remainder of the session making a visualization tape for Melissa in which I guided her in nurturing and reparenting her inner child. I also spoke on the tape about buried treasures and about exploring new rooms of her house that are filled with sensory delights. Lastly, I described a ballet, and how it feels to dance with another in harmony, grace, and balance on a light-filled stage. I asked Melissa to listen to the tape as often as she could for homework.

Session Eight:

At the next couples session, Melissa and Richard confessed that they had not practiced any active listening. However, they had been keenly aware of their use of critical parenting messages and each had only ended up paying the other one two dollars for those times when they had reverted to their old patterns. They were doing a much better job of expressing themselves using "I" statements. Furthermore, both had tried to offer daily compliments to their partners and they were willing to continue doing so.

We spent the rest of the session rehearsing active listening and also specifying the exact times and places when they would practice at home during the next weeks. They also agreed to continue exchanging dollars when they employed critical parenting messages.

Session Nine:

At the next individual session with Melissa, she reported that she had listened to the tape often and she was beginning to feel freer and less restricted. Melissa told me that in the past week, she had become aware that she had always pushed her own needs aside and pretended that they did not exist. She had not been making her needs known to Richard—or even to herself. I likened it to a sweatshirt that she had been wearing which proclaimed, "My needs and feelings don't matter!"

I had observed that Melissa was much more subdued and passive around Richard than she was during her individual sessions. Even her voice was more quiet and weak when she was in his presence. Melissa explained that she did not want to be an "aggressive bitch" like her mother was, so she tended to hold herself back from being too powerful when she was with her husband. I emphasized the difference between being assertive versus being aggressive, and Melissa used role playing to try out some new, more assertive ways of communicating with her husband. As homework, she agreed to address one need or want that she would normally just ignore. I also suggested that she read the books, *The Dance of Anger* and *The Dance of Intimacy*, by Harriet Goldhor Lerner (1985, 1989).

Session Ten:

At the next couples session, Melissa and Richard reported that they had not exchanged any dollars, and that they had followed through on the three sessions to practice active listening.

I asked Richard if he would be willing to help Melissa to heal the wounds of her past caused by her uncle's sexual abuse (which Melissa had told him about) and he indicated a desire to help her in any way he could. I told him that Melissa had learned to associate touching with pain and I explained that there were methods that he and Melissa could use to teach her to associate touching with love, tenderness, and pleasure, but that they would require a sacrifice on his part. Richard looked somewhat wary as he nodded at me.

I then explained that I wanted the two of them to set aside one hour at a time on two separate days in the next week when they could spend uninterrupted time together in the bedroom. During each one hour session, they were to make their bedroom environment as comfortable as possible, with nice lighting (maybe candles), beautiful music playing, and perhaps incense burning. Lying naked in bed, Richard was to take one-half hour to caress Melissa with his hands in ways that were pleasing to her—however, he was not to touch her genitals at all. During the second half-hour, Melissa was to caress Richard all over with her hands, without touching his genitals. They could let each other know if they particularly liked a certain kind of touch, and they could guide each others' hands with their own, but they were not to say anything negative to each other, like, "Don't do that." When it was their turn to give the caresses, it was important that they focus on the pleasure of touching their mate.

I stressed to them that during the next week it was of the utmost importance to refrain from having intercourse. They agreed to follow all instructions carefully. In addition, Melissa agreed to initiate physical contact with Richard three times during the week by hugging him, kissing him, or holding his hand.

Session Eleven:

During session eleven, we reviewed the results of the sensate focus exercises assigned during the previous session and I prescribed that they continue to follow the same procedure for two more weeks. Melissa indicated that the first session was especially difficult for her because she was concerned that Richard really didn't want to be participating, but that during the second session she was able to really relax and enjoy it. Melissa was surprised and delighted to discover that she was actually able to notice and enjoy the physical sensations in her body for the first time. Richard said that he was surprised that he enjoyed caressing Melissa as much as he liked being the recipient of her caresses.

Melissa had begun to initiate spontaneous hugs and kisses with Richard, though she confessed that it felt awkward at first. I asked her to continue to do so for the next two weeks.

Session Twelve:

During the last individual session with Melissa, she indicated that she had been getting out more and reaching out to both old friends and new friends. She felt as if she had begun to remove some of her protective armor and she was feeling really good about it. She was also practicing asserting herself more with Richard and others, although it was not easy for her.

I spent the remainder of the session making her another guided visualization tape in which she went to a beautiful sanctuary, walked across a bridge, and encountered a future self who had made many of her dreams a reality. Her future self was open, loving, healthy, and comfortable giving and receiving physical affection. She had developed to her fullest potential and she was confident and assertive.

At the close of the session I suggested that Melissa use the tape as a way of reinforcing the work that she had done in therapy and facilitating additional self-growth in the direction that she desired.

Sessions Thirteen through Sixteen:

I continued to assign sensate focus exercises with Melissa and Richard and gradually reintroduced genital touching and inter-course over time. We also continued to address Melissa's need to assert herself more in the relationship, as well as Richard's ten-dency to ignore her assertions or to assume that she didn't really mean it when she did state her desires.

During one session I talked to Richard and Melissa about their personality types. In particular, I focused on the ways in which they were different from each other. For example, as an Artisan, Richard was not interested in spending lots of time talking about the "deep, meaningful" subjects that captured the attention of his Idealist wife.

When we terminated counseling, both Melissa and Richard indi-cated that they were able to address conflicts without blowing up or withdrawing. They were not nagging each other anymore and they were appreciating their time together and with the children very much. Melissa reported that she was beginning to relax and enjoy making love with Richard and both agreed that the quality of their lovemaking had improved considerably.

CASE DISCUSSION

Melissa's Idealist temperament is apparent in both the nature of her work (teaching English) and in her description of what she likes best about it. As an NF, Melissa wants to *develop* her students' potential, *inspire* them, and *encourage* them to search for meaning. She enjoys reading about and discussing abstract ideas and also expressing her creativity through writing. In her pursuit of self-actualization, Melissa attends personal-growth classes and seminars whenever possible. As is typical of most Idealists, one of Melissa's top priorities as a parent is to see to it that her children develop healthy self-esteem.* Of the four NFs, Melissa is an INFJ, or Mentor/Diviner. She is a private person who needs a lot of solitary time to charge up her batteries. Evidence that Melissa is a J, as opposed to a P, is the ease with which she gives directives to her husband.

In contrast to his Idealist wife, Richard is the ESFP, or Player/Performer Artisan. Richard thrives on action and excitement in his work in the entertainment industry and in his sporting activities. He loves to be around people, gravitates towards team sports, and has extensive friendships with others. He is charming, gregarious, and playful. As a concrete-type person, Richard is not especially interested in having theoretical conversations with Melissa—in fact, they put him to sleep. In his parenting, Richard's focus is on playing with his children and enjoying them first, while discipline takes a back seat.

Initially, both Melissa and Richard are playing survival games. Of course, it is Richard's game of *Blackmail*—in particular, his escalation of *Outrage* to the point of physical violence—that moves Melissa to seek counseling.** In addition to his game of

---

* Certainly, most parents want their children to have positive self-esteem. But, it is the Idealist who is most likely to view self-esteem as being of *primary* importance, and who is therefore likely to base most of his or her parenting decisions on how a child's self-esteem will be affected.

** I have encountered very few cases of Idealist females who remain in relationships that are physically violent. In contrast, many SFJ's who are

Outrage, Richard is also engaging in *Binge* tactics when he plays team sports seven days a week. This survival game enables Richard to let off steam, avoid the uncomfortable situation at home, and also to get even with Melissa for criticizing him and refusing to have sex with him.

Melissa is playing the *Mind Reader, Statue,* and *Martyr* variants of the *Masquerade* game. Her false accusations that Richard is having affairs with other women are characteristic of the Mind Reader game. Melissa's Statue game is evident when she withdraws inside of herself and puts up a wall during disagreements with Richard and also in other uncomfortable social situations. Still another aspect of the Statue game is when Melissa becomes numb from the neck down during intercourse. When Melissa consistently sacrifices her own needs and wants in favor of Richard's, then she is playing the survival game of Martyr.

To handle the issue of physical violence, it was necessary for Melissa to let her Artisan husband know that there were consequences to his actions in the present and that there would be consequences in the future. Therefore, besides insisting that they attend marriage counseling, Melissa decided to inform Richard that she would take the children and leave for good if he ever hit her again.

Next, I arranged for Richard to spend more time at home with his family and also alone with Melissa, while also interdicting the critical messages that each of them used to try to control the others' behavior. By asking them to pay a dollar to the other every time they made certain critical comments, I was able to get Melissa and Richard to stop pushing each others' buttons. In addition, I taught Melissa and Richard ways of communicating more effectively about their differences using "I" statements and active listening.

In order to stop Melissa from playing the game of Mind Reader, I prescribed that Richard leave her five phoney clues, and that

---

playing Doormat and many SFP's who are playing Shocking end up staying in such destructive relationships for years.

she practice discerning the "real" clues from the phoney ones. This intervention stopped her game immediately—she never voiced another accusation after that.

Since Melissa began using the games of Statue and Martyr as survival tactics when she was sexually and emotionally abused as a child, I employed guided visualizations to help her begin transforming those old patterns into new, more satisfying ones. Specifically, I encouraged Melissa to nurture her wounded inner child, rewrite the traumatic scenes of her past, and to change early decisions that she had made regarding her relationships and her sexuality. In addition, I used numerous passport metaphors with Melissa about uncovering buried treasures, exploring new rooms of her house, and dancing a graceful ballet with a sensitive partner. I also introduced Melissa to her future self in order to instill her with hope, courage, and the belief that she could, indeed, accomplish the goals that she had set for herself. Many of these processes were recorded so that Melissa could play them repeatedly at home, thus enhancing their effectiveness.

Other therapeutic methods that I used in individual sessions with Melissa included the empty-chair exercise, assertion training, journaling, and the ritual of writing letters to her mother and uncle and burning them.

Once Melissa had begun to heal the wounds of her past, I gave her the opportunity to learn to enjoy sensual pleasures in the present by prescribing that she and Richard practice a series of sensate focus exercises. These exercises made it safe for Melissa to relax and tune into the delightful sensations in her body as her husband lovingly caressed her. They also taught Richard how he could assist his wife in finding greater pleasure in their lovemaking.

It is noteworthy that Melissa had already undergone several years of psychotherapy, but that she was unable to stop employing many of her game tactics by just talking about her feelings and what had happened to her. I believe that talking and insight are usually not enough to help clients to actually stop their game playing. In my experience, clients seem to demonstrate the greatest amount of improvement when they are given the opportunity to *do* something that is meant to be therapeutic—whether it is a guided visualization, a Gestalt dialogue with an empty chair, a sensate focus exercise, a sand-play picture, or a ritual. These therapeutic exercises seem to enable clients, like Melissa, to access their own powerful ability to heal themselves.

AFTERWORD

The case studies throughout this book provide numerous examples of how the Keirseyan Games Model can be used to illuminate and clarify the reasons why people behave in strange or abnormal ways, without labeling anyone as *crazy, bad, sick,* or *stupid.*

When I look through the lenses of the Keirseyan Games Model, I do not see mental illnesses or personality disorders. Rather, I see individuals who are defending themselves in unsafe territory. I also see new avenues which may be pursued for assisting those people in overcoming their difficulties.

It is my hope that the use of these lenses will foster greater tolerance of and appreciation for human differences. Too often, when people are dissimilar to us, we conclude there must be something wrong with them. What's more, we take it upon ourselves to try to change them—to mold them into our own image. This "Pygmalion Project" (as Keirsey and Bates call it) is not only doomed to fail—it is also a primary cause of survival game playing since it activates the defenses of the person who is being chiseled upon (Keirsey and Bates, 1978). In trying to sculpt our children or mates into our own likenesses, those of us who engage in the Pygmalion Project are sending such (implied) messages as "You are *not* okay just as you are," and "To be acceptable, you must want what I want, feel what I feel, think what I think, and do what I do!"

One of the greatest gifts we can give our family, friends, and associates is the freedom to be themselves. Whether at home, at work, or in a classroom, individuals reveal their most productive and creative selves when they are applauded for their unique contributions.

I have seen many desirable transformations occur in those couples and families in which people put down their chisels and begin to accept and appreciate each others' differences. Often game playing comes to a halt when each person stops trying to change the other.

In the workplace, the Keirseyan lenses can serve to foster greater cooperation and teamwork. Where there is an appreciation for differences, employees can better recognize and utilize the diverse strengths of the various members of the organizational team.

This model can also assist teachers, parents, and administrators in creating an educational milieu in which all types of children feel validated and valued. By addressing the needs of all four personalities, schools can more effectively nourish and develop the unlimited potential that exists within each student. Our society can benefit enormously when each child is inspired to express his or her special talents in creative and constructive ways.

We must abandon our Pygmalion Projects both at home and at work if we are to create nurturing and accepting environments that invite the people in our lives to thrive, rather than just survive.

BIBLIOGRAPHY

Alexander, Franz. *Psychosomatic Medicine*. New York: Norton, 1932.

Arapakis, Maria. *Softpower*. New York: Warner Books, 1990.

Assagioli, Roberto. *Psychosynthesis: A Collection of Basic Writings*. U.S.A.: Hobbs, Dorman, and Company, 1965.

Berne, Eric. *Games People Play*. New York: Grove Press, Inc., 1964.

Borysenko, Joan. *Minding the Body, Mending the Mind*. New York: Bantam Books, 1987.

Bradshaw, John. *Healing the Shame That Binds You*. Deerfield Beach, FL: Health Communications, 1988.

Bradshaw, John. *Homecoming: Reclaiming and Championing Your Inner Child*. New York: Bantam Books, 1990.

Dreikurs, Rudolph, and Vicki Soltz. *Children: The Challenge*. New York: Hawthorn/Dutton, 1964.

Ellis, Albert. *Reason and Emotion in Psychotherapy*. Secaucus, NJ: Lyle Stuart, 1962.

Faber, Adele, and Elaine Mazlish. *How to Talk So Kids Will Listen, and Listen So Kids Will Talk*. New York: Avon, 1980.

Glasser, William. *Reality Therapy*. New York: Harper and Row, 1965.

Gordon, Thomas. *Parent Effectiveness Training*. New York: Peter Wyden, Inc., 1972.

Haley, Jay. *Strategies of Psychotherapy*. New York: Grune and Stratton, 1963.

Haley, Jay. *Advanced Techniques of Hypnosis and Therapy: Selected Papers of Milton Erickson, M.D.* New York: Grune and Stratton, 1967.

Haley, Jay. *Uncommon Therapy*. New York: Ballantine Books, 1973.

Haley, Jay. *Ordeal Therapy*. San Francisco: Jossey-Bass, 1984.

Haley, Jay. *Conversations With Milton H. Erickson, M.D.* 3 vols. Rockville, MD: Triangle Press, 1985.

Hendrix, Harville. *Getting the Love You Want: A Guide For Couples*. New York: Henry Holt and Company, 1988.

Imber-Black, Evan, Janine Roberts, and Richard Whiting. *Rituals in Families and Family Therapy*. New York: Norton, 1988.

James, Muriel, and Dorothy Jongeward. *Born to Win*. Reading, MA: Addison-Wesley, 1971.

Jung, Carl. *Psychological Types: The Collected Works of C. G. Jung*. Vol. 6. Princeton: Princeton University Press, 1971.

Jung, Carl. *Man and His Symbols*. New York: Dell Publishing Company, 1964.

Kalff, Dora. *Sandplay: A Psychotherapeutic Approach to the Psyche*. Boston: Sigo Press, 1980.

Keirsey, David, and Marilyn Bates. *Please Understand Me*. Del Mar, CA: Prometheus Nemesis Book Company, 1978.

Keirsey, David. *Portraits of Temperament*. Del Mar, CA: Prometheus Nemesis Book Company, 1987.

Keirsey, David. *Abuse It—Lose It: A Drug-Free Method of Teaching Self-Control to "Hyperactive" Children*. Del Mar, CA: Prometheus Nemesis Book Company, 1991.

Kretschmer, Ernst. *Physique and Character.* London: Harcourt Brace, 1925.

Landis, Richard. *Parts Work: Interactive Imageries for Habit, Feeling and Behavior Changes.* 1989. Available at: 780 N. Euclid, Suite 110, Anaheim, CA 92801.

Lerner, Harriet Goldhor. *The Dance of Anger.* New York: Harper and Row, 1985.

Lerner, Harriet Goldhor. *The Dance of Intimacy.* New York: Harper and Row, 1989.

Levy, David. *Maternal Overprotection.* New York: Columbia University Press, 1943.

Madanes, Cloé. *Strategic Family Therapy.* San Francisco: Jossey-Bass, 1981.

Madanes, Cloé. *Behind the One-Way Mirror.* San Francisco: Jossey-Bass, 1984.

Madanes, Cloé. *Sex, Love, and Violence.* New York: Norton, 1990.

Mahrer, Alvin. *Dream Work in Psychotherapy and Self-Change.* New York: Norton, 1989.

Miller, Alice. *For Your Own Good: Hidden Cruelty in Child-Rearing and the Roots of Violence.* New York: Farrar, Straus, and Giroux, 1983.

Myers, Isabel Briggs. *Gifts Differing.* Palo Alto, CA: Consulting Psychologists Press, 1980.

Myers, Isabel Briggs, and Mary McCaulley. *Manual: A Guide to the Development and Use of the Myers-Briggs Type Indicator.* Palo Alto, CA: Consulting Psychologists Press, 1985.

Nelsen, Jane. *Positive Discipline.* New York: Ballantine Books, 1981.

Norwood, Robin. *Women Who Love Too Much.* New York: Jeremy Tarcher, 1985.

Perls, Frederick. *Gestalt Therapy Verbatim.* Moab, UT: Real People Press, 1969.

Rogers, Carl. *Counseling and Psychotherapy.* Cambridge, MA: The Riverside Press, 1942.

Rosen, Sidney. *My Voice Will Go With You.* New York: Norton, 1982.

Rossi, Ernest. *Collected Papers of Milton Erickson.* Vols. 1-4. New York: Irvington Publishers, 1980.

Small, Jacquelyn. *Awakening In Time: The Journey From Co-dependence to Co-Creation.* New York: Bantam Books, 1991.

Smith, Manuel. *When I Say No, I Feel Guilty.* New York: Bantam Books, 1985.

Spränger, Eduard. *Types of Men.* New York: Johnson Reprint Company, [1928] 1966.

Stone, Hal, and Sidra Winkelman. *Embracing Our Selves.* Marina Del Rey, CA: De Vorss and Company, 1985.

Wallas, Lee. *Stories For the Third Ear.* New York: Norton, 1985.

Wallas, Lee. *Stories That Heal: Reparenting Adult Children of Dysfunctional Families Using Hypnotic Stories in Psychotherapy.* New York: Norton, 1991.

Watzlawick, Paul, John Weakland, and Richard Fisch. *Change: Principles of Problem Formation and Problem Resolution.* New York: Norton, 1974.

Weinrib, Estelle. *Images of the Self.* Boston: Sigo Press, 1983.

SUGGESTED READINGS

On Personality Types and Temperament Theory:

Berens, Linda A. *Comparison of Jungian Function Theory and Keirseyan Temperament Theory in the Use of the Myers-Briggs Type Indicator. Dissertation Abstracts International*, 1985.

Giovannoni, Louise, Linda Berens, and Sue Cooper. *Introduction to Temperament*. Huntington Beach, CA: Telos Publications, 1987.

Jung, Carl. *Psychological Types: The Collected Works of C. G. Jung*. Vol. 6. Princeton: Princeton University Press, 1971.

Keirsey, David, and Marilyn Bates. *Please Understand Me*. Del Mar, CA: Prometheus Nemesis Book Company, 1978.

Keirsey, David. *Portraits of Temperament*. Del Mar, CA: Prometheus Nemesis Book Company, 1987.

Kretschmer, Ernst. *Physique and Character*. London: Harcourt Brace, 1925.

Montgomery, Stephen. *The Pygmalion Project: Love and Coercion Among the Types*. Vol. 1, *The Artisan*. Del Mar, CA: Prometheus Nemesis Book Company, 1989.

Montgomery, Stephen. *The Pygmalion Project: Love and Coercion Among the Types*. Vol. 2, *The Guardian*. Del Mar, CA: Prometheus Nemesis Book Company, 1990.

Myers, Isabel Briggs. *Gifts Differing*. Palo Alto, CA: Consulting Psychologists Press, 1980.

Myers, Isabel Briggs, and Mary McCaulley. *Manual: A Guide to the Development and Use of the Myers-Briggs Type Indicator.* Palo Alto, CA: Consulting Psychologists Press, 1985.

Spränger, Eduard. *Types of Men.* New York: Johnson Reprint Company, [1928] 1966.

On Therapeutic Methods:

Assagioli, Roberto. *Psychosynthesis: A Collection of Basic Writings.* U.S.A.: Hobbs, Dorman, and Company, 1965.

Blatner, Howard. *Acting In: Practical Applications of Psychodramatic Methods.* New York: Springer Publishing Company, 1973.

Breggin, Peter. *Toxic Psychiatry.* New York: St. Martin's Press, 1991.

Ellis, Albert. *Reason and Emotion in Psychotherapy.* Secaucus, NJ: Lyle Stuart, 1962.

Glasser, William. *Reality Therapy,* New York: Harper and Row, 1965.

Haley, Jay. *Strategies of Psychotherapy.* New York: Grune and Stratton, 1963.

Haley, Jay. *Advanced Techniques of Hypnosis and Therapy: Selected Papers of Milton Erickson, M.D.* New York: Grune and Stratton, 1967.

Haley, Jay. *Uncommon Therapy.* New York: Ballantine Books, 1973.

Haley, Jay. *Ordeal Therapy.* San Francisco: Jossey-Bass, 1984.

Haley, Jay. *Conversations With Milton H. Erickson, M.D.* 3 Vols. Rockville, MD: Triangle Press, 1985.

James, Muriel, and Dorothy Jongeward. *Born to Win.* Reading, MA: Addison-Wesley, 1971.

Keirsey, David. *Abuse It—Lose It: A Drug-Free Method of Teaching Self-Control to "Hyperactive" Children.* Del Mar, CA: Prometheus Nemesis Book Company, 1991.

Imber-Black, Evan, Janine Roberts, and Richard Whiting. *Rituals in Families and Family Therapy.* New York: Norton, 1988.

Jung, Carl. *Man and His Symbols.* New York: Dell Publishing Co.,1964.

Kalff, Dora. *Sandplay: A Psychotherapeutic Approach to the Psyche.* Boston: Sigo Press, 1980.

Landis, Richard. *Parts Work: Interactive Imageries for Habit, Feeling and Behavior Changes.* 1989. Available at: 780 N. Euclid, Suite 110, Anaheim, CA 92801.

Madanes, Cloé. *Strategic Family Therapy.* San Francisco: Jossey-Bass, 1981.

Madanes, Cloé. *Behind the One-Way Mirror.* San Francisco: Jossey-Bass, 1984.

Madanes, Cloé. *Sex, Love, and Violence.* New York: Norton, 1990.

Mahrer, Alvin. *Dream Work in Psychotherapy and Self-Change.* New York: Norton, 1989.

Mills, Joyce, and Richard Crowley. *Therapeutic Metaphors For Children and the Child Within.* New York: Brunner/Mazel, Inc. 1986.

Oaklander, Violet. *Windows to Our Children.* Highland, NY: Gestalt Journal, 1989.

Perls, Frederick. *Gestalt Therapy Verbatim.* Moab, UT: Real People Press, 1969.

Rogers, Carl. *Counseling and Psychotherapy.* Cambridge, MA: The Riverside Press, 1942.

Rosen, Sidney. *My Voice Will Go With You.* New York: Norton, 1982.

Rossi, Ernest. *Collected Papers of Milton Erickson.* Vols. 1-4. New York: Irvington Publishers, 1980.

Steiner, Claude. *Scripts People Live.* New York: Grove, 1974.

Stone, Hal, and Sidra Winkelman. *Embracing Our Selves.* Marina Del Rey, CA: De Vorss &Company, 1985.

Wallas, Lee. *Stories For the Third Ear.* New York: Norton, 1985.

Wallas, Lee. *Stories That Heal: Reparenting Adult Children of Dysfunctional Families Using Hypnotic Stories in Psychotherapy.* New York: Norton, 1991.

Watzlawick, Paul, John Weakland, and Richard Fisch. *Change: Principles of Problem Formation and Problem Resolution.* New York: Norton, 1974.

Weinrib, Estelle. *Images of the Self.* Boston: Sigo Press, 1983.

On Games and Their Origins:

Alexander, Franz. *Psychosomatic Medicine.* New York: Norton, 1932.

Berne, Eric. *Games People Play.* New York: Grove Press, Inc., 1964.

Levy, David. *Maternal Overprotection.* New York: Columbia University Press, 1943.

Miller, Alice. *For Your Own Good: Hidden Cruelty in Child-Rearing and the Roots of Violence.* New York: Farrar, Straus, and Giroux, 1983.

Miller, Alice. *Thou Shalt Not Be Aware: Society's Betrayal of the Child.* New York: New American Library, 1986.

Shapiro, David. *Neurotic Styles.* New York: Basic Books, 1965.

On Relationships and Communication:

Arapakis, Maria. *Softpower.* New York: Warner Books, 1990.

Hendrix, Harville. *Getting the Love You Want: A Guide For Couples.* New York: Henry Holt and Company, 1988.

Lerner, Harriet Goldhor. *The Dance of Anger.* New York: Harper and Row, 1985.

Lerner, Harriet Goldhor. *The Dance of Intimacy.* New York: Harper and Row, 1989.

Norwood, Robin. *Women Who Love Too Much.* New York: Jeremy Tarcher, 1985.

Smith, Manuel. *When I Say No, I Feel Guilty.* New York: Bantam Books, 1985.

On Parenting:

Briggs, Dorothy. *Your Child's Self-Esteem.* New York: Doubleday and Compay, 1970.

Dreikurs, Rudolph, and Vicki Soltz. *Children: The Challenge.* New York: Hawthorn/Dutton, 1964.

Faber, Adele, and Elaine Mazlish. *How to Talk So Kids Will Listen, and Listen So Kids Will Talk.* New York: Avon, 1980.

Gordon, Thomas. *Parent Effectiveness Training.* New York: Peter Wyden, Inc., 1972.

Nelsen, Jane. *Positive Discipline.* New York: Ballantine Books, 1981.

On Self-Healing:

Bass, Ellen, and Laura Davis. *The Courage to Heal: A Guide for Women Survivors of Child Sexual Abuse.* New York: Harper and Row, 1988.

Barbach, Lonnie. *For Yourself: The Fulfillment of Female Sexuality.* Garden City: Anchor Press, 1975.

Borysenko, Joan. *Minding the Body, Mending the Mind.* New York: Bantam Books, 1987.

Bradshaw, John. *Healing the Shame That Binds You.* Deerfield Beach, FL: Health Communications, 1988.

Bradshaw, John. *Homecoming: Reclaiming and ChampioningYour Inner Child.* New York: Bantam Books, 1990.

Forward, Susan. *Toxic Parents: Overcoming Their Hurtful Legacy and Reclaiming Your Life.* New York: Bantam Books, 1989.

Jeffers, Susan. *Feel the Fear and Do It Anyway.* New York: Fawcett Columbine, 1987.

Ross, Ruth. *Prospering Woman.* Mill Valley, CA: Whatever Publishing, 1982.

Siegel, Bernie. *Love, Medicine, and Miracles.* New York: Harper and Row, 1986.

Siegel, Bernie. *Peace, Love, and Healing.* New York: Harper and Row, 1989.

Small, Jacquelyn. *Awakening In Time: The Journey From Co-dependence to Co-Creation.* New York: Bantam Books, 1991.

Tattlebaum, Judy. *You Don't Have to Suffer: A Handbook for Moving Beyond Life's Crises.* New York: Harper and Row, 1989.

Hanh, Thich Nhat. *Peace is Every Step: The Path of Mindfulness in Everyday Life.* New York: Bantam Books, 1991.

TRAINING
ACTIVITIES

For more information about the classes, seminars, and casework consultation groups conducted by Dr. Eve Delunas, contact:

Delunas and Associates
225 Crossroads Boulevard #237
Carmel, CA 93923
Phone (408) 626-3325
Fax (408) 625-3770

Also Available . . . .

Bridges Across Time   A guided visualization tape by Dr. Eve Delunas, accompanied by beautiful and relaxing piano music written and performed by Lee Ann Lakin.

> *Side One*:   Meeting Your Future Self
> *Side Two*:   Healing the Wounds of Childhood
> $15.00

BOOKS
AND TAPES

Please Use This Form To Order Books or Tapes:

Name (Please Print)_____

Street Address_____

City_____ State_____ Zip_____

Phone_____ Fax_____

	Unit Cost	#	Total Cost
Survival Games Personalities Play	$15.00	_____	_____
Bridges Across Time (Tape)	$15.00	_____	_____
		Subtotal	_____
CA Residents add tax of 7.25% of Subtotal			_____
*Shipping and Handling (See Below)			_____
		Total (U.S. $) $	_____

*Please add $3.50 for the first book or tape, and $1.50 for each additional one. For international orders, please include $5.50 for the first book or tape, and $1.50 for each additional one.

Payment Enclosed: __Check   __Money Order
Please Charge My: __VISA   __MasterCard

Credit Card No._____Exp. Date_____

Signature as on card_____

Mail this form and your check or money order to:
Delunas and Associates
225 Crossroads Blvd. #237
Carmel, CA 93923
Phone # (408) 626-3325 Fax # (408) 625-3770